HOUSING SUBSIDIES IN THE UNITED STATES AND ENGLAND

HOUSING SUBSIDIES IN THE UNITED STATES AND ENGLAND

By

DANIEL R. MANDELKER

Professor of Law

Washington University, St. Louis

THE BOBBS-MERRILL COMPANY, INC.
A SUBSIDIARY OF HOWARD W. SAMS CO., INC.
PUBLISHERS • INDIANAPOLIS • KANSAS CITY • NEW YORK

Copyright © 1973 by THE BOBBS-MERRILL COMPANY, INC.
Library of Congress Catalog Card Number: 73-7690
ISBN 0-672-81871-X
Printed in the United States of America
All Rights Reserved

TO MY MOTHER

Preface

This comparative review of housing subsidy programs in England and the United States is published at a time when housing subsidy policy in both countries has come under searching legislative scrutiny. In England, a Conservative government has just enacted the most far-reaching reform of housing subsidy legislation to be adopted in recent history. In the United States, a Republican administration has proposed a comprehensive codification of existing housing subsidy programs, which though not requiring many substantive changes, has been stymied by a reluctant Democratic Congress. Widespread abuses in America accompanying the expansion of housing subsidies in recent years, especially those subsidies that have been made available to private owner-occupied and rental housing, now suggest that even more substantial legislative changes may be in the making. These legislative initiatives in both countries indicate that housing programs which had a decidedly ambiguous beginning are coming under increasingly careful scrutiny, and that their purposes and policies are being thoroughly reexamined.

This current examination of housing subsidy issues has focused alternatively on the geographic and on the income distribution aspects of housing subsidy policies. Many strategists in the United States are concerned about the impact which housing subsidies have on the location of housing serving different racial and income groups. For example, recently adopted policies at the federal level in the United States have required the dispersal of housing subsidized with federal funds. The English have not been as concerned about the impact of their subsidy programs on the location of subsidized housing units. Nevertheless, housing subsidies in both countries play an obvious and important role in a national strategy for housing dispersal, slum clearance, and neighborhood maintenance and renewal in general.[1] Other critics in both countries, who are more concerned with the role of housing subsidies in a larger income support policy, see these subsidies as one method of redistributing income in societies which

---

[1] *See, e.g.,* Downs, *The Future of American Ghettos,* DAEDALUS, at 1331 (Fall, 1968).

still suffer from widespread poverty. From this perspective, many would argue for the elimination of housing subsidies as a separate income strategy, or at least for changes in housing subsidy policy which would structure these subsidies in the form of direct income grants. These grants would either be made on an independent basis, or absorbed into a larger income support program.

This interest in the relationship between housing subsidies and income support programs illustrates the fact that the housing problem is increasingly viewed as a question of financial ability to pay for adequate housing, rather than the improvement of physical housing standards on a nationwide basis. A continuing improvement in housing conditions undoubtedly contributes to this change in emphasis. But subsidy programs aimed at improving the ability to pay for housing create problems with which the existing housing subsidy system is not entirely equipped to cope. How these problems are resolved at the legislative and administrative policy levels will have an important bearing on the success of any strategy for the improvement of housing and the relief of poverty among the very poor in our society.

The emergence of income support issues in housing subsidy programs has also coincided with a series of other developments which have made solutions to the housing problem more, not less, difficult. In the United States, continued deterioration of ghetto and inner city neighborhoods has accompanied the general improvement in housing standards and the massive construction of new housing in suburbia. Signs of inner city abandonment have occurred in some areas of northern England as well. These symptoms have also signalled a widespread paralysis and collapse of the private rental housing market, especially in England, where fully one-third of the population now lives in subsidized and publicly owned rental housing. At the same time, annual national expenditures for housing subsidy programs, which have been expanded to cover a larger segment of the population, have been rising rapidly in both countries. These expenditures may be marginal to giant-sized national budgets. Nevertheless, neither country appears willing to accept an expenditure for housing subsidies which takes as much as five percent of a national budget strained by competing and equally urgent priorities, especially when these subsidies are widely available and when the level of housing demand is rising and shows no signs of abating.

Subsidies for housing needs are thus likely to be made available only at a level which provides no real assistance in the improvement of household housing standards. The experience with income and housing grants in the welfare programs of both England and the United States bears testimony to this observation, and it is only the continuing and accelerating drift of welfare recipients into subsidized, publicly owned rental housing in England that has avoided serious difficulties on this score in that country.

It is the purpose of this book to contribute to this growing debate over the future of housing subsidies, with a special emphasis on subsidized housing that is both publicly owned and rented, and which serves the lowest income groups in our population. However, while this book concentrates on the financial and related policy problems that are raised by housing subsidy programs, the impact of these policies on housing dispersal, renewal, and rehabilitation, and the related elements of a total housing strategy is not neglected.[2] Attention is directed where essential to these issues.

My interest in housing subsidy problems was stimulated by an earlier visit to England, during which I concentrated on problems of housing improvement strategy.[3] I followed up this interest with later visits to England in the summer of 1971 and the spring of 1972, during which I concentrated especially on housing subsidy issues. Time for evaluating my English research, and for pursuing my analysis of American public housing, was made available to me during my appointment as Walter E. Meyer Research Professor of Law and Social Problems at the Columbia University School of Law during the 1971-72 academic year.

It is difficult to acknowledge the contribution of the many people who have assisted me in this study. The library staff at the English Department of the Environment, the British Information Service in New York City, the School of Law and Department of Urban Planning at Columbia University, and the School of Law and Urban Documents Collection at Washington Uni-

---

[2] D. MANDELKER & R. MONTGOMERY, HOUSING IN AMERICA: PROBLEMS AND PERSPECTIVES (Bobbs-Merrill, 1973), contains a selection of edited readings which present a comprehensive review of housing policies and programs in the United States.

[3] *See* Mandelker, *Strategies in English Slum Clearance and Housing Policies,* 1969 WIS. L. REV. 800.

versity, provided substantial assistance in locating important documentary and other materials. National and local officials in both countries were especially helpful in making their time available for interviews, and many of these officials also read and reviewed several of the chapters of this book. While most of these officials have asked me not to be identified, I would especially like to thank Mr. Aleksander Shlahet, Research Director of the Newark Housing Authority, whose insights on the problems of American public housing were especially valuable, and who made a considerable contribution to my understanding of the intricacies of public housing administration.

Professor Barry Cullingworth[4] of The Planning Exchange, West Central Scotland, and Professor Victor Moore, College of Estate Management, University of Reading, England, both read several of my chapters and contributed many helpful comments and suggestions. Professor Cullingworth has noted the omission of any reference to Scottish housing in my book, and so my book cannot strictly be termed a book on *British* housing subsidies. This omission is intentional, though certainly not meant to slight the importance of Scottish housing, and was prompted by the fact that the housing situation in Scotland has distinctive characteristics, especially as owner-occupation there is only one-half of what it is on the English side of the border. Moreover, although the Scottish program of publicly owned rental housing is in most respects similar to the English, it has enjoyed a somewhat different tradition, especially as rents in Scottish public housing have always been substantially lower than the English. The Scottish program is also operated under separate though substantially similar legislation, and the fair rent principle, to take one example, is not to be applied (at least for the moment) to Scottish public housing.

In the United States, I am especially grateful to Mr. Timothy Naegele, legislative assistant to Senator Edward Brooke; Miss Mary Nenno of the National Association of Housing and Renewal Officials; and Mr. Jeffrey Schwartz, legal counsel to the National Tenants Organization, who all provided valuable information and documentation on the Brooke Amendment and its implementation. The staff of the National Center on Social

---

[4] *See* J.B. CULLINGWORTH, HOUSING AND LOCAL GOVERNMENT IN ENGLAND AND WALES (1966), at that time the leading text on English housing policies and programs.

Welfare Policy and Law in New York City likewise provided important materials dealing with welfare problems in public housing, and with the impact of the Brooke Amendment on welfare recipients. Mr. Harry Schwartz, of Abeles, Schwartz, and Associates, New York City, made available the report of his firm on the impact of the Brooke Amendment on public housing. Professor Leonard Ross of the Columbia University School of Law reviewed the first part of the chapter on rent regulation, while Professor Roger Montgomery of the planning department at the University of California, Berkeley, reviewed both the introductory and concluding chapters. Mrs. Susan B. Rothschild, J.D., Columbia University, 1973, served as my research assistant on this project. My wife read the entire manuscript and proved a very severe editorial critic. Mr. Allen Anthony, a student at the Washington University School of Architecture, prepared the diagrams in Chapters III and VI. The manuscript was typed by Mrs. Gertrude Koch and Mrs. Janis Lapp of the Washington University School of Law, and by staff in the Secretariat at Columbia University School of Law.

Since this book concentrates so heavily on legislative policy, a final comment on legislative history and how legislation is enacted in both countries is in order. Hearings before congressional committees, committee reports on legislation, and congressional debate are the standard sources for the history of congressional legislation in the United States. However, there is no point in debate at which the meaning and purpose of statutory clauses are debated in detail, and while legislative purpose is explained in committee reports this explanation usually is not substantial.

In England, by way of contrast, legislation is subjected to careful, clause-by-clause debate at the committee stage in both houses of Parliament. However, there are no regularly constituted substantive standing committees, as in the United States Congress. Instead, legislation in the House of Commons is assigned to a special committee assembled to consider each bill. This committee usually contains spokesmen on the policy area in question from the opposition party as well as Cabinet representatives from the majority party. These committee debates are reported verbatim, and form an important source of legislative history. They are not included in the Hansard parliamentary reports, however. In the House of Lords, a comparable debate occurs at committee stage, but the House resolves itself into committee to consider legislative bills and these debates are reported verbatim in Hansard. Important substantive debate may also occur when the bills are reported for debate on the floor of both houses, but much debate at this stage is political rather than substantive. English courts, unlike their American counterparts, will not consider legislative history when they are asked to interpret legislation, but I have followed the American judicial tradition and have consulted parliamentary legislative history wherever possible.

Some important differences in customary parliamentary procedure characterized the enactment of the most recent housing legislation which is reported in this book, however. One is that most of the substantive debate occurred in the House of Commons committee, and this debate is primarily relied upon in textual discussion of the law. The House of Lords, which often makes important substantive contributions to legislation, was less in evidence in this instance. One reason may have been that the bill was placed under what is known as a "guillotine" procedure in the House of Commons after debate in the committee stage had gone on for some time. That is, the bill was subjected to a timetable and debate was limited. In the committee stage in the House of Lords debate was limited by agreement. One result of this procedure was that floor debate in both houses was less helpful than usual. In addition, only Cabinet ministers from the majority party were permitted to speak during proceedings in the House of Commons committee, which lasted an unduly long time due to intense Labor Party opposition.

It is a political paradox that, even as housing conditions improve in both England and the United States, housing problems are attacked with greater initiative and housing issues more than ever before receive public attention. This increasingly political debate on housing policy, and the involvement of a wider range of interest groups in the policy-making process, have combined to make decision-making on housing issues more difficult to achieve than ever before. Only the next decades will tell us whether and to what extent we have succeeded in dealing with this all-important public issue.

Daniel R. Mandelker

St. Louis, Missouri
March 7, 1973

Table of Contents

Preface vii

CHAPTER I. INTRODUCTION: PERSPECTIVES ON HOUSING SUBSIDY PROBLEMS 1

    A. The Subsidy Framework: Scope, Availability and Distribution 5
    B. Housing Supply Problems and Housing Subsidies 13
    C. Housing Tenure and Rent Control ... 17
    D. Summary 21

CHAPTER II. POLICY PROBLEMS IN HOUSING SUBSIDY PROGRAMS 25

    A. Housing Standards and Housing Expenditures 27
    B. Housing Costs and Subsidy Strategies . 32
    C. The Impact of Welfare Programs .. 35
    D. National and Local Responsibilities in Housing Subsidy Programs 38
    E. Summary 41

CHAPTER III. PUBLIC HOUSING SUBSIDIES IN THE UNITED STATES 45

    A. An Introduction to the Program 45
    B. The Legislative Structure for Subsidies and Rents 47
        1. The Federal Contribution to Public Housing Costs 47
        2. Rent and Admission Requirements 49
        3. Summary 52
    C. Rent Policies in Public Housing Projects: Herein of Welfare Rents 53
        1. Rent-Setting Practices of Public Housing Agencies 53
        2. The Welfare Rent Problem 58

TABLE OF CONTENTS

    3. Welfare Rents in Public Housing   62
    4. Legal Attacks on Welfare Rents ..   70
  D. Summary 79

CHAPTER IV. THE BROOKE AMENDMENT TO THE PUBLIC HOUSING LAW: MEETING THE CHALLENGE OF COSTS 81
  A. The Roots of the Financial Crisis 83
  B. Congress Responds: The Brooke Amendment—First Round 84
  C. HUD Responds: Regulations Under the 1969 Law 92
    1. Substantive Scope of the Subsidy .. 93
    2. The Impact of the New Rent Limitation 95
    3. The Welfare Rent Problem 98
  D. Reaction: The Welfare Crisis 99
  E. Congress Responds: The Brooke Amendment—Second Round 104
  F. Postscript: Congressional and Administrative Action Since the 1970 Changes 108
  G. Summary 110

CHAPTER V. COUNCIL HOUSING IN ENGLAND 119
  A. An Overview of the English Program . 119
    1. The Economic and Political Background 119
    2. The Legal and Administrative Background 124
  B. Basic Features of the English Program 126
    1. Subsidies, Rents and Rebates 126
    2. Scope of Program, Tenant Admissions, and Restrictions 131
  C. Summary 136

CHAPTER VI. RENT REGULATION IN ENGLAND 139
  A. The Nature of the System 140
    1. An Overview of the Problem ... 140

TABLE OF CONTENTS

    2. The Fair Rent Standard 143
    3. Operation of the System in Practice 154
  B. Conversion of Controlled to Regulated Tenancies: The Problem of Housing Improvement 156
  C. Fair Rents for Local Authority Dwellings 161
    1. Policy Problems 161
    2. The Statutory Fair Rent Formula as Applied to Council Housing .. 166
  D. Summary 170

CHAPTER VII. A "FAIR DEAL FOR HOUSING": THE HOUSING SUBSIDY SYSTEM IN ENGLAND 173
  A. Elements of the Rent Rebate System. 174
    1. The Rent Rebate and the Minimum Rent 175
    2. Rebates to Tenants on Supplementary Benefit 180
    3. Relationship of Rent Rebates to Other Income Support Programs. 183
  B. Housing Subsidies to Local Authorities 188
  C. The Distributive Impact of the Housing Subsidy System 197
  D. Summary 203

CHAPTER VIII. CONCLUSIONS AND PROSPECTS 207
  A. The Quality Level and Rent Determination Problems in Housing Subsidy Programs 208
    1. The Quality Problem 208
    2. The Rent Problem 210
  B. The Direct Housing Allowance and Freedom of Choice Issues 213
    1. The Nature of the Problem 213
    2. The Home Ownership Problem .. 214
    3. The Concentration-Dispersion Issue 216

C. Some Policy Alternatives for Housing
   Subsidy Programs 218
D. Conclusion 226

Selected Bibliography 227

Index 243

Chapter I

INTRODUCTION: PERSPECTIVES ON HOUSING SUBSIDY PROBLEMS

A few years ago, English television decided to dramatize housing issues in that country. "Cathy Come Home," now a legendary television drama, told the dramatic yet tragic story of a family which, initially self-supporting and on the brink of home ownership, fell on sadder days. As the family moved to increasingly inadequate housing, they were finally separated because their last dwelling was too small to hold them all. Thus the title—and the meaning—of their story.

"Cathy Come Home" galvanized English public opinion on housing issues. In response to public outcry over the program, a private national organization was formed to lobby on housing, and housing became, even more than before, a priority political topic. A similar incident occurred in recent American history. Shortly after the Second World War, during Congressional debate over housing legislation, a national mass circulation magazine published a full-page picture of slums in Washington, D. C., with the Capitol building as background. This dramatic portrayal of slum conditions helped consolidate public opinion behind the enactment of new national housing legislation.

Both of these episodes dramatize the public concern over housing that has been typical of England and the United States, for much of this concern has centered on the problems of substandard housing and on housing shortage. In recent years, however, while shortages still remain critical in some areas, they have lost some of the national urgency and prominence which they held earlier. Both countries have also seen a substantial improvement in their housing supply, and many of the worst slums have disappeared. The slums in back of the United States Capitol building, for example, are no longer there, and many of the worst English slums are also gone.

As housing conditions have improved, however, changes have also occurred in the way in which the housing issue has been defined. An initial concern with housing shortages and with physical conditions in slum areas came from a deep public concern over the environmental degradation that slum dwellers experienced in slum areas. But bad housing conditions simply masked deeper economic factors which were instrumental in slum formation. Instead of viewing slums simply as a physical blight which needs to be eradicated, analysts now look deeper and trace the presence of slums to poverty conditions, and to income deficiencies. When incomes are low, they cannot support the maintenance and construction of an adequate housing supply. Homeowners with inadequate incomes are unable to keep their dwellings in good condition. Landlords faced with a group of poor tenants let their buildings deteriorate when they find that they cannot recoup in rents the cost of making necessary repairs and improvements. Routine maintenance at adequate levels becomes impossible, and the condition of the dwelling unit deteriorates as repairs and improvements are repeatedly deferred. Undermaintenance and slum formation results.

More recently, economic stress in the housing market has been aggravated by other factors which have led to an increase in housing costs. One of these factors is a higher public expectation about housing standards, as the public expects housing to meet increasingly higher space and facility requirements. While not so long ago, demands for better housing centered on the provision of minimum sanitary facilities for each dwelling, now even subsidized housing is considered inadequate if air conditioning is not provided in warm climates. Higher standards mean higher housing costs. The more widespread adoption of housing improvement programs has also led to increased costs for existing housing, while extensive slum clearance has increased costs whenever newer housing has replaced older housing that commanded lower prices and rents because it was lower in quality.

These changes in the pattern of housing standards and housing costs might not have caused the dislocation they produced if personal incomes had kept up. What has happened in recent years in both countries, however, is that the rate of increase in housing costs has moved ahead of the rate of increase in personal incomes.[1] Should this pattern continue, and there is no indication that it will soon abate, the housing problem will extend beyond the impoverished slum dweller. Inadequate incomes force many families into substandard and overcrowded housing. But other families, even in income groups substantially above the poverty line, manage to purchase adequate housing only by overspending for the housing they consume, and the overspending group is not a small one. Popular estimates in the United States, for example, suggest that over half of the families in the market for new homes have been priced out of that market under conventional standards that allot one-fourth of family income for housing.[2] Similar tendencies have also appeared in rental housing. The same trends have developed in England, and these estimates may be conservative.

This growing disparity between the housing that the public demands and the personal incomes that are available to pay for

---

[1] In recent years, personal incomes have grown at an average rate of three percent. *United States Housing Needs, 1968-1978,* in REPORT OF THE PRESIDENT'S COMM. ON URBAN HOUSING, TECHNICAL STUDIES, Vol. I, at 20 (1967). At the same time, the average annual increase in the price of new homes, to take one example, has been twice as great. Schechter & Schlefer, *Housing Needs and National Goals,* in PAPERS SUBMITTED TO SUBCOMM. ON HOUSING PANELS, HOUSE COMM. ON BANKING AND CURRENCY, 92nd Cong., 1st Sess., pt. I, at 54 (1971).

As statistical references will be made throughout this book, a word on the use of statistics is in order here. Since most housing statistics are presented in terms of national aggregates which can be misleading, and since statistics grow out of date quickly in any event, most statistical references in this book will be made in terms of qualitative rather than quantitative comparisons. When specific figures are given they will usually be placed in footnotes.

[2] For example, under conventional assumptions which require a home purchase price not to exceed two-and-one-half times annual income, an income of $10,000 would have been required to purchase the median price house in 1969. Yet even by 1978, only 40 percent of all households are estimated to earn this much, and by this time the average cost of housing will have increased even more. REPORT OF THE PRESIDENT'S COMM. ON URBAN HOUSING: A DECENT HOME 42 (1968).

that housing has created an expenditure gap which has increasingly attracted government attention. A variety of strategies can be adopted to deal with this problem. Housing standards could simply be lowered, for example. But if society considers housing standards to be properly set, yet still finds that expenditure for housing at that standard is excessive, then a housing subsidy to meet some of that expenditure may be justified. Of course, the level of housing standards will also affect the level of the subsidy. This is a problem to which we will return later, but at this point we might begin by defining just what a subsidy is. In its most elementary terms, a housing subsidy is nothing more than an income transfer. Some of the housing costs that would be borne in the absence of subsidy by a limited segment of the population are transferred by means of the subsidy to a wider population. If the subsidy is national, the wider public to which the subsidy is transferred is national, and the subsidy is met by the national system of taxation and revenue-raising. From this perspective, a housing subsidy is primarily a social instrument for resource allocation.

While not minimizing the importance of social and related issues as they affect the housing problem, this book will consider the increasingly important economic aspects of housing policy, with the housing subsidy problem as its central theme. Experience with housing subsidies in England and America has been selected for a comparative review of two different answers to the issues that have been, and are still, posed. We will find that both countries share a history of confusion over the role that housing subsidies should play in a strategy for solving housing problems. English subsidies were first adopted in response to an inflation in costs which began after the First World War. American subsidies received an ambiguous charter during the depression of the 1930's, when there was as much concern over providing employment as there was about solving housing problems. As pressures for more extensive subsidies have mounted in the face of unclear tradition, political influence has merged with social pressure to create programs in which basic purposes still remain undefined.

Even more explicitly, this book will concentrate on housing subsidies in the rental sector of the housing market. There are important reasons for this choice. We have already indicated that we will focus on the economic dimension to housing problems, and that economic pressures on housing consumption are most severe among low-income families. They are most in need of subsidy, and their housing need is often inversely related to the amount of income they have available for housing expenditure. Developing a housing subsidy program to meet the needs of low-income families, therefore, has the highest priority and presents the greatest challenge to public policy. But low-income families usually rent, and for this reason housing subsidies have usually been provided for the rental sector of the housing market. This interest in the housing problems of low-income families thus explains our concentration on rental housing subsidy programs.

Within this framework, moreover, we will limit our focus even further. Subsidies for rental housing have historically been provided in both countries in the form of housing units that are publicly owned and managed, and so it is on the provision of subsidized and publicly owned housing that we will concentrate. However, this limitation does not mean that our analysis will only be important to public housing programs. Public housing has been an active program in both countries for a long time. A study of its operation should help us to evaluate, not only this program, but subsidies for privately owned and rented housing, as well as the newly emerging subsidies for homeowners.[3]

In the remainder of this chapter, we will sketch some of the basic issues which must be faced in the development of a housing subsidy policy. Attention will especially be paid to the scope and breadth of the subsidy, and to the method of distribution through which it is made available. This discussion will be followed by an analysis of the relationship of the housing subsidy to and its effect on housing markets, the type of housing that these markets make available, and patterns of tenure within these markets. The next chapter will consider the all-important problem of rents, and the way in which rental policies determine the allocation of responsibility for housing expenditure between tenants and the subsidy program. In the remaining chapters the American and then the English program of housing subsidies will be given detailed consideration.

A. The Subsidy Framework: Scope, Availability and Distribution

One fundamental question must be considered at the very beginning of any discussion of subsidy problems. As we have sug-

---

[3] For discussion see P. MARCUSE, HOMEOWNERSHIP FOR THE POOR: ECONOMIC IMPLICATIONS FOR THE OWNER/OCCUPANT (1971) (U.S. Urban Institute).

gested, American public housing serves a narrowly defined income group, and is limited to the lowest income groups in the population. In order to reduce housing costs for this group, American subsidies to public housing have been very generous. English public housing, on the other hand, is not limited to the poor, but the subsidies available to this housing are much less generous than public housing subsidies in the United States. Until recently, when both countries decided to meet the operating costs of subsidized housing, the Americans met two-thirds of housing costs in public housing through a national subsidy,[4] while the English met only 25 percent.[5]

This important relationship between scope and breadth of subsidy is indicated in Figure 1. American public housing subsidies fit alternative D; the subsidy is generous, but it is limited to comparatively few units in the market. Nationally, only about three or four percent of all rental housing is publicly owned, although the ratio may be twice that in some cities. As a result, while the subsidies have a dramatic effect on the housing costs of those who receive them, the restricted availability of the subsidy both limits its impact on housing consumption and forces eligible households to compete for a limited number of subsidized housing vacancies. Extensive social stratification is another consequence of the American public housing subsidy structure. Since these subsidies are limited to the very poor, they place an economically stratified population in the housing projects. While initially this population was an upwardly mobile group—a submerged middle class—the characteristics of the public housing population have changed radically since the Second World War. Increasingly, the projects have been filled with welfare families, and with marginal workers who have not shared in the economic advance enjoyed by most of the population.

---

[4] F. DE LEEUW & S.H. LEAMAN, THE SECTION 23 LEASING PROGRAM 24 (1971) (U.S. Urban Institute).

[5] Minutes of Evidence Taken Before Subcomm. B of the House of Commons Estimates Comm., Sess. 1968-69, Vol. II, at 89, 137.

FIGURE 1. ALTERNATIVE HOUSING SUBSIDY PATTERNS BASED ON SCOPE AND BREADTH OF SUBSIDY

	Scope of Subsidy	
Breadth of Subsidy	**Limited**	**Substantial**
Broad	A. The housing subsidy is limited and is available to a high proportion of the population.	B. The housing subsidy is substantial and is available to a high proportion of the population.
Narrow	C. The housing subsidy is limited and is confined to a small proportion of the population.	D. The housing subsidy is substantial and is confined to a small proportion of the population.

Much of the concern about American public housing has been a reaction to these trends. Economic—and racial—segregation in the projects has aggravated management problems and, in extreme cases, has led to total breakdown. In England, on the other hand, social concern over the program has been exactly the reverse. English housing subsidy policy fits alternative A in Figure 1; the subsidy is limited but is available to a high proportion of housing units in the rental housing market. Two-thirds of all rental housing in England is publicly owned. The impact of the subsidy on the housing market is magnified but, as the subsidy is not as generous, its effect on the housing costs of those who receive it is more limited. Since no income qualification is placed on admission to the projects, the tenants living in public housing have about the same income distribution as tenants living in private rental housing, although all tenants generally have lower incomes than owner-occupiers.[6] While persons receiving welfare assistance also make up a substantial portion of English public housing tenants, most of these are elderly. Unlike the United States, chronic unemployment has not been a problem in England, and incomes of tenants in public housing have tended to rise with the incomes of the rest of the population, providing a sounder economic base for the program.

---

[6] *Id.*, at 960.

At the same time, concern has been expressed that the wide availability of English housing subsidies has extended its benefits to tenants who could afford to pay unsubsidized rents. Until legislation passed in 1972 made rebates mandatory, English housing authorities were encouraged but not required to adopt a system of rent rebates for their poorest tenants.[7] This advice was not always followed. Some authorities would simply keep rents low generally in order to avoid a rebate program.

What has happened in recent years is that housing subsidy policies in both countries have, to some extent, crossed paths. Beginning in 1961, the United States adopted subsidies applicable to private rental housing which followed the English system. On each unit, the subsidy was less, but eligibility was extended by substantially raising the qualifying income limits.[8] As in England, contentions have been made that the subsidy is so wide that problems of selection have occurred,[9] although arguments that income limits are too high have not yet been prominent. On the other hand, legislation in England has now substantially altered that program. Admission is still open, but the legislation requires rebates, yet limits them to lower income groups. Eligibility for rebate disappears rather quickly as incomes rise above welfare budget levels.

These changes in housing subsidy policy in the two countries suggest additional reasons for comparison. Will narrowing the English subsidy lead to the kind of social and economic stratification that has been experienced in the American public housing program? An examination of the American public housing subsidy experience may provide some answers to this question. Would broadening the American subsidy lead to the problems of selection and distribution that the English have experienced? Again, an examination of the English housing subsidy may provide some insight on this problem.

Questions like these are all the more important to pose in view of growing pressures in both countries for a more general social strategy which would alleviate poverty through a public guarantee of a minimum income. In England, for example, the introduction

---

[7] This policy was restated in a recent WHITE PAPER, THE HOUSING PROGRAMME 1965 TO 1970, CMND. NO. 2838 at par. 41 (1965).

[8] *See* A DECENT HOME, *supra* note 2, at 68-9.

[9] *See* Kummerfield, *The Housing Subsidy System*, in PAPERS SUBMITTED TO SUBCOMM. ON HOUSING PANELS, *supra* note 1, at 451.

of a minimum income guarantee in the form of a negative income tax now seems imminent.[10] Minimum income guarantees are an alternative to a specific housing subsidy, since presumably the minimum income level will be set high enough to allow recipients to rent and purchase adequate housing in good condition. We will not look in detail at all of the issues which a choice between a more specific housing subsidy and a more general income subsidy present. But we can acquire some notion of the magnitude of the housing support element of a guaranteed income program by looking closely at the housing subsidies that are now available. Moreover, we already have a minimum income support program in the form of public welfare assistance. Welfare programs support housing as well as other family expenditures, giving rise to problems of coordination with housing subsidies. These problems are similar to those that would arise under a more expanded program of income support, and will be considered here.

Closely tied to decisions affecting the scope and availability of housing subsidies are related issues concerning the method through which the subsidy is distributed. In the United States and in England, housing subsidies are presently distributed by an intermediary that lies between the subsidy and the housing consumer, and in both countries this intermediary has been a designated local government agency. This situation has been changed in England to the extent that tenants in private rental housing now receive a housing allowance which they may use to help pay the rent for their housing. But even this housing "allowance" is distributed by the local government authority, and is available only so long as the tenant stays in the rather restricted private rental market. So the English housing allowance is not that much of an innovation.

There are differences, however, in the governmental network through which the housing subsidy is distributed. In England, any general purpose local authority may and most do provide public housing units. Both rural and urban governments are in the program, and so the public housing network is nationwide. More public housing per capita tends to be provided in the older and larger cities, but the public housing program is not limited to the inner cities of metropolitan areas as it is in much of the

---

[10] *See* Brown, *Negative Income Tax and the Incentive to Work*, 20 NEW SOCIETY, 461 (1972). On American possibilities see Holden, *The Nation's Income Maintenance Policies*, 15 AMER. BEHAVIORAL SCIENTIST 665 (1972).

United States.[11] In this country, the public housing function has been entrusted to special purpose local government authorities that usually have no other function. These authorities are almost always urban, and their boundaries coincide with the boundaries of the parent municipalities that create them.

Using an intermediary such as a public housing agency to distribute housing subsidies has important consequences for those who receive the subsidy.[12] When an intermediary such as a public housing agency has the responsibility for distributing the subsidy, then the intermediary and not the housing consumer decides where the subsidized housing will be located. For example, mobility patterns will be affected by the availability of housing units at costs that those seeking housing can afford. But if it is the housing agency that determines locations, families in the public sector will, to this extent, have their housing location choices made for them.[13] For example, federal directives in the United States now dictate a location pattern which is aimed at breaking up the concentration of public housing in the ghetto areas of inner cities.[14] Note also that when an intermediary, such as a public housing agency, is selected to distribute housing subsidies, it is this agency which makes critical decisions on such important questions as costs, rentals, and admission policies. Some of this responsibility may be centered in the national agency responsible

---

[11] The difference lies partly in differences in the legal character and distribution of local government units in the two countries. In England, every part of the country is organized into what Americans would call an incorporated local governmental unit of some type. Consequently, since all local governments may build public housing, all areas of the country may be available for public housing construction. Differences in program size and initiative do make for differences in public housing locations, however. For example, suburban metropolitan local governments, like their American counterparts, have small public housing programs.

In the United States, areas not within the jurisdiction of some incorporated local government unit fall under the control of county governments. Counties may be given the authority to create public housing agencies, but few American counties have done so. Public housing may be built within the area of incorporated municipalities only if the municipality chooses to create a public housing agency. Within metropolitan areas, these agencies have largely been created by inner cities which have large minority populations and extensive areas of substandard housing.

[12] For a discussion of these problems in the American setting see Frieden, *Improving Federal Housing Subsidies: Summary Report*, in PAPERS SUBMITTED TO SUBCOMM. ON HOUSING PANELS, *supra* note 1, at 473.

[13] For an exploratory cross-national comparison see J.B. CULLINGWORTH, HOUSING AND LABOR MOBILITY (1969).

[14] *See* 37 FED. REG. 203 (1972).

for distributing the subsidy rather than the local agency which administers the program. Nevertheless, the decision-making responsibility in these important areas of the program still resides in the public sector.

The local housing authority charged with the administration of the program must also make important distributional decisions affecting the scope and generosity of the subsidy and the extent to which it is available. Since housing expectations have been rising faster than the income levels needed to support them, the pool of eligibles who are entitled to a subsidy tends to be larger than the subsidies that are available to distribute. Even in the United States, where the public housing subsidy is limited to a comparatively narrow population group, the program has never been large enough to support more than a small proportion of those who are eligible to enter it. Selections must then be made from the pool of potential eligibles, and the method used to make this selection carries with it important policy judgments on such important social values as privacy and freedom of choice. As the housing problem is increasingly defined in terms of income deficiency, the most important eligibility determinant is income, and the ability of income in relation to family size to support what is considered to be a reasonable housing expenditure.

At this point, the nature of the distribution method which is used in the subsidy system gains added significance. Since the subsidy is attached to housing units owned and managed by local authorities, entitlement to the subsidy requires admission to the project. This decision on entry is crucial, and the amount of discretion which the agency is permitted to exercise when making this selection becomes critical. While housing need would seem to be the most important factor to be considered in making this decision, the fact that most eligible applicants are in serious housing need will mean that other tests will also have to be used. Depending on the test selected, the housing agency may be able to admit only the most suitable candidates from the pool of eligibles, and this selection process may not only bias the population in the projects themselves, but the characteristics of those eligibles who are not admitted and who must find housing in the private market. For example, the tendency of the English authorities to favor long-term residents has often excluded immigrant families from public housing, even though these families may have more severe housing problems.

Critics of the existing system have pointed out these practices, and have urged that a direct subsidy to eligible recipients in the form of a housing allowance would avoid these objections.[15] (A housing allowance is simply a more limited alternative to a more expansive minimum income guarantee.) While eligibility for the subsidy would still require a means test, since it would be based on income, they argue that direct distribution of a housing allowance would permit greater freedom on the part of recipients in their choice of housing, greater mobility among subsidy recipients, and a more positive impact on housing conditions. The last conclusion follows, so the argument runs, because the housing subsidy will not be limited to the publicly owned sector, but will be distributed to individuals throughout the housing market. As those receiving the subsidy would be able to pay more for the housing they obtain, they will be able to purchase better housing than what they previously had and all housing will be upgraded.

This argument is attractive, and since it is gaining in popular acceptance it deserves consideration here. One problem is that it does not consider some of the political consequences of a direct housing allowance. Limitation of the subsidy to specified subsidized dwelling units restricts it to those units that are available at any one time, and so total spending for the subsidy can be controlled. Direct distribution of the subsidy would automatically make eligible all those who are entitled to it, once the authority of the housing agency to select from competing applicants has been eliminated. Political pressure to expand the scope of the subsidy to meet housing needs fully may then lead to counter-pressures to curtail the program. This has been the experience in the American welfare system, and it should not be ignored.

Distribution of housing subsidies directly to the recipient, however, should open up freedom of choice in the housing market, at least in theory. Whether that choice is more apparent than real is another question, and will depend on the character, location, and age of the housing stock. It will also depend on the system of housing tenure, and on the distribution of housing units among those tenures, especially as between rental and owner-occupied housing. For example, if the age of the housing supply is weighted on the older side, the quality of housing will generally

---

[15] See Frieden, *supra* note 12.

be lower and so will prices and rents. Housing subsidies will go further, but the ability of the direct payment subsidy system to affect the quality of the housing stock will depend on the willingness of owners to upgrade and maintain the housing supply. Some new housing will be supplied in any event, and the impact of this new construction must also be considered.

Likewise, the ability of a direct payment subsidy to affect housing conditions will depend on what housing tenures are available on the market. Again, if a substantial amount of the housing supply is owner-occupied, subsidy recipients will be restricted to rental housing unless some method can be found to move them into the owner-occupied sector. Opportunities for making this move would seem to be restricted in view of the fact that most of these recipients will come from lower income groups, and may not have the equity or the income necessary to sustain the payments required for home ownership, even with the subsidy.

We will return later to a more detailed consideration of the housing allowance alternative to existing housing subsidy programs. At this point, these observations on the possible impact of a direct housing allowance suggest other factors which must be considered in evaluating the existing housing subsidies which are distributed through governmental agencies. We have just noted that the impact of a housing allowance on the market will depend directly on the quality and character of the housing that happens to be in that market at any one time. Some of the same comments apply to a housing subsidy that is governmentally distributed, and we will now turn to an examination of this aspect of the housing subsidy problem.

B. Housing Supply Problems and Housing Subsidies

Different sets of public strategies can be adopted toward the maintenance and provision of the housing supply, and each of these strategies will have different effects on housing costs and quality, and on the scope and impact of the housing subsidy program. Some appreciation of the nature of public concern over housing strategies can be obtained by returning briefly to the examples we used at the beginning of this chapter. They indicate that both America and England have demonstrated a concern over housing conditions and the programs that are needed to improve them. But each country has historically approached this problem from a different perspective.

For example, in the United States the early emphasis was on remedial action to improve substandard housing.[16] At first through the early tenement house laws, and more lately through the widespread adoption and enforcement of housing codes, the hope was that local governments would be able to upgrade the quality of the existing housing supply through corrective regulation. In England, on the other hand, housing shortages have been uppermost as a housing concern.[17] National housing policy has historically been oriented toward measures which alleviate housing shortage by stimulating new construction, which in turn produces an improvement in housing conditions. Especially in the postwar years, electoral campaigns have been fought over national housing programs which have been expressed as production targets for the construction of new housing.[18]

What is of considerable interest, within the framework of this study, is that national priorities in both countries have been changed. In the United States, housing code enforcement programs have encountered severe difficulties, and interest in slum abatement has diminished. Housing problems have increasingly been stated in terms of housing shortage, and the ability of housing production to meet these needs. Indeed, debate over housing in recent years has been dominated by the 1968 finding, publicized by a prestigious Presidential committee, that America needed 26 million new units in the next decade.[19] Housing improvement is accepted as a method of meeting these housing needs, but the legal difficulties and social and economic costs which close pursuit of a rehabilitation program would entail have not been rigorously considered.

On the other hand, the English, having concluded that their housing shortage has been eliminated, recently redirected much of their housing effort toward improvement efforts in what the

---

[16] This theme is carefully elaborated in L.M. FRIEDMAN, GOVERNMENT AND SLUM HOUSING: A CENTURY OF FRUSTRATION (1968) (American experience).

[17] D.V. DONNISON, THE GOVERNMENT OF HOUSING ch. 1 (1967).

[18] See, e.g., THE HOUSING PROGRAMME 1965 TO 1970, CMND. NO. 2838 (1965) (Labor government).

[19] See A DECENT HOME, supra note 2, at 40. For a critique of this estimate see Renshaw, *The Demand for Housing in the Mid-1970's*, 47 LAND ECON. 249 (1971).

English call their "twilight," or older residential areas.[20] Much recent English legislation, including an important new housing act in 1969, has been directed toward this objective.[21]

The important point to make about these historical trends is that the type of policy that is selected for dealing with the housing supply can have an important bearing on housing subsidy programs.[22] While the observation may oversimplify, housing programs that emphasize housing improvement over new construction tend to retain older units in the housing supply longer. We noted earlier that weighting the housing supply on the older side will reduce the price, rents, and quality of the housing that is available. Now we should note that these characteristics of the housing supply are very much affected by the public strategy that is selected for housing programs.

At the same time, decisions about housing subsidies will also affect housing quality and cost. These decisions are extremely important. For example, a decision could be taken to subsidize only housing units that are in a socially acceptable condition. This decision could be expected to have a beneficial impact on housing improvement programs, but some owners might simply elect to stay out of the subsidy system altogether. As an alternative, housing condition could be taken into account when subsidies are set and subsidies reduced for unsatisfactory dwellings. But this approach would require a reduction in rents or prices proportionate to the degree of disrepair, unless the market can be expected to react to lower subsidies by lowering its price and rent levels. Uncertainty about this kind of market response would probably lead to a system of rent control, which is not generally in effect in the United States, but which has been imposed nationwide in England. The impact of these controls will be considered shortly.

In view of these observations, it is of some interest that the need for subsidy in both countries was at first recognized only in the case of new construction. The comparable need to subsidize

---

[20] This change in policy has been documented in Des Wilson, *How Labour Lost its Grip (Housing)*, 81 NEW STATESMAN 799 (1971), where it is much criticized. Wilson's analysis is corroborated by testimony of government officials before a select Parliamentary committee. See Minutes of Evidence, *supra* note 5, at 159-62.

[21] *See* Housing Act, 1969, ch. 23.

[22] *See* W.G. GRIGSBY, HOUSING MARKETS AND PUBLIC POLICY 283-335 (1963).

the costs of housing improvement came much later. Yet housing improvement requires the investment of new capital in the dwelling, and in many cases rents must go up to recoup these costs unless a subsidy is available.

More recently, improved and rehabilitated housing has been brought within the subsidy system. Under one approach, the housing subsidies that are generally made available throughout the housing market are simply utilized to reduce the rents of rehabilitated dwellings. For example, American subsidies for privately owned rental dwellings are available for rehabilitated units.[23] Some existing housing is also taken into the English publicly owned housing supply, and subsidies for existing housing units are also made available in the American public housing program.[24] Nevertheless, this housing forms only a small portion of public housing in each country, and extensive rehabilitation of existing housing that is taken into the program is not a major emphasis. In addition to the fact that housing subsidies in the direct subsidy programs are to some extent made available for existing housing, both countries also have related programs which provide direct grants and, in the United States, loans for housing improvement. To the extent that these direct grants and loans provide subsidies for improvement costs, they should be considered a part of the housing subsidy system.

Another factor having an important bearing on cost and quality levels are the standards to whom both the new and rehabilitated dwelling units must comply. For example, rehabilitation of existing housing will tend to raise the quality and thus the cost of housing units in the market. But the degree to which costs are raised will be determined by the standards which are adopted for housing improvement. The same comment applies to new construction.

Housing standards are determined in a variety of ways. In the United States, local housing maintenance codes set the standards for housing improvement, but the federal housing statute has also contained additional standards applicable to the federal loan and grant programs.[25] Legislation in England likewise indicates the kinds of improvements for which housing improvement

---

[23] 12 U.S.C. § 17122-1 (1970).
[24] Unit costs in this segment of public housing are less than in newly constructed units. F. DE LEEUW & S.H. LEAMAN, *supra* note 4.
[25] 42 U.S.C. § 1466 (1970).

grants will be given.[26] Local building and related codes in the United States, and a national code in England, determine the standards to be applied to new construction. In addition, when rehabilitated or newly constructed units are taken into the subsidy program, the question arises whether separate quality standards should be applied to these dwellings within the subsidy program, as an alternative to those standards which are usually applicable.

This issue has many dimensions, and is tied very closely to the nature of the housing subsidy that is made available. American and English subsidies have been tied to the capital cost of subsidized housing, and the statutes enacting the housing program have independently set housing standards which are applicable only to subsidized housing.[27] This method controls the amount of the subsidy by controlling the cost of the housing that is made available. Collateral problems may then arise if the standards applied to subsidized housing affect other objectives. In America, for example, cost limitations in the federal housing subsidy programs have made it difficult to build on inner city sites. In England, cost standards have been calibrated so that they make it difficult to build one- and two-bedroom units, even though this type of unit may be required to fulfill housing needs.

C. Housing Tenure and Rent Control

Another important issue to be faced when developing criteria for housing subsidy programs is the relationship of the subsidy to housing markets and to housing tenure patterns. Housing economists tend to divide the housing market into a series of submarkets, and one of the most important divisions lies between the rental housing market, on the one hand, and the home ownership market on the other. We have already indicated that the ability of housing subsidy recipients to move between rental and home ownership is one measure of freedom of choice within the housing system. Now we need to consider the extent to which the nature of the subsidy system will affect this choice.

In both countries, owner occupancy has been on the increase, and presently about half of all dwellings in England are privately owned, while in America the proportion is around 65 percent. Yet we have noted that housing subsidies have historically been

---
[26] Housing Act, 1969, pt. I.
[27] E.g., 42 U.S.C. § 1415(5) (1970).

limited to the rental sector. Of course, indirect public subsidies for home ownership have been available for some time in both countries, as homeowners buying homes on mortgage have been able to deduct the interest charges on their mortgage from their income tax. These indirect subsidies to home ownership have been substantial, but the indirect interest deduction subsidy has not materially benefited low-income groups. Either low-income families cannot afford to own housing, or they have little or no income against which the interest deduction can be offset.

Both countries now also have direct subsidies for home ownership which are explicitly directed to low- and moderate-income families. In each case, the subsidy takes the form of interest payments to the mortgagee which reduce the interest cost of home purchase to the home buyer. We should also note that welfare benefits in both countries are payable to welfare recipients who happen to own, or are buying, homes. Even so, the English have decided to confine to renters their new housing subsidy which is payable directly to individuals.

In addition, while direct subsidies have largely been restricted to rental housing, the subsidies for rehabilitation which were outlined earlier have primarily been used by homeowners. This situation has largely been the result of administrative practice, for the rehabilitation subsidies in both countries have legally been available both to owner-occupiers and to owners of housing which is rented out. In England, however, landlords have been reluctant to take improvement grants for their housing, partly because the grant only meets half the cost of their outlay and the statutory recovery rate on this amount is limited.[28] In the United States, federal assistance for local housing improvement programs has largely been limited to areas of home ownership for much the same reason, while many owners of rental housing have been excluded from the program because of statutory limitations on income.[29] The result is that rehabilitation subsidies are generally not available to rental housing at the same time that rental housing makes up the larger share of the subsidized housing supply. This pattern does not provide the best subsidy match.

Since direct housing subsidies are so largely confined to rental housing, subsidy policy must also consider the impact which these

---

[28] Housing Act, 1969, ch. 33, pts. I, III.
[29] Only owner-occupiers are entitled to grants. 42 U.S.C. § 1466 (1970). For the loan provision see 42 U.S.C. § 1452b (1970).

subsidies have on the overall level of housing rents. Here the legal situation in the two countries differs, for England has had some form of rent control since the First World War. Since rents on the American private market are usually not controlled, the separate existence of a subsidized rental sector has led to wide disparities in the rents paid by families of similar income for similar accommodations. For example, rents in public housing are set at 25 percent of income, while in privately owned but federally subsidized private housing rents are controlled by a statutory formula that requires a comparable payment.[30] Rents tend to be substantially lower in this housing as well because statutory cost limitations hold rents down, and because a large portion of the principal and interest payments on this housing is met by the federal subsidy. To make one comparison, rents paid by welfare recipients in public housing may be as much as 30 to 50 percent below the rents paid for welfare recipients on the private, unsubsidized market.

These problems would be aggravated if widespread housing allowances paid directly to tenants were to be made available as an alternative to the present system of housing subsidies to public agencies and to private developers. Without rent control, much of the subsidy will be dissipated by rent increases brought about by the increase in housing demand which the housing allowance creates. While the studies done on the problem can only estimate the impact, they suggest that as much as one-half of any housing allowance paid to individual housing consumers will be absorbed by rent increases.[31] In other words, a shift to a direct system of housing allowances would remove some of the rigidities of the present system, under which housing subsidies are distributed through intermediary public agencies and private owners. But it would carry its own inefficiencies as well, and a loss of subsidy on the scale indicated cannot be tolerated.

In England, on the other hand, a long history of rent control has brought public control of rental housing to a degree not experienced in the United States. All but the very small portion of the rental housing market which is available at the highest rents

---

[30] For a case refusing judicial review of rent increases approved by the federal agency see Hahn v. Gottlieb, 430 F.2d 1243 (1st Cir. 1970).

[31] *See* F. DE LEEUW & N.F. EKANEN, THE SUPPLY OF RENTAL HOUSING (1971), also reported in de Leeuw & Ekanen, *The Supply of Rental Housing*, 61 AMER. ECON. REV. 806 (1971).

is rent-controlled to some degree. These rent control systems confer a sizeable subsidy on tenant families, apart from the direct subsidy system, because they limit rents to levels considerably below what landlords could charge in a free market. Moreover, due to the structure of the rent control law, rents charged will differ with the size of the unit, the time at which it came under control, and the length of time the tenant has been living in the unit. Often the only explanation for differences in rent paid can be found in the impact which the rent control legislation has had on the dwelling.[32]

Rent controls of long standing, together with other economic disincentives, have substantially curtailed investment in rental housing in England. Perhaps the most important of these other disincentives is the failure of the English income tax law to allow landlords a deduction from taxable income for depreciation on the rental housing they own. This deduction is available in the United States.[33] Since the depreciation deduction is based on an assumed amount which represents a reserve against replacement, and does not require a cash outlay, the unavailability of this deduction is a severe disincentive to the ownership of rental housing. In addition, interest on mortgages entered into to buy rental housing is not deductible from income tax, as it is in America.

As a result, there has virtually been no new construction of rental housing in England in recent decades, except (to a very limited extent) in the small and uncontrolled luxury market. Much rent-controlled housing is old, and a good portion of it is subject to clearance and demolition. Continuing construction of subsidized housing by local authorities has led at the same time to a situation in which more than one-half of all rental housing is publicly owned in England, and this proportion is likely to increase as private rental housing ages and is not replaced. Similar problems may have to be faced in the United States. Even though construction for the private rental market is strong in suburban and other good quality residential areas, recent studies testify to

---

[32] For the situation in a typical inner London borough see Centre for Urban Studies, *Report on the Housing Rents Study*, in HOUSING IN CAMDEN, Vol. II, at 3 (1969).

[33] For discussion see R.E. Slitor, *The Federal Income Tax in Relation to Housing* (Research Rep. No. 5, National Comm'n on Urban Problems, 1968).

the accelerating abandonment of privately owned rental housing in the inner cities.[34]

What we have discovered, then, is that direct housing subsidies have most generally been available in the rental sector of the housing market, but that this sector is the least healthy portion of that market and is subject to severe economic stress, particularly in England. Any subsidy program for rental housing will have to take these factors into account. At one extreme, for example, the disappearance of the private landlord as a supplier of housing could lead to the complete public take-over of the rental market, unless some alternative form of quasi-public or cooperative ownership could be developed. So far, experiments in this direction have not been noticeably successful.

We can only hint at a solution to these problems in these pages, for the issues are difficult to face and have not received as much public attention in either country as they deserve. Yet rental housing cannot be allowed to disappear completely, for home ownership is beyond the reach of many families and in many circumstances is not the most desirable housing solution. What is hoped is that this book will provide some insight into the rental housing issue, as well as the problems arising in subsidy systems which make housing available at affordable rents for those who need financial assistance in securing adequate accommodation.

D. Summary

This book is intended as an analysis of the legal and institutional problems that arise in the development of housing subsidy systems, and in this chapter we began our analysis of these problems by examining the different assumptions about the scope and breadth of a subsidy which underlie the English and American programs. These assumptions are crucial to the character and effect of a subsidy system, a point well illustrated by our analysis of English and American public housing, on which we have concentrated. For example, while the English have made a small subsidy contribution to each public housing unit, their public housing has been more widely available and there has been no

---

[34] On New York City, see G. STERNLIEB, THE URBAN HOUSING DILEMMA: THE DYNAMICS OF NEW YORK CITY'S RENT CONTROLLED HOUSING (1970). See generally, NATIONAL URBAN LEAGUE, THE NATIONAL SURVEY OF HOUSING ABANDONMENT (1971).

income limit on entry. As a result, English public housing has served a wider income group than the American, there has been little stratification within the projects, and tenant rents have been sufficient to support project costs and expenses.

In the United States, on the other hand, while the subsidy contribution to each public housing unit is much greater, this housing has by statute been limited to the lowest income groups in the population. They have not shared in the general increase in personal incomes, and so tenant rents have not been sufficient to support project operations. Social, economic, and racial stratification within public projects has also led to other severe management problems, and in some cases to total breakdown.

Recent trends in both countries suggest that their housing subsidy policies may be moving closer together. The English have taken legislative steps to narrow eligibility for subsidy payments, while at the same time eligibility for admission to public housing remains unrestricted. In the United States there is considerable interest in improving the social and economic mix within subsidized housing projects, and even in a wider housing allowance which would be made directly available to recipients. As policies in the two countries coalesce, an analysis of the subsidy experience in each country may well point the way to common problems and approaches.

In the balance of this chapter we examined some of the other major issues to be faced in a subsidy program, such as the method of subsidy distribution, and the impact which housing costs and quality levels can have on subsidy support. We were also interested in the relationship between types of housing tenure and subsidy programs. Home ownership has been growing at the same time that subsidy policy has emphasized rental housing. Yet weaknesses in the rental market, especially in England, suggest that severe stresses have and will continue to develop in this sector, especially in rental housing that is privately owned. Subsidy policy, therefore, will have to be concerned about the effect it has on owning or renting as the preferred type of housing pattern.

In the next chapter we turn to some of the decisions about the structure of a housing subsidy that have to be made within the subsidy program. We will especially be concerned with decisions about rents and rent levels, and with the effect that these decisions have on the distribution of housing expenditure between the occupant of subsidized dwelling and the subsidy system. The issues may appear largely technical, but we shall see that they require highly important policy decisions on income distribution, and on what should be considered as appropriate levels of housing expenditure.

Chapter II

POLICY PROBLEMS IN HOUSING SUBSIDY PROGRAMS

Consumers spend more on housing than on any other item in their personal budget, yet they have very little influence over many of the elements that enter into housing costs. As a result, subsidy programs face real dilemmas. If they fully subsidize consumer income at levels which permit tenants to rent adequate housing, they may face insupportable subsidy burdens if costs continue to mount. On the other hand, cost subsidies may not provide housing at rents that tenants can afford, if they do not bring rents down to low enough levels.

These comments bring us back to our previous chapter, in which we noted that housing subsidy programs vary in the degree to which they subsidize housing expenditure and housing need. Now we need to examine this problem from the point of view of the housing consumer. Housing expenditure for rental housing is usually expressed in the form of a rent/income ratio, a statement of housing outlay in which the rent paid is given as a percentage of income. Subsidy needs can be determined in relation to this ratio, for arguably any housing cost which the tenant cannot meet at an acceptable rent/income level should be met by the subsidy system. While the subsidy can take the form either of an income or a cost supplement, English and American subsidy programs have traditionally subsidized costs. With this tradition in mind, we need to review the options that are available when costs are subsidized, and how this subsidy can be translated into rents which fall within a rent/income ratio that society finds acceptable.

This consideration of rent/income ratios, and of the strategies through which housing expenditure is subsidized in the housing program, leads us on to consider the impact on housing subsidies of a related program of income support, the welfare system. Many tenants in publicly owned housing also receive welfare payments. These payments include a budgeted amount for housing, which meets the share of the rent which the tenant would ordinarily pay out of his own income. Welfare budgets for housing must thus be coordinated with the subsidy structure, so that all tenants receiving subsidized rents are treated in a similar fashion. Since the welfare system differs from the housing subsidy system in its method of administration, however, we will find that problems of coordination have arisen which have been difficult to resolve.

Finally, another issue to be faced in evaluating the impact of housing subsidies on income is to consider how subsidy costs are financed. This inquiry leads us into a consideration of the division of governmental responsibility within the housing subsidy system itself, for we have already noted that the national government in both countries meets the largest share of subsidy costs, while the actual administration and management of the program is in the hands of local housing agencies. Just how these financial costs and administrative responsibilities are allocated has an important bearing on the economic impact of the program. To the extent that the subsidy burden is shifted downward to the local level, for example, recipients of the subsidy are taxed to pay their own subsidy. Understandably, considerable intergovernmental tension has arisen over the way in which the housing program distributes these economic burdens and administrative responsibilities, and we need to look closely at the way in which the issues have been resolved through the political and legislative process.

A. Housing Standards and Housing Expenditures

We should begin with the housing expenditure issue, for one of the first problems to be faced in any housing subsidy program is to find agreement on the appropriate level of housing expenditure. How much rent is generated in subsidized housing depends on two factors, the incomes of tenants admitted to the projects, and the proportion of income which they are required to pay toward the rental cost of their housing unit. While rental income can of course be increased by increasing the number of tenants who need little or no subsidy, the amount of rent to be paid by those tenants needing a subsidy is always a critical issue. We will therefore begin with a discussion of the rent/income ratio, which defines the extent to which tenants in the housing program will need to receive subsidy support.

Estimating rent/income ratios presents formidable problems, however. On the income side, difficult problems are presented in determining how much of the tenant's income should be applied to his housing costs. To take one example, effective disposable income varies with size of family. Most family budget specialists would argue that appropriate adjustments should be made for differences in family size when determining how much of its income a family should set aside for housing purposes. Problems also arise in determining just what expenses should be attributed to housing costs, in addition to the basic net rent. Property taxes and the cost of repairs and utilities are additional costs associated with housing which also deserve consideration. Which of these additional costs should be included is a matter of judgment, however. We have not included repairs, for example. Maintenance on rental property available to lower income groups is often deferred and, when undertaken, is frequently subsidized by government loans and grants. This leaves utilities and taxes.

Whether utility costs should properly be considered a part of housing expenditure is very much wrapped up with the question of housing standards, since if housing standards differ, utility expenditures will differ too. For example, renting a house with central heating is usually more expensive than renting a house without it. Levels of housing standard also determine the quantity and quality of housing that housing expenditures buy. Equal expenditures for housing are not comparable if they do not purchase the same amount of housing "service."

Our analysis of rent/income ratios ought to begin, then, with the standards problem, and when we look at housing standards in the two countries we can begin with this central observation: extensive slums of the American variety, in which environmental conditions have been inhumanly degraded, are rare in England, yet housing standards in the United States are much higher. Especially is this true of space standards, for the average American home is at least 50 percent larger than its English counterpart.[1] In addition, American houses are better equipped,[2] and if statistics for inner London are any guide, there are even serious shortages of dwellings with self-contained sanitary and cooking facilities on the English scene.[3] Substantial slums do remain in both countries, but the proportion of this housing in the total housing supply has been declining, and is probably no greater than ten percent in either place.[4] Nevertheless,

---

[1] COLIN BUCHANAN & PARTNERS, THE PROSPECT FOR HOUSING 70 (1971). The American figures are 1480 square feet as of 1967, the English, 900 square feet as of 1969. Differences in space standards, and in the provision of household facilities, make costs of construction difficult to compare. Average costs for a two-bedroom publicly owned apartment in London ran between $20,000 and $22,500 in mid-1971, about one-third less than the cost of a comparable unit in New York City, but only slightly less than the cost of a comparable unit in Kansas City. Many housing experts have commented to the author that the United States is the only country in the industrialized west in which housing space standards have improved since the Second World War.

[2] UNITED NATIONS, THE HOUSING SITUATION AND PERSPECTIVES FOR THE LONG-TERM HOUSING REQUIREMENTS IN EUROPEAN COUNTRIES 55 (1968). For example, practically all American urban dwellings have a fixed bath or shower, but only about three-fourths of English urban dwellings have such facilities.

[3] Camden is an inner London borough which ranges from the upper middle-class housing of Hampstead Village to the slums of St. Pancras. Careful analysis of housing conditions in the borough indicate that only two out of five households in the private sector have a fully self-contained home which contains its own cooking and sanitation facilities. Centre for Urban Studies, *Report on the Housing Rents Study*, in HOUSING IN CAMDEN, Vol. II, at 33 (1968). A similar survey in New York City found that only a small number of dwellings presently do not have their own sanitary facilities. RENTAL HOUSING IN NEW YORK CITY: CONFRONTING THE CRISIS, Vol. I, at 3 (I.S. Lowry ed. 1970).

[4] Unfortunately, the 1970 American housing census made no attempt to determine whether housing was dilapidated, as did earlier surveys. But a 1968 sample census indicated that about nine percent of all housing was substandard, and that most of these units also lacked plumbing facilities. U.S. DEP'T OF COMMERCE, BUREAU OF THE CENSUS, HOUSING UNITS BY PLUMBING FACILITIES AND CONDITIONS IN THE UNITED STATES, AUGUST, 1968 (Series H-121, No. 17, 1970). A survey of English housing conditions undertaken in 1971 indicated a modest decline in substandard housing. *See Housing*, 20 NEW SOCIETY 413 (1972).

these figures can be misleading. In both countries, housing conditions are undoubtedly more severe in the older cities, and in the United States there is every indication that urban housing may be much worse than aggregate statistics indicate.[5] These statistics suggest that English housing expenditure needs to be considered in view of the generally lower quality of English housing, and that utility costs as well should reflect the smaller size of English dwellings and the lack of extensive household facilities.

With these qualifications in mind, we can now examine housing expenditure patterns in more detail. We first need to recall the differences in the character of the rental market which are characteristic of England and the United States. As so much English rental housing is publicly owned, rents paid in the public sector need to be considered separately from rents paid to private landlords. Until 1972, rents for publicly owned housing had been set under a wide variety of local practices, while rents in the private sector had been controlled by statute. In the United States, practically all rents in the private sector are uncontrolled, while the number of public housing units is proportionately quite small.

These differences make comparisons difficult, but some general observations are still possible. One is that rent/income ratios vary with income levels, and tend to be heavily regressive. That is, lower income tenants pay a greater share of their income for rental accommodation than middle and upper income tenants do, and this regressivity is perhaps the most striking characteristic of the rental market. Public policy appears to be insensitive to this distribution. Most discussions of housing expenditure center on the problem of defining an absolute maximum or minimum for all subsidized housing, and little attention is paid to the variations in rent/income ratios which presently exist.

When we turn to a comparison of actual rent/income ratios, we find that the English appear to spend less. At median wage earner levels, the average rent/income ratio in England for an

---

[5] While this book will concentrate on urban slums, the equally poor housing conditions in many rural areas of the United States should not be forgotten. Some of the issues involved in dealing with substandard rural housing are discussed in Cochran & Rucker, *Every American Family Housing Need and Non-Response*, in PAPERS SUBMITTED TO SUBCOMM. ON HOUSING PANELS, HOUSE COMM. ON BANKING & CURRENCY, 92nd Cong., 1st Sess. 525 (1971).

unfurnished, publicly owned dwelling is around 13½ percent, while for an unfurnished privately owned dwelling it is around 12¼ percent.[6] In the United States, at similar income levels, the median rent/income ratio is around 18 to 20 percent.[7] At the lower end of the income scale, the percentage of income paid for rent can range as high as 35 percent for private accommodation in the United States, and as high as 23½ percent for unfurnished, publicly owned housing in England.

Even these figures must be carefully evaluated. For example, they do not reflect regional variations, and in England alone the highest rentals for publicly owned housing are twice as high as the lowest. In addition, lower rents for privately owned rental housing in England probably reflect the fact that this housing is both older than publicly owned housing and inferior in quality. Finally, rents vary by type and age of dwelling, and aggregate statistics hide these differences.

These figures also include a payment for local property taxes, and so the tax burden in each country needs to be considered in order to determine whether the property tax share of what we have called rents is comparable. Our conclusion is that the share of rents which goes toward taxes is about the same, but that differences in tax policy affect the distribution and incidence of the tax burden.

One difference is that the national government in England makes a larger contribution toward local government revenue than national and state governments do in the United States, the English national contribution currently averaging around 60 percent.[8] Since there are no states intervening between national and local government in England, this proportion holds throughout the country. Moreover, welfare and health expenditures, a

---

[6] Dep't of Employment, Family Expenditure Survey Report for 1971, at 8-11 (1972). In recent years, rents in publicly owned housing have been on the increase while controlled rents in the private sector have remained stationary. *Id.*, Family Expenditure Survey Report for 1969, at 8-9 (1970). The calculations in the text are based on rental costs that include heat and utility expenditures. *Cf.* note 7, *infra*.

[7] *United States Housing Needs, 1968-1978*, in REPORT OF THE PRESIDENT'S COMM. ON URBAN HOUSING, TECHNICAL STUDIES, Vol. I, at 1, 13-15 (1967). These estimates include utilities and heat as part of rental costs. *Id.*, at 33. English statistics ordinarily do not. *See also* Newman, *Housing the Poor and the Shelter to Income Ratio*, in PAPERS SUBMITTED TO SUBCOMM. ON HOUSING PANELS, *supra* note 5, at 555.

[8] *See* THE FUTURE SHAPE OF LOCAL GOVERNMENT FINANCE, CMND. NO. 4741, at 2 (1971).

very high proportion of local government spending in the United States, are financed entirely by the national government in England. In the United States, the insertion of state government between the federal and local levels produces a widely variant contribution pattern. Despite extremes, the proportion of total local government expenditure which is contributed by national and state governments presently averages around 35 percent, a ratio directly the converse of what prevails in England.[9]

Beyond these differences in national allocations of revenue and expenditure burdens, there are other differences between the American and the English local property tax systems worth noting. One is that public housing in England is fully taxable, while public housing in the United States has been exempt from local property taxes and makes a payment in lieu of these taxes, usually estimated at one-fifth to one-third of what the tax payment would be if the housing were not exempt.[10] Another difference is that the English tenant pays his taxes directly, even the tenant in public housing.

Subject to these qualifications, studies indicate that property taxes normally account for about 19 percent of the rent of non-farm housing in the United States, net before taxes, rising to as much as 30 percent in urban areas like New York City.[11] Expressed as a percentage of income, if rents at median income levels are 20 percent of income, then the property tax burden as a proportion of income is about four percent, assuming that all of the tax is passed on to the tenant. English property tax payments as a percentage of income tend to be slightly higher,[12] but they are reduced to about the same average level by a national system of property tax rebates to lower income groups. Only a few states in the United States have enacted such programs,[13] although their number is increasing. In some areas of England, however, property taxes are higher than the national

---

[9] *See* ADVISORY COMM'N ON INTERGOVERNMENTAL RELATIONS, URBAN AMERICA AND THE FEDERAL SYSTEM 7-17 (1969).

[10] F. DE LEEUW & S.H. LEAMAN, THE SECTION 23 LEASING PROGRAM 20-21 (1971) (U.S. Urban Institute).

[11] *See* D. NETZER, IMPACT OF THE PROPERTY TAX: EFFECT ON HOUSING, URBAN LAND USE, LOCAL GOVERNMENT FINANCE 22-30 (National Comm'n on Urban Problems, Research Rep. No. 1, 1968).

[12] A.R. ILERSIC, RATES AS A SOURCE OF LOCAL GOVERNMENT FINANCE 13 (1969).

[13] *See* Wittman, *Property Tax Relief: A Viable Adjunct to Housing Policy,* 1972 URBAN L. ANN. 171.

average. London is one such area, and recent surveys carried out in one inner London borough indicate that property taxes may often equal or exceed rents exclusive of taxes in all income ranges.[14] In such areas, the national property tax rebate may not reduce the tax burden to average national levels, and the rent portion which is applied toward property taxes is much higher.[15]

We have included this much discussion of rents and property taxes in relation to income simply to indicate how rough a measure of housing expenditure the rent/income ratio really is. Although this ratio is widely used as the basis for evaluating the housing burden, its limited usefulness as a measure of housing effort should be kept in mind throughout this discussion. Moreover, as we have suggested, the extent to which this ratio truly measures housing costs can easily be manipulated. Indeed, the lack of agreement over what is an acceptable rent/income ratio has usually led to intense conflict on this issue when the costs, incomes, and services that are used in determining the ratio are legislatively considered. Arguments over these definitions simply reflect the pressures and counterpressures which are exerted on legislation to adjust housing expenditures to levels which the protagonists consider appropriate.

B. Housing Costs and Subsidy Strategies

Assuming, however, that the tenant share of housing costs can be agreed upon, the remainder of the cost of rental housing has to be met from subsidy, and the next question is to determine how that subsidy is to be applied. If the subsidy is not paid as a direct supplement to the tenant's rental expenditure, it is usually tailored to meet a share of housing costs. These costs are usually divided as follows: property taxes, on the average, represent about 20 percent, and another 50 percent must be applied toward the cost of construction, which includes the

---

[14] *See* L. Rowley, *Introduction to the Housing Rents Study*, in HOUSING IN CAMDEN, Vol. I, at 22 (1969).

[15] It should be noted that changes in methods of financing local government expenditure can have important consequences for local property tax levels, and thus for the amount of property tax which renters must pay. In the United States, for example, current efforts to shift the financing of elementary and secondary public education to other tax sources may have a substantial impact on the level of local property tax collections. These decisions on tax policy, we should note, are not taken with their impact on housing costs clearly in mind.

original costs of the land and the dwelling, and the debt service on this cost—payments on principal and interest. Operating costs and maintenance make up the remainder.[16] A subsidy could absorb some or all of these expenses. Property taxes could be waived or reimbursed, or all or a part of capital and operating costs could be subsidized.

Tax exemption for public housing has only been tried in the United States, and neither country has subsidized operating costs until recently. As we have noted, housing subsidies have traditionally been available only for capital costs, and in the United States all of the capital cost has been subsidized while in England the capital subsidy has not been total. As a result, some of the capital cost of publicly owned English housing has to be met from rents, while in the United States rents need only cover operating costs and the payment in lieu of taxes. Problems may then arise if the capital cost subsidy does not bring rents down to low enough levels. Either tenants will have to pay more than they should, or the mix of tenants will have to be adjusted so that the poorer tenants within the project are balanced by the more affluent. Presumably the rents of tenants who are better off would then subsidize the rents of those who are not as fortunate. We will note both of these tendencies in the English and American programs.

The problem of matching capital subsidies to rent levels is further compounded by difficulties that must be faced when the aggregate subsidy is divided among housing units, which are then matched to the needs of each occupant. This problem is especially acute when, as is presently the case, the subsidy is distributed by an intermediary in the form of a local housing agency. It does not disappear, however, when the subsidy is paid directly to the housing consumer, since comparable adjustments must then be made in the amount of the subsidy to reflect the varying housing needs of subsidy recipients.

Let us look at this problem as it presently arises within housing projects managed by housing agencies. There are four major variables to be considered: unit size, family size and income,

---

[16] REPORT OF THE PRESIDENT'S COMM. ON URBAN HOUSING: A DECENT HOME 118 (1968). English costs are similar when an additional allowance is made for property taxes paid by the tenant. Fourth Report from the Estimates Comm., H.C. Sess. 1968-69, at 21. No allowance for profit on investment need be made for publicly owned rental housing.

and unit quality. These may be matched in a variety of ways. For example, a decision may be made to give each subsidized family the unit its family size requires, charging it only the rent it can afford to pay under the accepted rent/income ratio. This system often prevails in American public housing. Since large families require large units, poorer large families will tend to receive a better rent bargain unless the housing agency offsets their higher space needs by giving them a lower quality unit. This kind of trade-off is difficult to carry out in American public housing, however, where only operating costs and the payment in lieu of taxes must be met from rents. These costs do not tend to vary that much from one project to the next within any housing agency's jurisdiction. If the capital subsidy does not make up all of the difference between the rents paid by these poorer families, and the cost of providing the dwelling, then the housing agency must either limit the number of low-income families in the project, or shift some of the cost of their housing to tenants with higher incomes.

The other alternative is to set rents on a unit basis, so that all comparable units carry the same rental. In this case, rents will be proportionately higher for the larger units, and large families with low incomes will not be able to afford them. The problems that this kind of rent system creates can be illustrated by the American housing subsidy system which is available for housing units which are privately owned and rented.[17] In this subsidy program, the subsidy is based on the capital cost of the housing. The federal government makes a subsidy payment equal to the difference between the market interest rate at which the mortgage on the housing project was executed, and the interest that would have been payable had interest been charged at one percent. This assumed one percent interest charge, together with all other housing costs, must be met from rents. These costs include taxes, since the projects are not exempt from local tax charges.

Under this system, rents are apportioned among dwelling units according to their size, and the larger units carry a correspondingly higher rent. As a result, large families must have a proportionately higher income in order to afford the rents

---

[17] C.L. EDSON & B.S. LANE, A PRACTICAL GUIDE TO LOW AND MODERATE INCOME HOUSING ch. 2 (1972).

for the larger units. There is another limitation in the program, in that all families in these units must pay a *minimum* of 25 percent of their income toward rent. There is no statutory *maximum*, although the practice within the program is to treat the minimum rent as a maximum as well. Since rents within the projects are apportioned to each unit on the basis of size, large families with low incomes may also find that they have to pay more than 25 percent of their income for rent, even assuming that they are admitted.

C. The Impact of Welfare Programs

Rent-setting and subsidy allocation problems in housing subsidy programs are complicated even more by the existence of a parallel system of income support, the welfare system, which subsidizes housing costs along with all other family expenditures. These relationships between the more general welfare support programs and the more specific housing subsidy program are critical to our study, since by concentrating on housing subsidies in the publicly owned sector we have focused our attention on that part of the housing supply which serves the poorest tenants. This group must also seek help, in many cases, from the welfare system, and the problems posed by overlapping requirements and criteria can be very complex. They are especially complex in that part of the welfare program which supports families out of work, or who have incomes below the support level which the welfare program guarantees.[18] Of all welfare families, this group has the most acute income and housing problems.[19] Their

---

[18] We should also point out that many of those living in publicly owned housing in both countries are elderly. Not only will these individuals be receiving social security and pension benefits, but they may be receiving welfare assistance as well, or they may be entirely dependent on welfare support. We have omitted detailed attention to elderly welfare recipients—and to the blind and disabled—partly for purposes of simplification. Many of the problems that arise under the programs which cover the unemployed or the working poor also apply to these other groups. In addition, the problems posed by the housing needs of the elderly are not as complex. Their housing needs are more clearly defined, they do not vary over time, and incomes received by the elderly are not affected by changes in the unemployment level.

[19] However, while welfare recipients make up an increasing proportion of public housing residents in the United States, less than five percent of the residents of privately owned but federally subsidized housing were on welfare as of 1970. *Overview Hearing on Operations of the Department of Housing and Urban Development Before a Subcomm. of the House Comm. on Government Operations*, 92nd Cong., 1st Sess., at 21-2 (1971). *See also* M. Rein, Welfare and Housing (1972) (unpub. ms. on file at Harvard-M.I.T. Joint Center for Urban Studies).

housing need does not decline when they receive welfare, and they are most susceptible to changes in employment levels, which can put heavy pressures on the welfare system when unemployment rises too high.

While the needs of the unemployed are met within the framework of an all-encompassing welfare program in England, in the United States they are met primarily through the program of Aid to Families with Dependent Children (AFDC).[20] This program was primarily intended for families with absent fathers. Mandatory extension of this part of the welfare system to the working poor as well as the unemployed has long been proposed as a welfare reform. Presently, the application of the AFDC program to this group is optional with the states, and some have enacted this extension of the law.[21]

Welfare assistance must cover all of the recipient's housing needs. But, as in the housing subsidy program, controls have been placed on welfare costs, including housing costs, which limit the potential burden of welfare expenditure. Welfare agencies exercise this control through regulations which determine what items are to be recognized in the welfare budget, and how much should be allowed for them. In the case of subsidized housing, the decision on housing costs could be straightforward. Welfare agencies could recognize in the welfare budget the rents fixed by the local housing agency, and a transfer payment could then be made from one program to the other. In practice, however, the problems are not that simple.

One problem is that the legal and administrative systems that have been developed to administer the two programs are very different. In the United States, while public housing subsidies are provided by the national government, considerable discretion in the administration of the program is delegated to local housing authorities.[22] No state agency is involved. By way of comparison, responsibility for welfare assistance is divided among national, state, and local governments. Federal statutes and regulations set criteria to which state plans for administering assistance must conform,[23] but much of the detail of the program is left to the

---

[20] *See* F.F. Piven & R.A. Cloward, Regulating the Poor: The Functions of Public Welfare (1971).

[21] *See* R.J. Levy, T.P. Lewis, & P.W. Martin, Cases on Social Welfare and the Individual 430-32 (1971).

[22] For the statute see 42 U.S.C. § 1401 et seq. (1970).

[23] For the statute see 42 U.S.C. § 601 et seq. (1970).

state plan. It serves as the basis on which welfare assistance is distributed by the appropriate local government unit.

In England, national and local responsibility for administration of publicly owned housing is divided along lines comparable to the American. But welfare assistance has been nationalized, and the administration of the program has been placed with a national agency. As a result, relationships between the two systems are not as complicated as they are in the United States.

Most of the coordination problems that have arisen between these two programs can be attributed to these differences in administrative organization. Coordination must be carried out by the operating agencies at the local level, but there has usually been no formal legal machinery for implementing a method of cooperation. As a result, local welfare and public housing agencies have been left to negotiate with each other, and public housing authorities in both countries have usually been successful in pushing a disproportionate share of their housing costs on to the welfare system. For example, local authorities in England sometimes placed welfare families in their more expensive units.[24] This problem has now been largely resolved there, but it still remains critical in the United States.

Another complicating factor is that each program has very different statutory objectives, and these differences have led to substantive differences in key statutory criteria. These problems are especially acute in the United States, and they are most critical in the case of those welfare recipients who have an earned income in addition to their welfare grant. For example, the federally supported program of Aid to Families with Dependent Children has been very concerned about its impact on work incentives. To encourage welfare recipients to work, they are permitted by statute to keep a substantial share of their earnings, in addition to the welfare grant.[25] Public housing regulations which define income for purposes of rent are not so generous. As a result, some of the incentive provided by the welfare system is lost whenever the public housing agency bases its rent on the income earned by the welfare recipient as well as the welfare grant which he receives.

These differences in administrative structure and substantive requirement lead in turn to serious equity problems. Not all

---

[24] *See* R.A. PARKER, THE RENTS OF COUNCIL HOUSES ch. 7 (1967).
[25] 42 U.S.C. § 602(a)(8) (1970).

welfare recipients are in public housing, and not all public housing tenants are welfare recipients. Especially in the United States, where public housing rents are substantially below rents in the private market, those welfare recipients who are in public housing get a better rent bargain. At the same time, rent differentials have arisen between those tenants within the project who are on welfare and those who are not, because public housing agencies usually charge a different rent to welfare recipients than they do to other residents. These disparities have attracted considerable attention, and raise important constitutional and statutory questions which have not yet been fully resolved here. The English settled some of these conflicts by standardizing their programs in national legislation, and the problems are simplified because the administration of welfare assistance is only a national responsibility. In addition, the housing subsidy program has been extended to tenants in private housing. Nevertheless, we shall see that some difficulties still remain.

D. National and Local Responsibilities in Housing Subsidy Programs

These divisions of governmental responsibility for income support between the housing subsidy and welfare programs are paralleled by a comparable division of governmental responsibility within the housing subsidy program. Now we need to examine more closely the way in which this allocation of authority affects the scope and content of the housing subsidy program, and its impact on the housing costs of tenants within the subsidy system.

The major task is to find a method for allocating substantive responsibility for the administration of the housing subsidy on the one hand, and financial responsibility for the support of the subsidy on the other. The two issues are of course intertwined. Whichever level of government has the responsibility to determine substantive standards, for example, will determine to a large extent the financial costs that will be generated. At one extreme, to place financial responsibility for the program on one level of government, while allowing the other level to make all of the critical substantive decisions, would create a questionable division of authority.

One answer to this problem would have been to make the financing and administration of the housing subsidy program entirely a national responsibility, just as welfare assistance and the health service have been nationalized in England. But strong traditions of local autonomy argued against such an approach there, while an adverse court case in America ended a nationally-administered public housing program which had been initiated in the mid-1930's. What has happened in both countries is that both substantive and financial responsibilities for the housing subsidy program have been divided, and how the dividing line should be drawn remains a matter both of considerable importance and intense political conflict.

First, let us look at problems of substantive responsibility. American public housing since 1959 has been operating under what has been called a federal "autonomy" amendment,[26] which is intended to maximize the scope of local control. Nevertheless, the number of new units to be built annually remains a national responsibility, the national housing agency reserves the right to review public housing locations, and the national statute imposes income, cost, and rent limitations, among other criteria. Responsibility for deciding on tenant admissions and rents still rests with the local housing authority, however, subject to fairly broad national legislative guidelines.

Somewhat the same pattern exists in England,[27] with the exception that income limitations for admission are not imposed anywhere in the program and location decisions are made locally. Annual production targets are set nationally, however, and the national housing department must also approve local building programs. Moreover, rents and the amount of the subsidy to be given to each tenant are now governed by national legislation. This last distinction is perhaps the principal difference from the American system. The result is a mixed pattern of administration in both countries, which makes it difficult to determine the precise impact of the programs on a national basis, and which aggravates the problem of arriving at political decisions on the content, scope, and character of the housing subsidy system.

There is yet another aspect to this problem. Conflicts between the national housing department and local authorities partly arise from the fact that the local authority may have an identity of interest with its own tenants. Local authorities are often

---

[26] See 42 U.S.C. § 1401 (1970).
[27] See MINISTRY OF HOUSING AND LOCAL GOVERNMENT, COUNCIL HOUSING: PURPOSES, PROCEDURES AND PRIORITIES (1969).

willing to agree to tenant demands for increased services, for example, if they know that the cost of these services will be absorbed at the national level. Indeed, in many English local authorities, where publicly owned housing makes up a large proportion of the housing supply, tenant interests are heavily represented in the council of the local authority administering the program, and their point of view may dominate. An increase in the proportion of subsidized public housing in American cities can have the same consequence.

We need to turn, then, to the way in which financial responsibility for housing subsidies has been allocated. Here there is a strong case for placing the full financial responsibility for the housing subsidy on the national government, although full national assumption of subsidy cost may well argue for fairly complete national substantive control as well. The case for this position runs about as follows: It is usually difficult to argue that housing needs arise out of economic conditions which are limited to any one locality, for local employment and job opportunities are more directly determined by a series of economic decisions made at the national rather than at the local level. This case for a national assumption of housing subsidy costs is especially persuasive in England, a smaller country in which there is also more national intervention in and control of the economy. There is also more national control of the planning and land development decisions which determine the places where people live.

In fact, however, policies in the two countries appear to be going in a direction which is opposite to what would be expected. The United States appears to be moving toward full national assumption of housing subsidy costs, while in England the localities are being asked to bear a larger share. The reasons for these contrary policies probably relate to the very different structures of government finance which we have already observed. Not only is a larger share of local government expenditure met from the local property tax in the United States, but the older, metropolitan cities in which much public housing is located are least able to bear the cost of providing an additional subsidy to the program. As we have suggested, all of the subsidy for public housing has been contributed by the national government, except to the extent that localities contribute a share by accepting a payment in lieu of taxes which is less than what the normal property tax ordinarily would be. Indications are that even this tax exemption may soon be eliminated.

While much the larger share of local government expenditure in England is borne by the national government, local property taxes, at least as a percentage of personal income, do not appear appreciably lower. But the healthier financial condition of local governments leaves room for their assuming a larger portion of the housing subsidy; local tax contributions to the subsidy program have had a varied history in England, and are now required. Probably the fact that publicly owned housing makes up a large part of the housing supply in many local government areas also lends credit to the view that subsidies for this housing are, at least partially, a local responsibility.

The difficulty with shifting a portion of the housing subsidy cost to the local level is that the incidence of the subsidy then becomes regressive, to the extent that recipients of the subsidy who are entitled to receive it must also pay a share of the subsidy burden. While publicly owned housing is more evenly distributed in England, it is more concentrated in the older cities, where the population is poorer. Yet continuing increases in the level of housing subsidies suggest that political pressures to shift some of that cost from national budgets will continue to increase.

E. Summary

Let us now see how far we have come. In these first two chapters we have examined a series of issues which must enter into the policies which are adopted for a housing subsidy program. Most of these aspects of the program are portrayed in Figure 2, which indicates how the different parts of the housing subsidy network relate to each other. Decisions made at any point in the subsidy system have an impact on other components within the program. But we have also seen how difficult it is to arrive at a comprehensive assessment of the entire system. Decisions on each element tend to be made separately, with little consideration for their wider impact, and we have noted these tendencies in our discussion. For example, an emphasis on housing rehabilitation would lower overall housing costs to the extent that an extensive rehabilitation program would keep older housing in the housing supply, and these lower cost levels would be reflected in lower subsidies. Yet rehabilitation

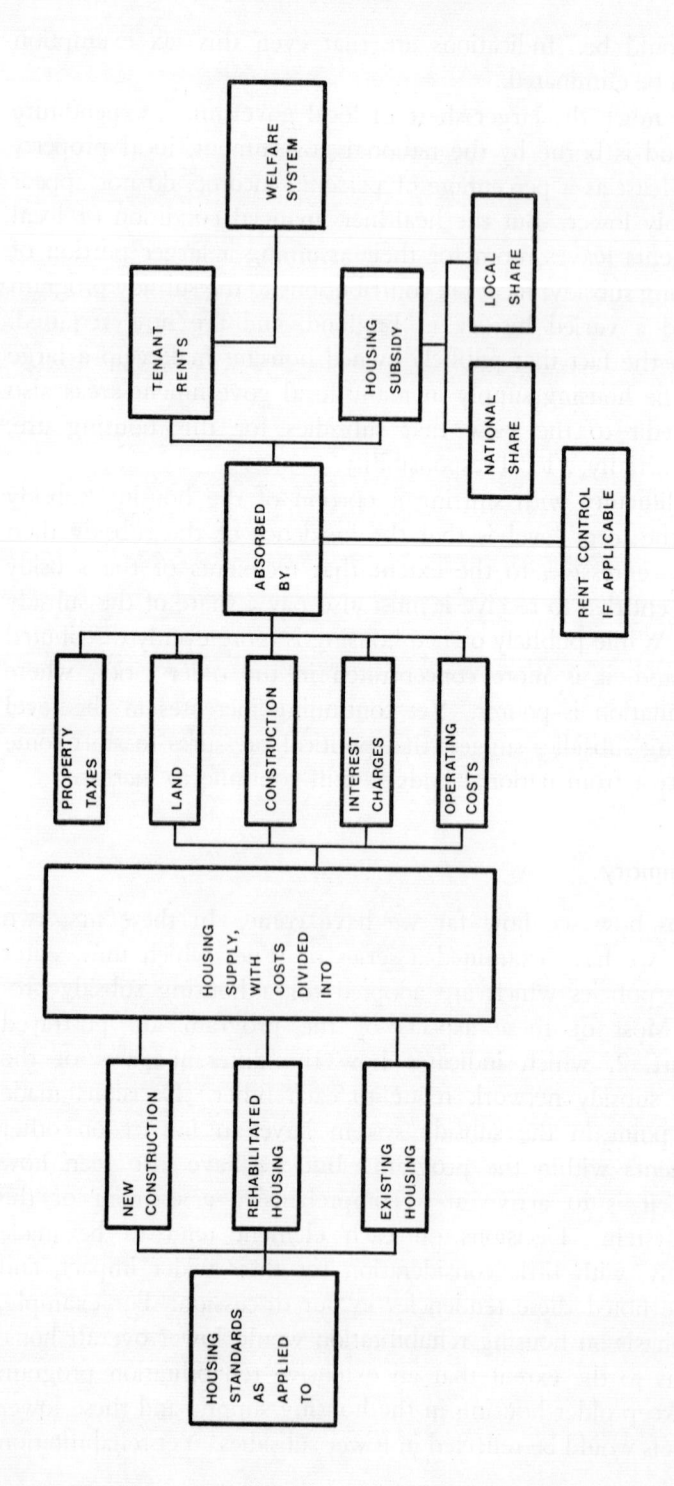

Figure 2. AN OUTLINE OF THE HOUSING SUBSIDY SYSTEM

programs are usually adopted to achieve independent objectives, such as the need to remove or repair slum housing, and the effect of a rehabilitation strategy on the subsidy program may not be considered. Other areas of decision lie outside the housing subsidy program entirely; welfare policy and tax policy are two examples.

Moreover, decisions taken within the system tend to work in both directions, a relationship which the diagram seeks to illustrate. To return to our rehabilitation example, we have noted that an emphasis on housing rehabilitation will have important effects on the level of subsidy costs. But the type of subsidy program which is selected will also have an impact on the rehabilitation effort. To take one possibility, large unconditional grants to local housing authorities, to acquire and improve existing dwellings for addition to their subsidized housing supply, would encourage rehabilitation at the expense of new construction.

We will now examine, in some detail, the way in which the several components of a housing subsidy program have been structured and arranged, both in England and the United States. The discussion centers as much on the way in which the issues have been developed and resolved, as on the present statutory and administrative solution to the questions that have been raised. Housing legislation and practice is sensitive to shifting political pressures, and continuing legislative innovation can be expected. But the issues are universal, and they will endure as long as society sees fit to improve the housing conditions of its constituents through monetary supplements to the cost of housing accommodation.

Chapter III

PUBLIC HOUSING SUBSIDIES IN THE
UNITED STATES

A. An Introduction to the Program

We now need to look more closely at the legal structure under which the American public housing program is operated. The principal point to make by way of a beginning is that this program, until recently, was operated under a subsidy framework within which the division of financial responsibility was clearcut. Capital costs of construction were met in their entirety by federal subsidy. Operating costs and the payment in lieu of taxes[1] were left to be met out of project rents, subject only to the federal statutory directive that public housing be limited to families of low income.

This dual federal and local responsibility for the public housing program is reflected in the legal structure under which public housing is built and operated. Federal legislation determines the basis under which the federal subsidy is distributed, and contains

---

[1] However, property taxes are payable on housing units that are leased from private owners at market rents, and then leased by the local public housing agency to public housing tenants. *See* Note, *The Oakland Leased Public Housing Program,* 20 STAN. L. REV. 538 (1968).

additional requirements which are binding on local public housing agencies which receive that subsidy. We will see that the nature and scope of these requirements have varied, but have always permitted minimum federal control over important aspects of local program operation, such as rents and admission policies. These federal statutory requirements have also been given additional content through federal administrative regulations, some of which have taken the form of guidance and advice on various aspects of program operation to local public housing agencies.

While federal legislation controls the terms under which the federal subsidy is distributed, state[2] and not federal legislation[3] provides the legal authority for the operation of the public housing program. However, very little substantive restriction is usually provided by state legislation, and since no state administrative agency participates in the administration of public housing, the content of the program at the state level is largely determined by the rules and regulations adopted by local public housing agencies. Although the influence of federal directives has led to many common characteristics in these local regulations, they still vary widely in detail.

This chapter will look first at the content of the public housing subsidy system as it has developed under these federal statutory and administrative directives. Next we will look at the local administration of the program, paying special attention to rents and admission policies, and to the problems which the accommodation of welfare tenants has imposed on local public housing agencies. In the next chapter we will then consider those federal reforms that have led both to new federal subsidies, and to changes in public housing rent patterns.

---

[2] Public housing legislation at the state level was based initially on model legislation prepared by the national housing agency, and much state enabling legislation still conforms to the pattern set by the model bill. For a typical state-enabling act authorizing public housing see ILL. ANN. STAT. ch. 67 ½, § 1 et seq. (1959).

[3] Federal, rather than local ownership and operation, was originally contemplated by the federal public housing legislation. However, federal court decisions adverse to the federal construction and operation of public housing projects led to the shift in emphasis to local ownership and control. L.J. Woodyatt, The Origins and Evolution of the New Deal Public Housing Program 91-101, 123-24 (Ph. D. Thesis on file at Washington University Library, 1968; Univ. Microfilm No. 68-17213).

B. The Legislative Structure for Subsidies and Rents

1. The Federal Contribution to Public Housing Costs

Since public housing is built and managed by local agencies, while the subsidy itself is provided by the federal government, a legal method had to be found to distribute the subsidy to the operating agencies at the local level. The method chosen is an Annual Contributions Contract, which embodies the conditions under which the subsidy is payable. The content and scope of the subsidy are determined by this contract, and by the legislative provisions which authorize its execution and govern its terms.

Yet the selection of the Annual Contributions Contract as the method of subsidy distribution was partly accidental, and arose out of a political compromise in the enactment of the original public housing legislation. Sponsors of the federal legislation initially proposed that public housing be subsidized through a one-time federal grant which would meet all of its construction costs. Federal outlays under such a system would have been considerable, however, as the full cost of the project would have had to be met in the year of construction. As a legislative program requiring such heavy budget outlays was not politically acceptable, the Annual Contributions Contract was proposed as an alternative method of financing which could take advantage of the method through which the construction of public housing projects are locally funded. These projects are financed by long-term bonded debt[4] payable in annual installments,[5] and federal public housing legislation was written to provide for an annual contribution toward this debt which meets annual principal and interest costs, known as debt service. In this fashion, the federal subsidy is spread throughout the life of the project, avoiding high initial budget expenditures. These annual contributions are pledged by the local agency toward full payment of its debt, the federal statute authorizes the federal government to continue the annual contributions "so long as any of such obligations remain outstanding," and the full faith and credit of the United States is pledged as security for these obligations.[6]

---

[4] The bonds of public housing agencies are exempt from national and often from state income taxes. Tax forgiveness on public housing agency obligations confers an indirect subsidy to the extent that the nonliability of bond interest to taxation results in a lower interest rate on these securities.

[5] See Woodyatt, *supra* note 3, at 153-54.

[6] United States Housing Act, §§ 22(b), 22(c). References throughout will be made to the applicable sections of the federal public housing act. The statute may be found in 42 U.S.C. § 1401 et seq. (1970).

The original federal statute did not explicitly limit annual contributions to principal and interest charges on local public housing bonds, however, as it was written more broadly to authorize "annual contributions to public housing agencies to assist in achieving and maintaining the low-rent character of their housing projects."[7] The narrower construction of this statute was adopted by the federal public housing agency, which administratively limited annual contributions to amounts sufficient to cover annual payments on principal and interest.[8] This administrative construction of the federal agency's subsidy responsibility became an ingrown part of federal attitudes toward the program, and was prompted by fears that overextension of the federal subsidy would lead to demands on the scope of the program which the agency was politically unwilling to support.

This use of an annual contributions subsidy to support public housing costs has important effects on the public housing program. One important effect is budgetary. Budget amounts authorized in federal spending programs are usually subject to annual appropriation by congressional appropriation committees, which may not permit the spending of the full amount authorized. But sums due under annual contributions contracts fall in a different category. While Congress technically may not bind itself to meet a financial obligation assumed in earlier legislation, congressional failure to meet the sums promised in annual contributions contracts to meet debt service on local public agency debt is not likely.

Another important consequence of the use of the annual contribution method of subsidy is strategic. Since the public housing subsidy for debt service has been funded through annual contributions, the most likely way to change the level of the subsidy is through legislative or administrative definition of the scope of the contribution, especially as the only costs not covered

---

[7] *See* § 10(a). Until recently, the annual subsidy could not exceed the annual yield at the going federal rate, plus one percent, on the development cost of the housing. This limitation has now been repealed. Pub. L. No. 92-503, § 3 (Oct. 18, 1972).

[8] *See, e.g.,* Statement of Charles E. Slusser, Commissioner, Public Housing Administration, in *Hearings on Housing Act of 1959 Before the Subcomm. on Housing of the House Comm. on Banking and Currency,* 86th Cong., 1st Sess., at 117, 137 (1959). Federal public housing officials during this period repeatedly stated to the author that they relied for this administrative interpretation on expressions of congressional intent as they appeared in congressional hearings on public housing legislation and public housing appropriations.

by the annual debt service subsidy are recurring operating expenses and tax payments which are easily funded on an annual basis.

An additional control on the potential federal subsidy burden is provided by cost limits on public housing dwellings. Dwelling costs are administratively determined by the federal housing agency, based on "prototype costs . . . in the area suitable for occupancy by persons assisted under this Act."[9] The projects are to be of "good design," are not to be of "elaborate or extravagant design or materials," and are to be economically constructed.[10]

2. Rent and Admission Requirements

A policy for rents and admission, the other critical variables in a housing program directed to low-income families, were also addressed by the federal statute. It first required that admission be limited to applicants whose incomes were not in excess of five times the annual rental for the unit to be occupied.[11] As a result, the statute also imposed a minimum rent/income ratio, at least at the time when tenants were admitted to a project.[12] No tenant could be admitted whose rent was less than 20 percent of his income, for otherwise the statutory requirement, that the income limit for admission could not exceed five times the rental, would be violated.[13] Admission to public housing was also limited by the federal statute to "families of low income," and the federal housing agency interpreted the statute to give it the authority to advise local public housing agencies on rent and admission policies.

By 1959, however, growing pressure for greater local control of the public housing program led to a substantial change in the federal statute. In what is known as the local autonomy

---

[9] *See* § 15(5).

[10] For discussion of this issue in the context of another federal housing subsidy program see Welfeld, *Rent Supplements and the Subsidy Dilemma*, 32 LAW & CONTEMP. PROB. 465 (1967).

[11] Act of Sept. 1, 1937, ch. 896, § 2(1), 50 Stat. 888.

[12] *See* PUBLIC HOUSING ADMINISTRATION, U.S. HOUSING AND HOME FINANCE AGENCY, LOCAL HOUSING AUTHORITY MANAGEMENT HANDBOOK, pt. VII, § 1, p. 1 (1964). This handbook, now termed a guide, was issued by the predecessor agency to the Department of Housing and Urban Development. It has not been officially revoked.

[13] The statute reflected the fact that rents in public housing projects were first set according to dwelling unit size, and were not varied by income. *Id.*, Exh. 1, at 2. Thus dwelling rents became the constant variable from which income limits and, by indirection, rent/income ratios were calculated.

amendment, local control over the program was affirmed in the federal law's statement of purpose. In addition, the income limits requirement was dropped, and the statute was changed to read that, subject only to review by the federal agency, local public housing agencies were to set rents and income limits for admission:

> ". . . after taking into consideration (A) the family size, composition, age, physical handicaps, and other factors which might affect the rent-paying ability of the family, and (B) the economic factors which affect the financial stability and solvency of the project."[14]

Federal regulations do not elaborate significantly on this statutory mandate,[15] and the only additional statutory guidance is a provision in the same section authorizing the setting of rent and income limits, and which defines low-rent housing as "dwellings within the financial reach of families of low income."[16]

Beginning in 1949 the federal public housing statute also carried a provision designed to keep public housing noncompetitive with the private market. This section requires a 20 percent gap between the upper rental limits for admission to public housing and "the lowest rents at which private enterprise unaided by public subsidy is providing . . . a *substantial supply* of decent, safe, and sanitary housing."[17] (Emphasis supplied.) When amendments to the federal public housing law were introduced in 1959, the role of the 20 percent gap provision was further expanded, and local public housing rent and income limits were directly linked to the 20 percent gap provision.[18] While this direct linkage was removed from the statute as finally enacted, the legislative history makes it clear that the 20 percent gap requirement was

---

[14] § 2(1). This amendment was prompted by an action of the federal public housing administrator at that time, who threatened the position of local executive directors by sending federal audit reports to their commissioner.

[15] U.S. DEP'T OF HOUSING AND URBAN DEVELOPMENT, LOW-RENT HOUSING INCOME LIMITS, RENTS, AND OCCUPANCY HANDBOOK RHM 7465.1, par. 2 (1969). In short, the regulations simply repeat the statutory language.

[16] § 2(1).

[17] § 15(7)(b). There is another little known but interesting reason for this statutory provision. Senator Taft of Ohio, who was one of the sponsors of the 1949 housing legislation, expected the 20% gap to encourage the private sector to "build down" into this housing range, thus providing dwellings for public housing occupants once their incomes disqualified them from public housing.

[18] See *Hearings on Housing Act 1959, supra* note 8, at 19.

to define the maximum ceiling on rental limits for admission.[19] That is, maximum rents were to be placed at a point 20 percent below the rent level at which the private market could supply a substantial amount of adequate housing.

In practice, however, the 20 percent gap provision has never been enforced by the federal housing agency, and the reason lies in the italicized language in the statute. Because of a continuing inflation in private market rents, the rent level at which a *substantial* supply of unsubsidized yet adequate private housing can be made available has risen considerably, and is now more than 20 percent above the highest rents in public housing. As a result, the gap provision does not provide a meaningful ceiling on public housing rent levels.

One other federal statutory provision does have an indirect effect on the level of public housing rents. If a local public housing agency acquires a surplus the federal statute provides that any excess of receipts over expenditures must be applied to a reduction of the federal subsidy.[20] Federal regulations have softened this requirement somewhat, for they do allow local agencies to maintain contingency reserves sufficient to meet operating expenses for six months.[21] This surplus recapture provision can be expected to have an impact on local rent policies, since local public housing agencies would tend to keep their rent levels low enough to avoid the creation of any repayable surplus amount. In practice, however, the deficit crisis in public housing has made the surplus provision irrelevant to many public housing agencies.

On the state level, legislation may or may not provide an additional control on public housing admission requirements and rents. Many of the state laws contain no provisions affecting rents at all, while a surprising number of other state statutes still follow the language of the federal law as it was before the 1959 revision, and impose a limitation on admission which is

---

[19] On this basis, the then federal public housing commissioner dropped his opposition to the change. Compare *id.*, at 121, *with Hearings on President's Message Disapproving S. 57 Before a Subcomm. of the Senate Comm. on Banking and Currency,* 86th Cong., 1st Sess., at 108 (1959).

[20] *See* § 10(c).

[21] *See* U.S. DEP'T OF HOUSING AND URBAN DEVELOPMENT, LOW-RENT HOUSING FINANCIAL MANAGEMENT HANDBOOK, RHM 7475.1, ch. 2 (1969).

related to the rents charged for public housing dwellings.[22] Since this type of provision only places a maximum limit on income for admission as it relates to rent, it does not prevent public housing agencies from raising the rents they actually charge.

Within these federal and state statutory limits, local public housing agencies have a wide discretion in setting rent and admissions requirements, which is reflected in the national pattern of maximum income limits for admission. These income limits are ad hoc, vary widely around the country, and are not proportionately related to differences from city to city in median income levels.[23] Nationally, however, trends in the median incomes of public housing tenants reflect the deteriorating economic base of the program. While median incomes of public housing tenants have been increasing,[24] they have not been increasing as fast as the median income for all families in the national population.[25]

3. Summary.

In this section we have sketched the major outlines of the statutory structure that governs the public housing subsidy programs. Financial responsibility for meeting public housing costs is apportioned between the federal government and local public housing agencies by the federal subsidy formula, which has historically been limited to debt service, the principal and interest

---

[22] *E.g.,* CAL. HEALTH & SAFETY CODE § 34322(c) (West 1967) (follows present federal law); CONN. GEN. STAT. ANN. § 8-45 (1971) (rents within financial reach of low-income families); GA. CODE ANN. § 99-1117 (1968) (similar to original federal law); ILL. ANN. STAT. ch. 67 ½, § 25 (1959) (similar to Connecticut); MO. ANN. STAT. § 99.100 (1969) (similar to Georgia); N.J. STAT. ANN. § 55:14A-8 (1964) (similar to Georgia); N.Y. PUB. HOUSING LAW § 156 (McKinney Supp. 1972) (similar to Georgia); TENN. CODE ANN. § 13-812 (1955) (similar to Georgia); WASH. REV. CODE ANN. § 35.82.090 (1965).

[23] *See, e.g.,* the table reproduced in *Hearings on 1971 Housing and Urban Development Legislation Before the Subcomm. on Housing and Urban Affairs of the Senate Comm. on Banking, Housing and Urban Affairs,* 92nd Cong., 1st Sess., at 718 (1971). This table compares estimated median incomes in different cities with maximum income limits for federally subsidized private rental housing, but maximum limits in this housing are by statute based on public housing maximums.

[24] U.S. Dep't. of Housing and Urban Development, Annual Report on Maximum Income Limits and Rents in Low-Rent Housing as of Dec. 31, 1969, at 1.

[25] For example, the median income limit for average-size families increased by only $500 between 1954 and 1968. *Id.,* at 3. Median family income increased by $900 just between 1964 and 1966. Gladstone & Associates, *The Outlook for United States Housing Needs,* in REPORT OF THE PRESIDENT'S COMM. ON URBAN HOUSING, TECHNICAL STUDIES, Vol. I, at 65 (1967).

payments on public housing construction. All costs not met by the federal subsidy were originally to be paid out of local public housing rents, and the structure of these rents has in turn been affected by federal and state statutory provisions on rent and admission policies. We have seen that the present federal statute provides only the broadest of policy guides for local rent practices, and confers considerable discretion in the setting of rents on the local public housing agencies. Local rent policies thus determine the impact the public housing program has on individual tenants in the projects, and so it is to an analysis of these policies that we turn next.[26]

C. Rent Policies in Public Housing Projects: Herein of Welfare Rents

1. Rent-Setting Practices of Public Housing Agencies

As the introductory chapter has pointed out, public housing agencies may use variations of two basic methods to set dwelling unit rents. Either rents may be calculated on what is known as a space rent basis, with each unit of comparable quality carrying the same rent, or rents may be calculated under a graded rent method. This second method requires the use of a rent/income ratio under which a certain portion of income is allocated for rent no matter what the size and character of the dwelling happens to be. Most local housing agencies now use some variation of this method,[27] although space rents were popular early in the program.

Before the housing agency decides to use a graded rent system, however, it must make a series of additional policy decisions in order to arrive at a final rent structure. The first of these decisions

---

[26] For additional discussion of rent and income problems in public housing see COMMUNITY SERVICE SOC'Y OF NEW YORK, RENT AND INCOME POLICIES IN PUBLIC HOUSING (1968); COMPTROLLER GENERAL OF THE UNITED STATES, REVIEW OF ELIGIBILITY REQUIREMENTS, RENTS, AND OCCUPANCY OF SELECTED LOW-RENT HOUSING PROJECTS (1963).

[27] REPORT OF THE JOINT HUD-HEW TASK FORCE ON WELFARE RENTS IN PUBLIC HOUSING 20 (1971). New York City is the prime example of a major authority which uses a space rent system. For a description of various rent systems see MANAGEMENT HANDBOOK, *supra* note 12, pt. VII, § 3. For a summary of rent schedules in force in over 200 representative housing authorities studied in an intensive survey, see ABELES, SCHWARTZ & ASSOCIATES, THE IMPACT OF THE BROOKE AMENDMENT ON PUBLIC HOUSING TENANTS AND LOCAL AUTHORITIES: A REPORT TO THE JOINT HEW-HUD TASK FORCE ON WELFARE RENTS IN PUBLIC HOUSING, at VIII-14, VIII-15 (1971) [hereinafter cited as REPORT].

is to determine what variation of a graded rent scale to use. Here the choice lies between a constant rent/income ratio which is applied to all tenants, and a sliding scale which takes a different percentage for rent at different levels of income. Under a sliding scale system, the rent/income ratio is ordinarily reduced as income rises, following the regressive pattern in the private market. Federal regulations favored this method,[28] and one recent survey of 200 public housing agencies showed that it was used frequently.[29]

Having first decided on which rent method to use, many local agencies next impose both minimum and maximum rents in their rent structure. That is, no rents imposed under the application of the rent/income ratio used in the graded rent system may either fall below or rise above an established minimum and maximum rent. Minimums and maximums thus have a regressive effect on rents. Minimum rents are regressive because they put a floor on rent levels and force up the percentage of income paid for rent by the poorer families. Maximum rents are equally regressive, since they reduce the percentage of income paid for rent by families with higher incomes. These relationships are portrayed in Figure 1.

The history of rent maximums and minimums may help explain their purpose. They were first required in public housing at a time when the federal housing agency exercised direct authority over the structure of local public housing rents. Federal regulations required a rent minimum to help maintain the financial solvency of the projects, and stated that rents should be equal to two-thirds of operating costs plus all utilities.[30] To make certain that tenants could meet the minimum rent charge, however, the regulations also stated that the "minimum rent should be that appropriate to the income required to maintain a bare subsistence level of living."[31] Minimum rents set at this level were not nominal, and required substantial contributions toward rent from families of low income. Since the 1959 amendments, of course, local housing authorities may set their own rents subject only to federal review, and may dispense with minimum rents altogether.

---

[28] MANAGEMENT HANDBOOK, *supra* note 12, pt. VII, § 2, at 5.
[29] REPORT, *supra* note 27, at VIII-14, VIII-15.
[30] MANAGEMENT HANDBOOK, *supra* note 12, pt. VII, § 4, at 3; Exh. 3, at 3.
[31] MANAGEMENT HANDBOOK, *supra* note 12, pt. VII, § 1, at 3.

FIGURE 1. – EFFECT OF MINIMUM AND MAXIMUM RENTS ON A GRADED RENT SCHEDULE

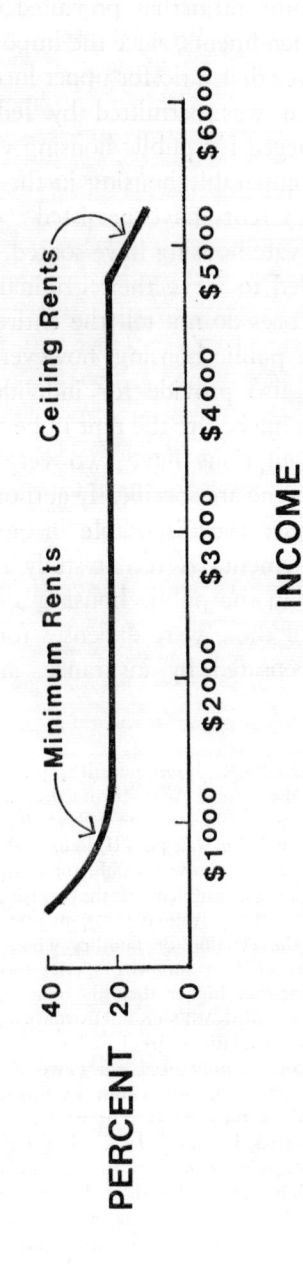

Source: Public Housing Administration, U.S. Housing and Home Finance Agency, Local Housing Authority Management Handbook, Pt. VII, § 3, at 3 (1964)

Maximum rents have a very different history. They were authorized by the federal housing agency as an exception to the minimum rent/income ratio that prevailed on admission before the 1959 federal amendments, since the imposition of a maximum would of course lower that ratio for upper-income tenants. Nevertheless, a maximum was permitted by federal policy so that maximum rents charged for public housing would not exceed the rents charged for comparable housing in the private unsubsidized market.[32] Maximum rents have persisted[33] even though rentals for unsubsidized private housing have soared, and rent maximums are no longer needed to serve their original function.

Rent-setting practices do not tell the entire story of rent levels and rent burdens in public housing, however. Most public housing rent schedules also provide for individual exemptions and deductions from income before the rent to be charged is calculated. Deductions and exemptions have two very different functions. Deductions from income are specifically authorized to reflect tenant expenses which reduce the disposable income actually available to meet the rent payment. A recent study found more than 82 different deductions in the public housing agencies surveyed, but the most common of these were expenses for child care, medical expenses not compensated by insurance, and work-related expenses.[34]

---

[32] MANAGEMENT HANDBOOK, *supra* note 12, pt. VII, § 4, at 3-5. Ceiling rents also date back to the World War II practice, attributed to rent control, of holding ceiling rents in public housing below the rent-controlled rents for comparable private accommodation. *Id.,* pt. VII, Exh. 2, at 3.

[33] Another problem that has proved troublesome since the inception of the public housing program is the problem of the over-income tenant. In order to avoid forcing families into the private housing market with insufficient income, and in order to avoid the eviction of families whose incomes rise marginally after admission, federal regulations authorize special income limits for continued occupancy which are somewhat higher than the maximum income limits which are applied on admission. MANAGEMENT HANDBOOK, *supra* note 12, RHM 7465.1, par. 2(c). These regulations are based on a statutory provision which provides that an over-income family need not move if "the family is unable to find decent, safe and sanitary housing within its financial reach." § 10(g)(3). The family may then stay in the project if it pays an "increased rent consistent with such family's increased income." *Ibid.* Housing professionals have long argued that allowing over-income tenants to stay in the projects would both stabilize them and afford leadership for those lower down on the economic and social scale. The issue is largely moot today, as so many public housing tenants are welfare recipients, or elderly people with fixed incomes.

[34] REPORT, *supra* note 27, at VIII-11, VIII-12. Prior to the 1959 autonomy amendment to the federal public housing law, these deductions were prescribed by federal regulation. *See* MANAGEMENT HANDBOOK, *supra* note 12, pt. VII, § 5, Exh. 1, at 3-5.

Exemptions from income, on the other hand, have a very different purpose. They function much as the exemptions for dependents do under income tax laws and recognize that expenditures for rent decrease when other family expenditures increase as families grow larger.[35] In recognition of this expenditure pattern, many public housing agencies authorize a flat monetary exemption for each child. Other exemptions from income are applicable only in determining eligibility for admission to the project. The most common of these exemptions are payments from federal economic opportunity programs, and payments from the federal government for disability or death in connection with military service. This distinction between income definition for admission purposes and income definition for determining rent has always been typical of public housing practice, and we might look briefly at the reason why this distinction has been made.

Perhaps the best explanation is that exemptions from income for the purpose of deciding on admission are made to determine whether or not the family belongs in public housing, while exemptions from income for the purpose of setting rent are intended to reflect its rent-paying capacity.[36] Consequently, exemptions for determining admission are more generous than exemptions used in calculating rent, partly so that families will not be forced to move from public housing when there is a change in circumstances.[37] Thus, the income of dependent children may be exempted so that the family will not be forced to move as children grow up and begin to earn money on their own. However, the exemption of military benefits from the definition of income in admissions criteria apparently derives from a federal statute which requires that a preference be given to disabled

---

[35] For discussion see von Furstenberg, *The Impact of Rent Formulas and Eligibility Standards in Federally Assisted Housing* in REPORT OF THE PRESIDENT'S COMM. ON URBAN HOUSING, TECHNICAL STUDIES, Vol. I, at 103 (1967).

[36] MANAGEMENT HANDBOOK, *supra* note 12, pt. VII, § 5, at 3. Prior to the 1959 autonomy amendment, these exemptions were specified by federal statute, but were set comparatively low. For example, there was a deduction of $100 for each minor, and a deduction of $100 for each dependent adult without income. *Id.*, Exh. 2, at 1.

[37] The 20% gap provision does not apply to elderly families or to families displaced by urban renewal or other governmental action. §§ 2(2), 15(7)(b)(ii). The practical effect of this exclusion is that maximum income limits for displaced and elderly families are somewhat higher than they are for other families.

veterans.[38] How these deductions and exemptions for purposes of rent and eligibility determination operate in one public housing agency is indicated by Figure 2. Note that the exemptions from income which are applicable in the determination of rents are not really substantial enough to offset the increase in family expenditures, other than rent, which the larger family brings.

In short, then, rent-setting practices in public housing projects present a complicated pattern of standards and criteria, with most rents set under a graded rent system that takes a constant percentage of income at all income levels. Some modification of this uniform charge is provided by most public housing agencies, both by the practice of setting minimum and maximum rents, and by the allowance of deductions and exemptions from income before rents are calculated. Subject to this qualification, since dwelling units are assigned on the basis of housing need rather than on the basis of income, there are substantial intra-project income transfers within the program, as more affluent but smaller families pay larger rents in order to support larger but poorer families who need more space. Whatever the equities of this system, which will be explored later, the net effect of the rent charge pattern is to tax one group of the house-poor to support another. This generalization must be qualified, however, by the very different pattern of rents which are applied to welfare tenants in public housing, and which are discussed in the next section.

2. The Welfare Rent Problem

Welfare tenants—those receiving some form of welfare assistance—initially made up a small proportion of all tenants in public housing; some public housing agencies excluded them altogether. In the past several years, however, the proportion of welfare tenants in public housing has been increasing dramatically,[39] especially in the big cities, where welfare recipients often constitute a majority of the tenants in the public housing projects. Nationally, however, only about ten percent of all welfare

---

[38] The exemption is authorized by HANDBOOK, *supra* note 15, RHM 7465.1, par. 10, and is based on § 10(g)(2) of the statute. Disability benefits are counted as income, however, on the ground that the statute intended to provide an admissions preference to disabled veterans, but not a rent-free dwelling.

[39] For example, 23.4% of the tenants in Philadelphia public housing received public assistance in 1965. Five years later this proportion had risen to 69.8%. *See* REPORT, *supra* note 27, at II-5.

FIGURE 2. NEWARK, NEW JERSEY PUBLIC HOUSING AUTHORITY: METHOD OF DETERMINING INCOME FOR RENT AND FOR ADMISSION

AGGREGATE Gross Income Received by all members of the family regardless of source or type of such receipts.

LESS

ALLOWABLE DEDUCTIONS, such as:
  Compulsory Payroll Deductions (but not withholding tax).
  Occupational Expenses, not common to all workers, but necessary to the employment of the individual.
  Financial Assistance to legal or moral dependents of the immediate family.
  Medical Expense for Predictable and Continuing Illness in Excess of 3% of Aggregate Family Income where not specifically compensated for or covered by insurance.
  Serviceman's Expense Allowance for head of family away from home and in armed services not to exceed $100 a month.

EQUALS

NET FAMILY INCOME

LESS   LESS

EXEMPTION OF: EXEMPTION* OF:
$100 for each minor member
of the family, other than   (a) Total payment from U.S. Gov't. for Disability or Death occurring in connection with military service.
head or his spouse

                                         (b) Not in excess of $600 of the net income of each minor having income, (other than the Principal Income Recipient).

                                         (c) Not in excess of $600 of the income of each adult having income, (Other than the Principal Income Recipient).

                                         (d) $100 for each Minor having no income, (Other than the head or his spouse).

                                         (e) $100 for each adult having no income, (Other than the head or his spouse).

EQUALS   EQUALS

INCOME FOR RENT   INCOME FOR AD-
DETERMINATION   MISSION ELIGI-
                                         BILITY

*Total in (b) - (c) not to exceed $1,400.

recipients are in public housing. The pattern of welfare rents that applies to these increasing numbers of welfare tenants has been extremely mixed, many inequities have arisen, and constitutional challenges to the system have been brought in several cities. To understand in more detail how the problem of welfare rents came about, we must begin with a discussion of the budgeting process in the welfare program, and especially the program of Aid to Families with Dependent Children (AFDC), on which we will concentrate here.

Welfare agencies usually determine welfare need on the basis of a welfare budget, and a separate budget standard is established for each budget item, including housing. Most states enter housing costs into the welfare budget on an "as paid" basis, and an allowance is made for the amount of rent actually paid by the welfare recipient who rents his housing. The amount of family income is determined next. If there is no income the AFDC family is theoretically entitled to receive a grant equal to 100 percent of its budget. If there is any available income, it must be deducted from the family's budget, although federal law provides that the first $30 of income plus one-third of the remainder is not to be deducted from the budget amount.[40]

This straightforward method of computing the assistance payment must be qualified by the fact that most states do not attempt to meet budgeted need in full, and will in one way or another limit the amount of assistance that should be available. These limitations apply to all items in the family budget, but since we are most interested in the amount which the welfare agency does make available for housing we will concentrate on that item.[41] As the budget item for housing is usually called a shelter allowance, we will use this terminology here.

States may use several methods to reduce the shelter allowance. Some enter the rent as paid into the welfare budget, but then reduce the amount of rent which they will meet by an arbitrary percentage. For example, a state may decide to meet only 50 percent of the rent payment. Other states do not arbitrarily reduce the amount which is budgeted for the shelter allowance, but

---

[40] *See* 42 U.S.C. § 602(a)(8) (1970).

[41] This discussion is based on U.S. DEP'T OF HEALTH, EDUCATION, AND WELFARE, SHELTER POLICY BY PROGRAM AND STATES (Feb. 26, 1971); *Id.*, SUMMARY OF PAYMENT METHODS-AFDC (May, 1971). Limitations on shelter allowances may also be imposed by statute. *E.g.*, ILL. ANN. STAT. ch. 23, § 12-4.11 (Supp. 1972) ($90 monthly maximum).

place a maximum limit on the amount actually paid for housing. The two methods may be used in combination. The amount budgeted for housing may be reduced, and a maximum still imposed on the shelter allowance grant. Shelter allowance payments are complicated even further in some states by the presence of statutory or administrative maximums which the welfare administrator may waive in his discretion. This system can be quite refined when discretionary decisions are required from administrators higher and higher in the welfare hierarchy to authorize higher and higher exemptions from the shelter allowance maximum.

Shelter allowance payments are also affected by budgeting and payment adjustments which are made in the total welfare grant rather than just in the shelter allowance payment. Some states do not proportionately reduce any budget item, but simply limit the total AFDC grant by a maximum. Other states do not budget each item of expenditure separately. Instead, they provide a flat welfare grant varied by family size, which includes a sum equal to the amount considered necessary for each item had it been budgeted independently. In the case of housing, for example, a shelter allowance will be included in the flat grant equal to an average rental cost calculated from the rents actually paid by welfare recipients throughout the state.

In the private market, however the shelter allowance is calculated, it still may be substantially less than the amount the recipient needs. Since welfare recipients can seldom bargain over their rents, the rental charges in excess of their shelter allowance must be made up out of that part of the assistance payment which, technically, is not budgeted for shelter. As a result, welfare recipients often pay an excessive proportion of their welfare grant for the private housing they occupy.

Even this sacrifice may not place them in satisfactory private housing, for a variety of studies have indicated that most welfare recipients live in substandard housing conditions.[42] Some state

---

[42] For representative studies see COOK COUNTY DEPARTMENT OF PUBLIC AID, CASTLES OF THE POOR: A STUDY OF HOUSING CONDITIONS OF PUBLIC AID FAMILIES IN COOK COUNTY, ILLINOIS (1969); ECONOMIC CONSULTANTS ORGANIZATION, INC., RESIDENTIAL ANALYSIS FOR WESTCHESTER COUNTY, NEW YORK, VOL. 7, WELFARE: HOUSEHOLD AND HOUSING (1970); Frieden, *Improving Federal Housing Subsidies: Summary Report,* in PAPERS SUBMITTED TO SUBCOMM. ON HOUSING PANELS OF HOUSE COMM. ON BANKING AND CURRENCY, 92nd Cong., 1st Sess. 473 (1971).

statutes and regulations do impose minimum housing standards for welfare recipients,[43] but it seems clear from the studies mentioned above that insistence upon compliance with these standards is difficult if not impossible. Even though welfare payments for housing are running nationally at an annual rate of over $1,000,000,000,[44] the level of shelter allowance payments to individuals is too low to allow them to acquire adequate private housing. Public housing is an entirely different matter. Even assuming that rents for private and public housing are the same, accommodation in public housing is often much more adequate.[45] But the important advantage which public housing confers is the rent saving. A suburban New York City study of welfare clients found, for example, that the rents of welfare recipients in public housing were 20 percent lower than those paid by welfare recipients in the private market.[46] In some areas, the differential has been even greater.[47] However, welfare tenants in public housing may still pay more rent for their units than public housing tenants who do not receive welfare assistance. Let us turn to this problem next.

3. Welfare Rents in Public Housing

Before we look at welfare rents, however, we should begin with some background discussion of public housing admissions criteria as they affect the admission of welfare tenants. The content and application of these criteria determine, to a large extent, the proportion of welfare tenants living in public housing, and consequently the extent of the welfare tenant problem.

---

[43] U.S. DEP'T OF HEALTH, EDUCATION, AND WELFARE, THE ROLE OF PUBLIC WELFARE IN HOUSING: A REPORT TO THE HOUSE COMM. ON WAYS AND MEANS AND THE SENATE COMM. ON FINANCE, at 12 (1969). *But cf.* Padilla v. Health and Social Serv. Dep't, 84 N.M. 140, 500 P.2d 425 (Ct. App. 1972), holding that a state may constitutionally provide a lower shelter allowance for recipients living in housing which is substandard.

[44] *Id.,* at 3.

[45] For example, contrary to popular belief, the New York City public housing authority has had an excellent maintenance policy. C.P. Rydell, Factors Affecting Maintenance and Operating Costs in Federal Public Housing Projects 5 (Rand Inst. Rept. R-634-NYC, 1970).

[46] *See* RESIDENTIAL ANALYSIS FOR WESTCHESTER COUNTY, *supra* note 42, at 48.

[47] It has been alleged that welfare rents in public housing in New Jersey are at least 60% below rents in the private market. Moreover, about 14% of AFDC clients in this state are in public housing. Brief for Appellants at 48, New Jersey Welfare Rights Organization v. Cahill, 448 F.2d 1247 (3rd Cir. 1971).

While the federal public housing law has left admissions policies to local public housing agencies, and the state enabling acts are also usually silent on this issue, the federal statute did for a time contain provisions which biased public housing populations in favor of welfare families. For example, the federal statute once required that a preference in admission be given to families displaced by urban renewal and other governmental action,[48] and many of these families, as they came from the poorer sections of the city, were receiving welfare assistance. The same statute now requires only that the local public housing agency "give full consideration" to its responsibility to rehouse displaced families.[49]

Likewise, the federal statute for a time prohibited discrimination against families receiving welfare assistance.[50] This provision was later repealed, and some public housing agencies began to limit the number of welfare tenants, or to exclude them altogether. These discriminatory policies were at first accepted by the courts. Public housing agencies were given the same legal status as any other landlord, and their decisions on exclusion and eviction were usually honored by the courts.[51] Recent developments in welfare law have changed this judicial attitude, however. Cases have been brought in which restrictive admissions policies of public housing agencies have been challenged on various legal grounds, and the courts have increasingly been willing to review these exclusions for consistency with the purposes of the federal statute and with constitutional limitations.[52]

Nonetheless, while the courts have placed some limitation on the discretion of local public housing agencies in setting eligibility criteria for admission, it is not altogether clear that these agencies are fully prohibited from considering welfare assistance status when deciding whether the applicant may be admitted. Part of

---

[48] Act of July 15, 1949, ch. 338, § 302, 63 Stat. 423.

[49] See § 10(g)(2).

[50] Act of July 15, 1949, ch. 338, § 301, 63 Stat. 413, 423.

[51] An early leading case is Walton v. Phoenix, 69 Ariz. 26, 208 P.2d 309 (1949) (eviction). The early cases are discussed in L. FRIEDMAN, GOVERNMENT AND SLUM HOUSING 134-36 (1968).

[52] For discussion of the legal issues see ROSEN, TENANT'S RIGHTS IN PUBLIC HOUSING IN HOUSING FOR THE POOR: RIGHTS AND REMEDIES 154 (Project on Social Welfare, Supp. No. 1, 1967); Note, *Nonfinancial Eligibility and Eviction Standards in Public Housing—The Problem Family in the Great Society*, 53 CORNELL L. REV. 1122 (1968).

the problem is that the issue does not always come up in so blatant a form, since the local agency may settle on some behavioral characteristic associated with welfare status as the basis for refusing admission, rather than openly refusing admission on the basis of welfare status alone.

For example, in the leading case of *Thomas v. Housing Authority*,[53] the public housing agency in Little Rock, Arkansas, had adopted a policy excluding from admission any unwed mothers with children born out of wedlock. (Certainly it is no secret that many women qualifying for AFDC are not married and have children born out of wedlock.) This limitation on admission was held illegal by the federal district court as not consistent with the policy of the federal housing act. Nevertheless, the federal court emphasized the absolute nature of the prohibition, intimating that eligibility criteria drawn more explicitly to take account of tenant conduct might pass judicial scrutiny. While the holding of the *Thomas* case has not been substantially elaborated by subsequent decisions, the federal housing agency has followed the lead of that case by suggesting that local public housing agencies may establish admissions criteria which take past conduct of the applicant into account. A tenant could be excluded, for example, if his conduct suggests that he would materially interfere with other tenants.[54] Federal administrative policy is of course subject to change, but it is of interest that the federal housing agency has also urged local public housing agencies to accept more applications from "wage earner and two-parent families having greater potential for stability."[55] This directive would suggest restrictions on the admission of single-parent families receiving welfare assistance.

Many critics of public housing have been concerned about the increase in welfare recipients in the projects, as they believe that the all-too-common breakdown in project life can be traced to the large number of these families, and the unstable family pat-

---

[53] 282 F. Supp. 575 (E.D. Ark. 1967). *Accord,* McDougal v. Tamsberg, 308 F. Supp. 1212 (D.S.C. 1970). *But cf.* Sumpter v. White Plains Housing Authority, 28 N.Y.2d 420, 278 N.E.2d 892 (1972), holding that applicants denied admission to public housing are not entitled to a Due Process hearing.

[54] U.S. DEP'T OF HOUSING AND URBAN DEVELOPMENT, CIRCULAR 12-17-68, ADMISSION AND CONTINUED OCCUPANCY REGULATIONS FOR LOW-RENT PUBLIC HOUSING.

[55] U.S. DEP'T OF HOUSING AND URBAN DEVELOPMENT, CIRCULAR 6-2-71, HOUSING A CROSS-SECTION OF LOW-INCOME FAMILIES IN LOW-RENT PUBLIC HOUSING, par. 3(c).

terns they bring with them. Moreover, these same critics believe that local public housing agencies have been circumscribed by recent court decisions, like the *Thomas* decision discussed above, which have forced them to change their admissions policies to admit more welfare tenants. A dilemma is therefore posed: must public housing agencies allow an excessive number of welfare families in the projects, in the face of evidence that these families make public housing projects unattractive to more stable residents?[56] The evidence of the destructive impact of welfare tenants is not all that conclusive, but the current folklore about the role they play in undermining project stability has not been altered.

Let us now look at welfare rent structures, for these affect both the receptiveness of the public housing agency to admitting welfare tenants, and the effect which their admission has on the financial health of the program. Unfortunately, the need to accommodate the very different statutory objectives in the public housing and welfare programs has presented public housing agencies with some very real difficulties in the determination of public housing rents. For example, the federal housing agency has long recommended special agreements between public housing agencies and welfare agencies on welfare rents in public housing, primarily to prevent the federal housing subsidy from being used to reduce welfare expenditures.[57] But the federal housing agency has not prevented public housing agencies from unilaterally raising public housing rents for welfare tenants above the rents charged to other tenants, and then passing these higher rents on to the welfare program. Since continuing inflation has forced welfare agencies into constant upward revisions in budget standards and welfare payments, public housing agencies took advantage of these trends to increase the proportion of their total rents which they collect from welfare tenants. With continuing growth in welfare caseloads, however, especially in the AFDC category, welfare agencies have increasingly placed limits on their wel-

---

[56] This point of view has been put most forcefully in STARR, WHICH OF THE POOR SHALL LIVE IN PUBLIC HOUSING No. 23, at 116 (Public Interest, Spring, 1971).

[57] MANAGEMENT HANDBOOK, *supra* note 12, pt. VII, § 4, par. 2(a). There was also concern in the federal General Accounting Office that welfare grants in some states were so low that welfare recipients could not pay rents that were sufficient to cover operating costs. An agreement was needed with the welfare agency to obtain an assurance that costs would be covered by welfare rents, and a few states legislated such a provision. *Cf.* CONN. GEN. STAT. REV. § 8-48 (1971).

fare expenditures, often by imposing maximum limits on the welfare grant for the shelter allowance. These limits have prevented public housing agencies from shifting an excessive share of their housing costs to the welfare program.

In view of this background, it is not surprising to find from a recent study that over three-fourths of the public housing agencies surveyed attempted to deal with the welfare rent problem through special welfare rent schedules.[58] These separate schedules may either be set independently by the public housing agency, or based on an agreement, as the federal housing agency suggested.[59] When agreements are used they are often negotiated at the state level, between a statewide association of public housing agencies on the one hand, and a statewide association of welfare agencies on the other.[60]

The next step is to determine how the problem of setting public housing rents for welfare recipients has been handled, either with or without the benefit of an agreement with the welfare program. The first question is to decide which tenants will pay the welfare rent. Not all welfare recipients in public housing get all of their income from welfare. Many of them or the members of their family may hold jobs. One question is what the public housing agency should do in this situation. A recent survey showed that many of these agencies apply welfare rent schedules whenever the tenant receives a majority, or even when he receives only some of his income from a welfare grant.[61] The effects of this policy are startling, and should carefully be noted. Public housing tenants who work are usually allowed to deduct work-related expenses from their income before their

---

[58] See REPORT, *supra* note 27, at VII-3.

[59] See MANAGEMENT HANDBOOK, *supra* note 12, pt. VII, § 4, par. 2(a).

[60] For examples see Memorandum of Understanding Between Georgia Department of Family and Children Services and Atlanta Regional Housing Assistance Office of the Department of Housing and Urban Development, June, 1970; Memorandum of Understanding By and Between the Atlanta Regional Office of Housing Assistance Administration and the North Carolina State Department of Public Welfare, July 1, 1966. The history of the agreement that was reached between the New Jersey State Department of Public Welfare and the regional office of the federal housing agency is detailed in HOUSING AUTHORITY OF THE CITY OF NEWARK, WELFARE RENT CHRONOLOGY: EVENTS PRECEDING THE ESTABLISHMENT OF THE CURRENT WELFARE RENT SCHEDULE (1970). Similar arrangements in effect in Pennsylvania are detailed in Pennsylvania Ass'n of Housing & Redevelopment Authorities, Memorandum to Pennsylvania Housing Authorities, Dec. 27, 1963.

[61] See REPORT, *supra* note 27, at VII-4.

rents are assessed, but may be denied this deduction if they receive a supplemental grant of any size from the welfare agency.

When we turn to the structure of the welfare rent schedules, we find that federal regulations prior to the 1959 local autonomy amendment suggested a variety of approaches, but the thrust of federal policy favored flat rents for welfare tenants.[62] Rents were to be fixed either on the basis of unit size or family size, and graded rents were not encouraged.[63] In addition, welfare rents were to be no less than the rents charged to nonwelfare families with the same income, and they were to approximate the average rents allowed by the welfare agency for private housing. This policy is contradictory. Since welfare rents in the private market are usually higher than rents for comparable units of public housing, the public housing agency could not equalize its welfare rents with private market rents without at the same time charging higher rents to its welfare tenants.

When we look at local welfare rent schedules we see that they have varied even more widely than federal directives would indicate. A recent study of local public housing agencies reveals the following practices:[64]

1. A large proportion of these agencies charge welfare tenants a rent based on average operating costs per unit.
2. A somewhat smaller group—about half this number—charge the maximum permitted for rent in the welfare recipient's budget.
3. About the same number of agencies base their welfare rents on the number of persons in the household.
4. About the same number of agencies base the rent on the size of the unit.
5. Finally, many housing agencies charge a specially negotiated welfare rent unless the nonwelfare rent based on net income is higher.

---

[62] For the policies of the federal housing agency see MANAGEMENT HANDBOOK, *supra* note 12, pt. VII, § 4, par. 2; *Id.*, Exh. 1.

[63] A similar approach is urged by the federal welfare agency. U.S. DEP'T OF HEALTH, EDUCATION, AND WELFARE, STATE LETTER NO. 1015, STATEMENT OF FUNDAMENTAL PRINCIPLES FOR ESTABLISHMENT OF RENTALS FOR PUBLIC ASSISTANCE FAMILIES (Feb. 15, 1968).

[64] REPORT, *supra* note 27, at VII-7.

These are the major variations, even though they are not the only ones. For example, a few public housing agencies charge welfare tenants a rent equal to the average rent paid by welfare tenants for private housing.

These practices also do not reflect negotiated agreements under which some welfare agencies have assumed all or a major portion of that part of the debt service on public housing costs. Since debt service is paid entirely by the federal housing subsidy, the local public housing agency gains in these cases to the extent that welfare agency accepts this federally subsidized amount as part of the welfare rent.

Several inequities result from this ad hoc and negotiated system of welfare rents. One is that welfare rents may either be more or less than per unit operating costs, which are not subsidized by federal subsidy. (Some representative examples are presented in Table 1.) Welfare recipients are thus deficit tenants in some cities and surplus tenants in others. Additional inequities occur within the projects. A combination of flat rent schedules, minimum rent charges, and less generous income deductions usually means that welfare tenants pay substantially more of their income for their public housing unit than do tenants who are not on welfare. Some typical examples are presented in Table 2.

TABLE 1. WELFARE RENTS AND PUBLIC HOUSING OPERATING COSTS FOR SEVEN MAJOR PUBLIC HOUSING AUTHORITIES

City	Welfare Rent (a)	Operating Cost (b)	Difference
Atlanta	$ 33.00	$ 49.92	—16.92
Birmingham	23.00	44.40	—21.40
Milwaukee	50.50	54.75	— 4.25
Newark	110.00	80.58	+29.42
Philadelphia	88.00	73.36	+14.64
San Francisco	61.00	67.49	— 6.49
Seattle	58.00	64.91	— 6.91

(a) For a four-person AFDC family
(b) From Trend Statements for 1966-70

Source: Abeles, Schwartz & Associates, The Impact of the Brooke Amendment on Public Housing Tenants and Local Authorities: A Report to the Joint HEW-HUD Task Force on Welfare Rents in Public Housing, at VII-8 (1971).

TABLE 2. WELFARE GRANTS, WELFARE RENTS AND NON-WELFARE INCOMES FOR SEVEN MAJOR PUBLIC HOUSING AUTHORITIES

City	Monthly Welfare Grant (a)	Monthly Welfare Rent	Equivalent Non-Welfare Monthly Net Income (b)
Atlanta	$133.00	$ 33.00	$166
Birmingham	81.00	23.00	138
Milwaukee	201.00 (c)	50.50	215
Newark	396.00 (d)	110.00	504
Philadelphia	324.00 (d)	88.00	399
San Francisco	221.00	61.00	310
Seattle	321.00	58.00	257

(a) For a 4 person AFDC family.
(b) Maximum income permitted according to the regular rent schedule (gross) at the welfare rent level for a family of one adult and three minor dependents.
(c) Estimated.
(d) Assumes that recent welfare rent increases $23 in Newark and $49 in Philadelphia, were added on to welfare grants in that exact amount.

Source: Abeles, Schwartz & Associates, The Impact of the Brooke Amendment on Public Housing Tenants and Local Authorities: A Report to the Joint HEW-HUD Task Force on Welfare Rents in Public Housing, at VII-10 (1971).

This situation has been altered in those states in which rising welfare costs have led to changes in welfare budgeting practices. In New Jersey, for example, welfare agencies operated until recently under a statewide agreement with public housing agencies which set welfare rents high enough to absorb some of the federally subsidized debt service on public housing units. This agreement was unilaterally revoked when the state welfare agency changed its previous method of budgeting for each item of family need on an individual basis, and shifted to a policy of making a flat grant to each AFDC family. While each budget item, such as housing, was included in the flat grant on the basis of an average supposedly representing actual costs, welfare groups and public housing agencies have argued that some items were underbudgeted. As a result, the new flat grant policy has led to a substantial reduction in the public housing rents paid by welfare recipients, and has aggravated the financial crisis faced by public housing agencies in that state.

These wide disparities in public housing rent systems for welfare tenants raise important constitutional questions. But judicial attitudes toward welfare rents have been heavily influenced by the course of the law as it affects shelter allowance practices in welfare administration, and these must be considered first.

4. Legal Attacks on Welfare Rents

From the point of view of possible legal objections that might be made to the shelter allowance, the most important point to note is the prevalence of legal devices which restrict the amount available for housing in one way or another. As pointed out earlier, these restrictions are usually imposed after the housing need standard has been determined.[65] Some state welfare statutes, as in California, do require a shelter allowance which will permit the recipient to acquire satisfactory housing, and courts in that state have sometimes directed welfare agencies to comply with the statutory mandate.[66] Elsewhere, welfare recipients who find their shelter allowance inadequate have little recourse, and when they seek to challenge the amount of their shelter allowance in court, they may find judicial relief foreclosed. Since the decision to award a shelter allowance requires a discretionary decision by the welfare agency, courts will ordinarily be unwilling to grant specific relief to claimants who seek to compel welfare agencies to make higher awards to them.[67] Delegations of administrative discretion in the system affect the availability of court relief in other ways. When welfare agencies are authorized

---

[65] Provided they are imposed uniformly throughout the state, they do not violate the statutory federal provision requiring uniformity in administration. 42 U.S.C. § 602(a)(1) (1970).

[66] Ivy v. Montgomery, Civil No. 592705 (Calif. Super. Ct., filed Sept. 11, 1969), *reprinted in Hearings on Emergency Home Financing Before House Comm. on Banking and Currency*, 91st Cong., 2nd Sess., at 325-35 (1970). *Accord*, Bronson v. Barbaro, Index No. 6938/70 (N.Y. Sup. Ct., filed July 23, 1970).

[67] *In re* Ocasio, CCH Pov. L. Rep. New Dev. par. 9268 (N.Y. Sup. Ct., filed Dec. 18, 1968). For similar results in cases in which the recipient moved to more expensive quarters and then attempted to sue to force the welfare agency to pay the increased rent see Green v. Essex County Welfare Bd., Civil No. A-49-69 (N.J. Super. Ct., App. Div., filed Mar. 31, 1970); *In re* Kreminicer, 162 N.Y.L.J. No. 66, at 18 (Sup. Ct. 1969). *Compare* Davis v. Goldberg, Index No. 02822 (N.Y. Sup. Ct., filed Feb. 25, 1969), finding a violation of Due Process when the welfare agency denied any rent allowance to a recipient whose rent was more than the maximum.

to grant administrative exceptions to housing allowance maximums, for example, the litigant may be asked to exhaust his administrative remedy before the welfare agency before challenging in court the explicit maximum ceiling on his grant.[68] Administrative recourse, naturally, will be time-consuming, frustrating, and punitive.

Even more difficult problems are presented when welfare recipients challenge in court the limitations that have been placed on the amount of their shelter allowance. These limitations, as we have noted, may take several forms. Most commonly, the welfare agency either places a maximum limit on the budget allowance for housing need, or averages the shelter allowance into a flat grant. Let us look at the flat grant approach first.

In *Rosado v. Wyman*,[69] flat grants for special needs of AFDC recipients in New York state were challenged under an ambiguous 1967 amendment to the federal welfare statute which required the states:

> "[To] provide that by July 1, 1969, the amounts used by the State to determine needs of individuals will have been adjusted to reflect fully changes in living costs since such amounts were established and any maximum that the State imposes on the amount of aid paid to families will have been proportionately adjusted."[70]

What happened in *Rosado* was that New York state changed its budgeting procedure in the AFDC program to convert from a system in which individual expenditure items were separately budgeted to a flat grant system with maximum allowances per family, based on the number of individuals in the household. The shelter allowance was still budgeted separately. In making this change the state eliminated a budget item for special needs which had been part of the old system, and a sum equal to the average amount which had been previously paid to meet these needs was apparently not included in the flat grant. This change was alleged to have violated the 1967 amendment, and the Supreme Court agreed. While the Court noted that a state, consistent with the statute, could "consolidate items on the basis of statistical averages," it could not do so if in the process it

---
[68] *See, especially*, Metcalf v. Swank, 444 F.2d 1353 (7th Cir. 1971).
[69] 397 U.S. 397 (1970).
[70] 42 U.S.C. § 402(a)(23) (1970).

eliminated a budget item that was previously covered.[71] Otherwise, the state would have indirectly avoided the cost-of-living adjustment by eliminating a previously existing budget item.

How this decision might affect welfare shelter allowances is indicated by recent litigation in New Jersey. We noted that the state has adopted a flat grant system for AFDC, abrogating its previous system of individually-determined budgets. Litigation was filed attacking the flat grant system in federal court. Among other allegations, the suit contended that the flat grant for housing had been improperly calculated. Public housing rents were included in the calculation on a weighted basis, even though they are substantially below private market rents in New Jersey, and only a small percentage of welfare recipients live in public housing. As a result, the flat grant does not contain an amount sufficient to meet the housing needs of tenants not living in public housing. This action was unsuccessful,[72] and elsewhere flat grants including a fixed amount for rent based on fair averaging have also been upheld.[73]

The statute on which *Rosado* is based is only of limited usefulness in dealing with the other method used to limit shelter allowances, the imposition of maximum ceilings. While the Supreme Court interpreted that statute to prohibit the elimination of a budget item or a reduction in its amount, the statute considered in *Rosado* appears to offset this limitation by permitting states to reduce proportionately the amount of assistance paid to all recipients. This possibility was recognized by the Court, which interpreted the statute to permit a downward adjustment in the amount of assistance paid, but only after all components of need had been fully adjusted to reflect cost-of-living increases as of the 1969 date. Answering objections that this construction would allow states to frustrate the statute's intent, the Court pointed out that the amendment would at least force a state to accept the "political" consequences of a welfare cutback.[74] Presumably, the

---

[71] *See also* Boddie v. Wyman, 434 F.2d 1207 (2nd Cir. 1970), *aff'd per curiam*, 402 U.S. 991 (1971), requiring New York to justify regional differentials in its budget standards.

[72] New Jersey Welfare Rights Organization v. Cahill, 349 F. Supp. 491 (D.N.J. 1972). *But see* Housing Authority of Asbury Park v. Richardson, 346 F. Supp. 1027 (D.N.J. 1972), denying a motion to dismiss a similar action.

[73] Johnson v. White, Civil No. 14,620 (D.C. Conn., filed June 12, 1972). *See also* Bronson v. Barbaro, Index No. 6938/79 (N.Y. Sup. Ct., filed Oct. 19, 1971) (upholds averaging technique under which housing allowance determined).

[74] 397 U.S. at 413.

Court meant that a cut in welfare grants following an upward adjustment in standards would attract political attention to inadequacies in the program.

But maximum limitations on shelter allowance grants are also open to the challenge that they violate the constitutional Equal Protection requirement. Assume two AFDC families, each with the same number of children, with the exception that the children in family A are quite young, while the children in family B are much older. Older children in a family usually require separate bedrooms, at least when they are of different sexes, so that B family's housing need will be greater than that of family A. If a maximum limit on the housing grant prevents family B from occupying a dwelling unit sufficient to meet its needs, while family A is not so restricted, a denial of Equal Protection can be argued on the ground that the welfare payment has improperly been based on family size, without regard to need. This basis for the welfare grant cannot be accepted constitutionally unless some justification can be found for it.

Two tests have been applied by the United States Supreme Court when passing on Equal Protection challenges to legislative and administrative discriminations of this kind.[75] The first, the traditional Equal Protection test, has been used for most discriminations that have an economic basis. This test has not placed a heavy burden of justification on the challenged classification and, under the usual formulation, the discrimination will be sustained if there is any "imaginable basis" for making it. The second is the strict Equal Protection test under which the legislative classification under attack is viewed as suspect, and therefore requires a heavier burden of justification. When the strict Equal Protection test is applied, the challenged classification will not be saved unless it serves a compelling state interest. If the same test were applied to the classifications inherent in a maximum housing allowance restriction, there would be little doubt that the maximum limitation would be held unconstitutional.

Before the strict test is adopted, however, the court must find that a fundamental constitutional interest of the complaining

---

[75] See Note, *Developments in the Law—Equal Protection,* 82 HARV. L. REV. 1065 (1969). However, there are indications that the Supreme Court may be departing from this method of analysis. See Gunther, *The Supreme Court, 1971 Term—Foreword: In Search of Evolving Doctrine on a Changing Court: A Model for a Newer Equal Protection,* 86 HARV. L. REV. 1 (1972).

party is injured by the classification. While there were suggestions in United States Supreme Court cases that classifications adopted in the welfare program might fall in the special interests category,[76] any doubts on this score were laid at rest in the recent United States Supreme Court case of *Dandridge v. Williams.*[77] That case held constitutional a maximum limitation on the total welfare grant that had been imposed in the Maryland AFDC program. Vacated at the same time was a federal district court opinion in California, which had invalidated a shelter allowance maximum in that state.[78]

In *Dandridge,* the amount of the total welfare grant was limited once a family reached a certain size. As a result, large families were denied an increase in their grant to which they otherwise would have been entitled. Nevertheless, the Court held that the interests of welfare recipients did not fall within the fundamental interest category, applied the traditional Equal Protection rationale, and found an "imaginable basis" on which the grant limitation could be sustained.

Although the Supreme Court in *Dandridge* was somewhat reluctant to offer its own justification for the maximum grant limitation, a close reading of the case suggests that the Court accepted the state's argument, that a maximum limit on the welfare grant is necessary to achieve statutory objectives in the welfare program which encourage welfare recipients to work. Without a maximum limit on the amount of the welfare grant, that grant might bring the welfare recipient more money than a job. This justification overrode any discrimination against large families which was inherent in the maximum grant system.

A maximum limit on the shelter allowance is open to a comparable justification.[79] A maximum limit on the shelter allowance may be imposed as part of or result from a maximum

---

[76] *See* Shapiro v. Thompson, 394 U.S. 618 (1969), holding a residence requirement in welfare assistance unconstitutional as a violation of the right to travel.

[77] 397 U.S. 471 (1970). The case is discussed extensively in Dienes, *To Feed the Hungry: Judicial Retrenchment in Welfare Adjudication,* 58 CALIF. L. REV. 555 (1970).

[78] Kaiser v. Montgomery, 397 U.S. 595 (1970).

[79] Federal statutory objections to the maximum welfare grants raised in the *Dandridge* case do not appear applicable to shelter allowances. *See* Dienes, *supra* note 77, at 565-91. A state supreme court has now relied on *Dandridge* to justify a shelter allowance maximum. *In re* Devoid, —— Vt. ——, 287 A.2d 573 (1972).

limit on the total grant. This limitation on the shelter allowance can be justified as incidental to the larger objective of limiting the welfare grant to an amount which is less than what the welfare recipient would have earned. While a maximum limitation on the shelter allowance can also be imposed in a welfare program in which no limitation is placed on the total amount of aid which is given to the recipient, an argument consistent with *Dandridge* can support a maximum limitation on the shelter allowance in this situation as well. Without the limit, it can be argued that welfare recipients would be better housed than working families not on welfare, to the extent that the unlimited shelter allowance would exceed the amount that low-income working families could afford to spend on housing. This kind of argument accepts the "less eligibility" principle of the English Poor Law, which apparently found its way into the *Dandridge* case. As this principle is applied in welfare programs, less eligibility simply means that welfare recipients should not be made better off than working families not on welfare. The difficulty with this rationale is that the housing allowance maximum is not always related to market rents, and so does not advance the objective which is claimed for it. Nevertheless, a liberal application of the imaginable basis rule would no doubt sustain the shelter allowance as well. An argument that the welfare grant maximum in *Dandridge* did not always encourage working because it was applied to welfare recipients who in fact had no work opportunities was rejected by the Court. In any event, vacation of a lower court decree invalidating a shelter allowance maximum, at the same time that *Dandridge* was decided, suggests that the highest court also considers shelter allowance maximum to be constitutional.[80]

Whatever other impact *Dandridge* and *Rosado* have had on welfare administration, these cases have opened the way for budgeting practices in welfare programs which set severe limits on the amount of money budgeted to welfare recipients for housing purposes. If welfare tenants in public housing are then required to pay rents that are disproportionately higher than those paid by other tenants, and if budgeting practices in welfare programs do not give them a shelter allowance large enough to pay these rents, welfare recipients will find their public housing

---

[80] *See also* Groff v. Wolgemuth, 328 F. Supp. 1016 (E.D. Pa. 1971), upholding after *Dandridge* an allegedly discriminatory system under which utility grants were budgeted in the Pennsylvania welfare program.

an economic burden too heavy to bear. This pressure on welfare rents in public housing led, in part, to the Brooke Amendment, which limited public housing rents to 25 percent of income. Before we turn to a discussion of this amendment and its problems in the next chapter, it may be well to consider the Equal Protection problems raised by *Dandridge* from another perspective. Are the classifications made between welfare and nonwelfare tenants in public housing rent schedules also open to challenge on Equal Protection grounds?

The first question to ask is whether welfare tenants really suffer discrimination in the public housing program. The discussion so far has shown that welfare tenants in public housing may or may not suffer discrimination from the different rent schedules adopted by most public housing agencies.[81] When discrimination against welfare tenants does result, it may take place in one of several ways. Welfare tenants may pay rents fixed on a unit or family basis, while other tenants pay graded rents fixed on a rent/income basis. Or, working tenants may be allowed certain work-related expense deductions which may be denied both to tenants completely on welfare and to welfare tenants who get income from work as well. These are the most common potentially discriminatory differentials in rent systems which have been litigated in court.[82]

Some court challenges to differential rent schedules for welfare tenants have been based simply on the fact that welfare tenants are charged flat rents while working tenants are charged graded rents.[83] To the extent that flat rents mean higher rents for welfare tenants it is argued that they suffer discrimination solely on the basis of their source of income, in violation of the

---

[81] For a discussion of rent schedules discriminating *against* welfare tenants see Note, *Higher Rents for Welfare Recipients in Public Housing: An Analysis Under the Equal Protection Clause*, 45 U. SO. CAL. L. REV. 263 (1972).

[82] Note that welfare rents may be calculated to include debt service met in full by federal subsidy, even though the rents of working tenants exclude debt service. *See* page 69, *supra*.

[83] Other problems arise from the practice of public housing agencies of charging both minimum and maximum rents. For example, minimum rents would force tenants to pay proportionately more for their unit once their incomes fell below the level at which the minimum rent charge took effect. This practice was invalidated in a lawsuit which predated *Dandridge*. Solomon v. Housing Authority of New Orleans, Civil No. 70-12 (E.D. La., filed April 23, 1970). *Cf.* Tyree v. Housing Authority of Pleasanton, 2 Cal. App. 3d 130, 86 Cal. Rptr. 461 (1970), holding that the state public housing statute does not impose a *duty* to operate at a profit.

Equal Protection clause.[84] While these cases of discrimination have had some success in court, the argument can be made that source of income is relevant to rent-setting policies in public housing. Both the federal statute, and many state statutes which follow it, mandate consideration of the rent-paying capacity of the public housing tenant.

The above argument has been used by public housing agencies which defended differential rent schedules of this type in cases in which the application of graded rents to working tenants and flat rents to welfare tenants resulted in higher rent levels for the welfare recipients. These agencies argued that the generally lower rent level for working tenants compensated for work-related expenses which were not otherwise explicitly deducted from income before rent was determined. As these additional work-related expenses would be administratively impossible to document on a case-by-case basis, lower rents for working tenants were a way of inserting these expenses into the rent schedule without having to undergo the administrative burden of determining their amount in each case.[85] Welfare tenants might be unfairly treated by this method of classification, but the *Dandridge* case suggests that no method of treatment must provide perfect equity in all cases.

To this argument the reply was made that flat rents were also applied to welfare tenants who work, in effect denying them the allowance for work-related expenses which is built into the lower grade rents charged to working tenants who receive no welfare assistance at all.[86] As an alternative, some other system could be used which would take into account the pro rata share of income which some welfare tenants earn.

The arguments against discriminatory welfare rent schedules have been accepted to some extent in the cases. A federal district court in *Hammond v. Housing Authority and Urban Renewal*

---

[84] Luna v. Housing Authority of Los Angeles, Civil No. 969, 666 (Cal. Super. Ct., filed July 7, 1970), *appeal pending*, Civil No. 37539 (Cal. App. Ct.). *See also* Complaint of Plaintiff, Johnson v. Illinois Dep't of Public Aid, Civil No. P 3184 (S.D. Ill., filed Jan. 21, 1971).

[85] Ford v. Housing Authority of San Francisco, Civil No. 47921 (N.D. Cal., filed Feb. 20, 1969), at 4.

[86] In addition, tenants not working but receiving more than half their income from sources other than welfare were also entitled to the more favorable rental schedule. This exception would include tenants receiving more than half their income from social security.

Agency of Lane County,[87] a post-*Dandridge* case, held unconstitutional a public housing rent schedule which resulted in higher rents for welfare tenants. While the basis for making this higher charge was not disclosed, the court noted:

> "The propriety of an attempt by a housing authority to motivate welfare recipients to seek work by charging discriminatory rents is itself doubtful. Equally dubious is the attempt made by the housing authority to use state and federal moneys to subsidize the repayment of its housing loan."[88]

Yet another federal district court, while finding the housing authority's rent schedule unconstitutional in similar circumstances, indicated that the authority was entitled to make distinctions between welfare and working tenants so long as "source of income involves a factor affecting the rent-paying ability of tenants and the differential fairly reflects that factor."[89] This case was decided pre-*Dandridge*.

Whether these cases are a correct interpretation of *Dandridge* is open to question. It can be argued that the goals of the public housing program do not permit work-related incentives, so that the system of rents in public housing may not be manipulated with these incentives in mind. We should also note that the court in *Hammond* objected to a structure of housing rents that allowed welfare grants to subsidize the public housing program. In some cases the converse is true. Rents from working tenants subsidize welfare tenants and, indirectly, the welfare program. Would the court object equally in this situation?

The real difficulty in public housing is that welfare rents must always reflect the pressures that arise from an attempt to accommodate what would otherwise be a potential conflict between two income support systems. In many states, for example, welfare agencies base the housing allowance on the rent actually paid. Public housing agencies, on the other hand, may calculate their rent as a portion of income received. Thus, rent setting for

---

[87] 328 F. Supp. 586 (D. Ore. 1971). *Accord,* New York City Housing Authority v. Fields, 167 N.Y.L.J. No. 78, at 18 (Sup. Ct. 1972), discussed in City Cites Saving in Relief Housing, The New York Times, Aug. 6, 1972, § 1, p. 28, col. 1.

[88] *Id.,* at 588.

[89] Ford v. Housing Authority of San Francisco, *supra* note 85, at 8.

welfare tenants in public housing is highly subject to manipulation by welfare and public housing agencies. The former can lower the public housing rent simply by lowering the welfare grant, while the latter can increase the welfare payment simply by increasing their rent charge. The question arises whether courts will or should be willing to consider this circumstance when passing on the constitutionality of public housing welfare rent systems. Should they be sympathetic to the rent-setting policies that public housing agencies adopt or, even better, uphold a negotiated agreement between public housing and welfare agencies? The courts may have to intervene, however, in cases when these agreements do not reflect the constitutional protections that should be accorded to public housing tenants.

D. Summary

This review of subsidy formulas and rent policies in American public housing has concentrated on the distribution of that subsidy to public housing tenants through the rent system. While the share of public housing costs met by the subsidy is determined by the federal statutory subsidy formula, the impact of the subsidy on individual tenants is largely decided by the local public housing agencies charged with the operation of the public housing program. Little federal or state statutory guidance is provided to these agencies, so that the adoption of detailed operating policies for public housing falls largely within the realm of local administrative policy.

We have learned that most local public housing agencies adopted rent systems which attempted to meet the housing needs of tenants by basing rent on a portion of income, and that dwelling units were assigned to tenants on the basis of housing need. This system of rent determination has led in turn to substantial internal cross-subsidies within public housing projects, as the more affluent tenants in smaller units will have to pay proportionately higher rents than poorer tenants in larger units if the program is to remain financially solvent.

The rent determination problem is most acute in the case of welfare tenants. Pressures for reducing financial costs in the welfare program have come at the same time that the number of welfare recipients in public housing has increased substantially. Welfare agencies have responded to this situation by limiting shelter allowance grants at the same time that public housing agencies have attempted to shift more of their costs to their welfare tenants. While the legal acceptability of these strategies is not yet settled, the courts so far have been willing to accept policies which reduce the welfare budget for housing, but have been hostile to practices which increase the public housing rent burden on welfare tenants in some instances.

These judicial attitudes have contributed to the financial pressures which are threatening public housing. Increasing financial hardship among public housing tenants has come at a time when rapidly escalating operating costs have undermined the financial solvency of the program. Especially in view of the growing number of welfare tenants in the projects, the opportunity to finance public housing through continuing increases in rent levels has grown increasingly limited. The result has been a radical change in the nature of the program, a development to which we turn our attention in the next chapter.

Chapter IV

THE BROOKE AMENDMENT TO THE PUBLIC HOUSING LAW: MEETING THE CHALLENGE OF COSTS

In the last chapter, which concentrated on problems of local administration and rent practices in the public housing program, we saw that the federal subsidy formula originally placed the full burden of public housing operating costs and local tax payments on the local public housing agencies. These agencies, in turn, had to find the funds to meet these costs from the rents charged to project tenants. So long as there was enough rental income to meet operating costs and local tax payments, the federal subsidy, together with rents collected in the local projects, managed to support the expenditure of running the program without a serious crisis in program finance.

As the decade of the 60's came to an end, however, the entire structure of local rent charges began to be threatened by financial difficulties within the public housing program. Costs and tax payments began to outstrip rent receipts and, especially in the major cities, public housing agencies faced accumulating and disastrous operating deficits.[1] Local public housing administrators

---

[1] *See* Walsh, *Is Public Housing Headed for a Fiscal Crisis?*, 26 J. HOUSING 64 (1969).

turned for relief to rent increases, but they soon found that they had little margin in which to operate. Public housing tenants began to find that their rents were taking a larger and larger share of their welfare grants and wages, and protests over rent increases began to be heard more frequently. At the same time, rising rents did not provide enough revenue to meet rising costs in many cities, and the need for additional financial aid soon became apparent.

Just where this aid was to be found was not immediately clear. A few cities, such as San Francisco, helped with contributions from local taxes. But most cities, especially those in the older metropolitan centers in which much public housing was located, faced other serious financial problems at that time and therefore had little excess revenue with which to assist their public housing agency. The federal government had the resources to help the program, but its assistance was prevented by the scope of existing Annual Contributions Contracts, which were limited to debt service.

Federal officials in the national housing department were not anxious to come to the rescue either, and blamed lax and inefficient local management rather than rising costs for the financial troubles in the public housing program. Only Congress responded with some additional help for limited categories of public housing tenants, first by way of a new subsidy of ten dollars per month per unit for elderly families, and then by an extension of the same supplement to families displaced by governmental programs, and families that are large or unusually poor.[2] When these additional subsidies proved inadequate, demands mounted for even more federal financial relief. Federal housing officialdom resisted. Change came only after a pitched struggle, which required more than one congressional intervention in the way of remedial legislation. Rents were limited by Congress at the same time that federal subsidies were extended to cover project operating expenses. Since these changes largely grew out of an amendment to the federal public housing law sponsored by Senator Edward Brooke of Massachusetts, we will

---

[2] *See* United States Housing Act, § 10(a). The subsidy for the elderly was also intended to induce public housing agencies to provide more housing for elderly people. All of these subsidies are payable only if operating revenues of the public housing agency are insufficient to maintain solvency.

refer to this related group of changes as the Brooke Amendment, although more than one amendment was involved.

Because the Brooke Amendment illustrates so well the difficulties of legislating for a complex and highly controversial program such as public housing, we have recounted its history in some detail. This history reflects the more open nature of the political setting in which policy changes are made in important American social programs, and contrasts vividly with the more controlled political environment in which even more substantial changes in the English housing subsidy system have been adopted. Thus, it carries lesson beyond the issues that were at stake in this particular legislative battle.

A. The Roots of the Financial Crisis

Studies of public housing, though not conclusive, confirmed the complaints of local public housing administrators that rising costs were at the root of their financial problems. One such study, carried out by the Urban Institute, a federally funded research agency, covered 23 major public housing agencies.[3] Reviewing the period from 1965 to 1968, just before the Brooke Amendment was passed, the Institute found that price inflation had been responsible for 80 percent of the cost increase during that period. These inflationary pressures had been punishing. Costs had been rising at an average rate of eight percent per year,[4] at the same time that rents had been increasing at an average rate of three percent annually. A study of New York public housing reached the same conclusion.[5] While the annual increase in operating costs was smaller—about five percent—rents had been rising at the same rate as in the Urban Institute sample.

Some significant correlations were also discovered between cost increases and other factors which have usually been held responsible for the rising costs of project operation. The number of minors in a family correlated with costs, for example, a finding attributed to the impact on cost of dwelling size, as additional children require more rooms.[6] Similarly, in the New York study, a ten percent decrease in dwelling size reduced expenses per unit by

---

[3] F. DE LEEUW, OPERATING COSTS IN PUBLIC HOUSING: A FINANCIAL CRISIS (1969).
[4] *Id.*, at 12, 15.
[5] C.P. RYDELL, FACTORS AFFECTING MAINTENANCE AND OPERATING COSTS IN FEDERAL PUBLIC HOUSING PROJECTS (New York City Rand Institute, 1970).
[6] DE LEEUW, *supra* note 3, at 40.

4.3 percent. But changes in the quantity and efficiency of services accounted for only one percent of the average annual yearly increase in public housing operating expenses.[7] Moreover, in the Urban Institute study, no correlation was found between the number of welfare tenants in a project and rising costs.

Whatever their cause, these upward trends in operating costs placed heavy pressures on tenant rents. As the Urban Institute study pointed out, rent increases had been put into effect during the study period even though median incomes in the projects had not been rising.[8] These financial stresses in the public housing program soon led to rent strikes and tenant protests, and eventually attracted congressional attention.

B. Congress Responds: The Brooke Amendment—First Round[9]

The politics of the congressional committees which deal with substantive housing matters may often be a politics of personal leadership. When Senator Edward Brooke of Massachusetts was first elected to the Senate in 1966, and assigned to the subcommittee of the Senate Banking and Currency Committee that has jurisdiction over housing matters, he did not show a strong interest in the housing field. Events, however, conspired to motivate his interest, and to catapult him into a leadership position on housing, and especially on public housing legislation.

Brooke had gone on a routine tour of his state early in 1969, and returned from visits to local public housing projects shocked by what he had seen; maintenance was bad, and recreational facilities were nonexistent. His impressions from this tour led Brooke to question the federal financial base for the public housing program, and these impressions were reinforced by another development of national importance, the first successful rent strike in a public housing project, in St. Louis, Missouri. In the notorious and ill-fated Pruitt-Igoe public housing project, a series of high-rise structures had been increasingly abandoned and vandalized

---

[7] RYDELL, *supra* note 5, at v.

[8] DE LEEUW, *supra* note 3, at 52, 55.

[9] In many instances, statements made in the text are based on discussions with agency officials, congressional staff, and the staff of various organizations in the housing field, both in Washington and elsewhere. Those persons who have been interviewed have requested that they not be quoted directly. For a discussion of some of the background to enactment of the Brooke Amendment see Housing Association of Delaware Valley, Racism and Exploitation in Public Housing: HUD and the Brooke Amendment 2-5 (Special Memorandum No. 55, 1970).

by their tenants. In spite of the deteriorating condition of its buildings, however, rents in this project had risen dramatically; welfare tenants were paying 60 to 75 percent of their grant for rent. Low welfare budgets in Missouri contributed to this high rent/income ratio, but the tenants found it easier to strike the public housing agency for lower rents than to strike the welfare agency for higher grants.

The Pruitt-Igoe strike ended successfully in 1969 with substantial changes in the management of the St. Louis public housing agency. But the management and financial problems exposed by the strike led the only black Congressman from St. Louis to approach HUD for financial assistance for St. Louis and other stricken public housing programs. HUD, the federal Department of Housing and Urban Development, was the agency then responsible for the public housing program at the national level. As HUD was cool to St. Louis pleas for more financial help, the St. Louis group decided to act legislatively.

All of these problems in St. Louis surfaced just at the time the Housing Act of 1969 was making its way through Congress, an act which contained the usual group of annual technical and other minor modifications to the national housing legislation. Senator Brooke was persuaded to draft an amendment to the 1969 act that would provide the financial assistance which the St. Louis and similar situations elsewhere seemed to require.[10] He was influential enough with his committee to have the amendment attached to the housing act when it was reported to the Senate floor. It was changed substantially, however, before it was finally enacted.

Brooke's Amendment was quickly drafted, and he did not attempt to deal systematically with the complex system of federal subsidies and local public housing rents which we have detailed in the last chapter. Instead, he simply added a new section to the federal public housing title which covered both the problem of excessive rents and additional federal subsidies:

> Sec. 24(a). In order to enable public housing agencies to provide housing within the means of families of very low income and to provide improved operat-

---

[10] The bill is reproduced in *Hearings on Housing and Urban Development Legislation of 1969 Before the Subcomm. on Housing and Urban Affairs of the Senate Comm. on Banking and Currency*, S. 2761, 91st Cong., 1st Sess. 553-54 (1969) [hereinafter cited as *1969 Senate Hearings*].

ing and maintenance services, the secretary [of HUD] may make, and contract to make, annual rental assistance payments to public housing agencies with respect to any low-rent public housing project.

(b) The amount of the annual payment with respect to any dwelling unit in a low-rent housing project shall not exceed the amount by which the rental for such unit exceeds one-fourth of the tenant's income.

As Brooke's legislation was drafted, therefore, it left several major questions unanswered, and these were to return after the bill was enacted to plague the administration of the new subsidy which the bill authorized. One major problem arose from the fact that the bill put a ceiling on public housing rents, but did not indicate what the rent structure in public housing should look like below that ceiling. As a result, local rent structures were unaffected, and the important question of the relationship of welfare shelter allowances to public housing rents was left untouched.

This lack of attention to local rent problems may have been consistent with the decision made in the federal legislation to leave these matters to the local public housing agencies. But Brooke's bill, by imposing a rent ceiling for the first time, invaded this local autonomy. It opened up the entire question of local rent determinations, triggering a controversy over the administration of a program which previously had been almost fully delegated to the local level.

For example, we have seen that local public housing agencies authorize a wide variety of income deductions when making the determination of net income against which rent is to be calculated. Some national definition of the income against which rent is chargeable would seem to be a necessary part of a national rent ceiling, and by the time Brooke's Amendment left the Senate committee the authority to make this determination had been added. A new proviso at the end of paragraph (b) authorized the HUD secretary to define tenant income for purposes of applying the 25 percent ceiling.[11] This change was included in the legislation as finally enacted.

---

[11] S. 2864, 91st Cong., 1st Sess. § 211 (1969), *reproduced in* 115 CONG. REC. 26723, 26726 (1969).

Unfortunately, the new amendment was to be read in practice as imposing an income definition and rent calculation only for purposes of determining whether the federal rent limit was violated. Local rent schedules, with whatever inequities they contained, were still to be used in determining the actual rent to be paid. This system introduced new administrative complications at the local level, and left untouched those local rent-setting practices which discriminated between welfare and working tenants. Backers of the income definition provision had also assumed an expansive rather than a restrictive definition of income by HUD. This interpretation, as we shall see, was not forthcoming.

Other aspects of the Brooke Amendment were also troublesome, and later presented some of the more difficult and controversial problems in its interpretation. For example, a careful reading of paragraphs (a) and (b) of the proposed Section 24 leaves some doubt about the basis of the new subsidies which were provided. Were they to be provided solely to make up operating deficiencies resulting from the new rent ceiling, or could they be made available to local public housing agencies to make up operating deficiencies without regard to revenue gaps created by this ceiling? Paragraph (a) also raised the question whether subsidies were to be limited only to public housing agencies whose operating and maintenance services were *improved.*

Finally, professionals familiar with the public housing program were critical of the method selected to fund the new operating subsidies authorized by the Brooke Amendment. The subsidies were not to be funded within the framework of the Annual Contributions Contracts, for which federal appropriations were relatively certain. Another amendment to the public housing law had been introduced by Senator John Sparkman of Alabama, also a member of the subcommittee responsible for housing legislation, which would make it explicit for the first time that annual contributions need not be limited to debt service. This amendment was included in the 1969 law as enacted.[12] But the Sparkman Amendment was not tied directly into Brooke's proposal.

---

[12] Act of Dec. 24, 1969, Pub. L. No. 91-152, § 212(a), 83 Stat. 379, 388, presently codified in 42 U.S.C. § 1410 (b) (1970). This amendment was initially contained in a bill introduced by Sparkman, S. 527, 91st Cong., 1st Sess. § 5 (1969). It passed both houses without difficulty.

Sponsors of the Brooke Amendment were aware of the limitations of the amendment, and also of the fact that intensive lobbying before Congress was necessary if its enactment was to be assured. Brooke himself was a Republican, but party affiliation did not prevent leading figures in the national housing department of a Republican administration from opposing him. Opposition inside HUD was led by Sherman Unger, then General Counsel to the agency, and by Lawrence Cox, then assistant secretary for housing assistance. Unger had had no previous housing experience, but Cox had been housing and renewal director in Norfolk, Virginia. Just what the opposition of HUD officials to Brooke's Amendment was based on is not clear. Supposedly, Cox and Unger were worried about the effect that operating subsidies would have on local public housing agencies, and also about lax management and improper tenant selection practices at the local agency level. They were also concerned that making operating subsidies available to local public housing agencies would aggravate and not improve these problems. Some would also argue that Cox and Unger were simply hostile to the public housing program, deplored the change in tenantry which came about when large numbers of welfare recipients were admitted, and wished to avoid any step which would increase the number of so-called problem families in the projects. The Senate Report, in commenting on Brooke's Amendment, had indicated that the amendment was intended to apply to "all families who otherwise . . . would be barred from public housing because their income was inadequate."[13] A large family needing a four or five bedroom unit was cited as an example,[14] apparently on the basis that large families often find themselves with inadequate resources for decent housing.

As a result of HUD opposition, behind-the-scenes pressure was put on the congressional committees to make substantial changes in the Brooke proposal. This conflict, though not reflected in the written record,[15] was a critical influence in determin-

---

[13] S. REP. NO. 91-392, 91st Cong., 1st Sess. 19 (1969).

[14] The committee apparently assumed that all public housing rents were based on the size of the unit.

[15] However, in debate on the House floor, Congresswoman Sullivan of St. Louis, a member of the housing subcommittee, had indicated that the new subsidies authorized by the 1969 legislation were not automatic. Local housing authorities, she said, "must take necessary steps to upgrade management policies to assure tenant responsibility." 115 CONG. REC. 38778-779 (1969).

ing the final shape of the new subsidy. Indeed, differences between the Senate and House of Representatives version of the Brooke Amendment were one factor which finally sent the entire 1969 housing act to a Conference Committee. What finally emerged was a compromise which included substantial changes in the Brooke Amendment.[16] Having been introduced as an independent and additional section to the public housing law, the Brooke Amendment was now distributed into three parts. One part of the amendment imposed a 25 percent rent/income ratio as a maximum rent in the public housing program.[17]

Another part dealt with the welfare rent problem, an issue which had surfaced during congressional consideration of the bill as a factor to be considered in the new reform. Legislators became aware that shelter allowances in welfare programs varied considerably among the states, and that where shelter allowances met rents actually charged the Brooke Amendment would shift part of the housing costs of welfare tenants to the housing program. That is, public housing rents of welfare tenants would be reduced, the loss in revenue would be picked up by the new federal operating costs subsidy, and welfare agencies would benefit by reducing the amount of their shelter allowance by the amount of the rent reduction.

Several methods were suggested to handle this problem. Grass-roots organizations in the housing and welfare fields argued for a "pass-through" of the Brooke Amendment subsidy to welfare tenants. That is, welfare tenants in public housing would have their rents reduced while their shelter allowance would remain the same. The rent reduction would thus go into their pockets as extra income. Whatever the equities and constitutional problems of such a system, this proposal aggravates rather than solves the problem of allocating housing costs between the housing subsidy and welfare subsidy systems. The problem was handled in the 1969 legislation by adding a provision that prohibited a rent reduction under the Brooke Amendment unless the welfare agency

---

[16] Act of Dec. 24, 1969, Pub. L. No. 91-152, § 213, 83 Stat. 379, 389.

[17] 42 U.S.C. § 1402(1) (1970): ". . . [I]ncome limits for occupancy and rents (which may not exceed one-fourth of the family's income, as defined by the Secretary) shall be fixed by the" local public housing agency and approved by the federal agency.

agreed not to lower its shelter allowance by the amount of the rent reduction.[18]

Finally, major surgery was carried out on those provisions of the Brooke Amendment which had specifically authorized additional public housing subsidies. One of the changes, although technical, was significant. In response to criticisms from local public housing administrators, the independent statutory provision for an additional operating subsidy was deleted from Brooke's bill. Instead, two changes were made in the public housing law which were intended to incorporate the intent of the original Brooke provision, and to secure for it the more reliable funding available for the federal annual contribution to public housing subsidies.

To carry out this intent, the public housing law was first changed to authorize *amendments* to annual contributions contracts when necessary "to insure the low-rent character of the project."[19] This language complemented the Sparkman Amendment, which explicitly authorized annual contributions for more than debt service, and was written generally enough to include the proposed operating subsidy. Next, the new independent appropriation for an operating subsidy which had been authorized by Brooke's Amendment was transferred to and made a part of the budget item from which all annual contributions to local public housing agencies are paid, and the language explaining the purposes for which the operating subsidy was to be used was deleted from the bill. Instead, the report of the Conference Committee which handled the 1969 housing act explained in detail the purposes for which the new subsidy could be used.[20] This explanation was inserted into the Conference Committee report at the insistence of HUD officials who had opposed the Brooke Amendment initially, and became the basis for the HUD regulations under which the subsidy was ultimately distributed.

---

[18] Act of Dec. 24, 1969, Pub. L. No. 91-152, § 213(b), 83 Stat. 379, 389. This paragraph, apparently introduced at the request of Congresswoman Sullivan, was not codified. The Conference Report also called for a joint task force of HUD and HEW to study welfare rents. CONF. REP. NO. 91-740, 91st Cong., 1st Sess. 30-31 (1969) [hereinafter cited as 1969 CONF. REP.]. The report of the HUD-HEW task force far from settled these questions. *See* REPORT OF THE JOINT HUD-HEW TASK FORCE ON WELFARE RENTS IN PUBLIC HOUSING (1971).

[19] Act of Dec. 24, 1969, Pub. L. No. 91-152, § 213(c), 83 Stat. 379, 389, codified in 42 U.S.C. § 1414(b) (1970). *See also* 1969 CONF. REP., at 31.

[20] 1969 CONF. REP., at 31.

Legislation by Conference Report is unusual. In the case of the Brooke Amendment, it reflected the intense political pressures brought to bear on Brooke's proposal. These pressures are mirrored in the vague language in which the Report was written, especially the part authorizing annual contributions in excess of debt service. The Report authorized:

> (1) [P]ayments to cover existing operating deficits of public housing authorities and enable them to maintain adequate operating and maintenance services and reserve funds, and
> (2) additional payments to make up the amount by which the proportionate share of operating and maintenance expenses attributable to a public housing tenant's dwelling unit exceeds 25 percent of the tenant's income.

The Report stated that the second category of payments was not available unless the tenant was paying one-fourth of his rent for income. However, the Report also made it clear that the new 25 percent rent/income ratio only affected the payment of the subsidy, and was not intended as a requirement that all rents in public housing projects had to be raised to the 25 percent rent/income figure.[21]

In another paragraph which was later to become intensely controversial, however, the Conference Report expressed deep concern over lax management in public housing projects, reflecting the concern of Cox and other HUD officials, and attributed the need for additional subsidies to increasing vandalism and crime in public housing projects:

> Much of the blame for these conditions lies with project managers and local government officials. Too frequently individual projects have filled up with problem families to the exclusion of others with resulting vacancy rates which have caused local budget deficits.[22]

The language of the Report had been reinforced earlier by a warning from a high HUD official, for Cox had written a letter

---

[21] *Ibid.* The same point had been made by one of the House conferees in floor debate. 115 CONG. REC. 38778 (1969).

[22] *Ibid.* HUD was also asked to review its management policies.

in which he told local public housing agencies either to accept more self-supporting tenants or to face the consequences.[23]

C. HUD Responds: Regulations Under the 1969 Law

Though they were dismayed by the Conference Report, supporters of the Brooke Amendment were encouraged by the new legislation, and viewed it as an important breakthrough.[24] They turned with anticipation to the drafting of the HUD regulations for the new subsidies. This task was made all the more critical because the language of the Conference Report had not sufficiently clarified the purpose of the new subsidies, and the resolution of ambiguities in the Report was now left to HUD to interpret. Only three months were available for this work. Enactment of the 1969 housing act, containing the Brooke Amendment, had come in December, at the end of the legislative session, but Congress had specified that the new rent ceiling was to go in effect not more than three months later, on March 1, 1970. HUD regulations implementing the new rent ceiling and the new subsidies had to be available by that time.

Responsibility for drafting the necessary regulations was delegated to officials in HUD's housing assistance branch, and they took a step which has increasingly become part of HUD's operating policies by bringing several organizations active in the housing field directly into the drafting process. The oldest and best-established of these organizations was the National Association of Housing and Redevelopment Officials (NAHRO). Dating back to the resurgence of interest in housing in the mid-1930's, this national organization represents the interests of professional administrators in the housing and redevelopment field, and tended to take a liberal view of the newly-enacted legislation. Similar views were expressed even more actively by three other organizations, all of which have been organized in recent years to serve a newly emerging advocacy role in the administration of social

---

[23] Letter from Lawrence M. Cox, HUD Assistant Secretary for Housing and Renewal Assistance, to Ronald L. Brignac, NAHRO Housing Divisional Comm., May 26, 1969.

[24] See Nenno, *Housing and Urban Development Act of 1969*, 27 J. HOUSING 14 (1970). Brooke also sent a letter to all local housing authorities, explaining his amendment. It is reprinted, *Id.*, at 16. For this he was severely reprimanded by Secretary Romney of HUD! Letter from George Romney, Secretary of Housing and Urban Development, to the Honorable Edward W. Brooke, Jan. 2, 1970.

benefit programs.[25] These outside organizations were not very successful in advocating a liberal interpretation of the new subsidy. What HUD officials could not entirely accomplish through congressional influence they accomplished by placing limitations on the new subsidy program. Some of these limitations were subsequently removed by amending legislation which quickly followed in 1970, but the underlying problems have persisted.

With this background to the drafting of the regulations in mind, let us now look more closely at the issues that were raised, and the way in which they were resolved.

1. Substantive Scope of the Subsidy

As the 1969 changes in the structure of public housing subsidies finally took shape, congressional intent concerning the scope of the new subsidies that were authorized was unclear. Senator Sparkman's Amendment had made it explicit that annual federal contributions to public housing were not to be limited to debt service, but Senator Brooke's original amendment had not affected the annual contributions structure. Instead, it carried its own appropriation authorization to fund a subsidy aimed at improving operating and maintenance services in public housing projects. This arrangement was changed by the Conference Committee, which shifted the money authorization for the Brooke subsidies to the annual contribution appropriation, removed Brooke's statutory language defining the scope of the new subsidies, and then explained in its Conference Report just how these funds were to be spent. The Committee also changed another section of the law to authorize "amendments" to the annual contributions contract to insure the "low-rent character" of the project, and this change was intended to authorize amendments in existing annual contributions contracts in order to incorporate Brooke's operating cost subsidy. Finally, the rent limitation was enacted separately.

Just how these provisions were to be interpreted was something of a puzzle, and most of the controversy centered on the new subsidies which the Conference Report had authorized. HUD's

---

[25] These organizations were the National Tenants Organization (NTO), the National Welfare Rights Organization (NWRHO), and the National Housing and Development Law Project in Berkeley, Cal. The Berkeley organization was funded under a grant from the Federal Office of Economic Opportunity to provide assistance in research and litigation to legal aid attorneys around the country who are engaged in housing and economic development matters.

solution, hotly contested by its outside advisers, was to break the new subsidies into two types.[26] The first type of subsidy was to be a one-time payment to cover "existing operating deficits"[27] of public housing agencies, was payable in HUD's discretion, and was conditioned on a demonstration by the public housing agency that "satisfactory standards of management and tenant responsibility have been or will be achieved."[28] The second type of subsidy was to be made available "To make up the amount by which the proportionate share of operating and maintenance expenses attributable to a dwelling unit exceeds 25 percent of the tenant's income."[29]

HUD argued that limiting the first type of subsidy to existing deficits was justified by the Conference Report, which had authorized "payments to cover existing operating deficits of public housing . . . [agencies] and enable *them*" to maintain adequate services and reserves. (Emphasis supplied.) HUD lawyers interpreted the word "them" in this quotation to refer to the deficits and not to the agencies; thus the decision to limit the subsidy to the one-time removal of existing deficits. This interpretation was bitterly contested by the organizations advising HUD,[30] who argued that HUD's interpretation strained the Report's language. They pointed to other language in the Conference Report which indicated that operating costs of public housing agencies were to be "covered" on a permanent basis, without regard to deficits existing when the bill was enacted.[31]

HUD's outside advisers were also incensed that the subsidy for existing deficits was limited to those local agencies showing an improved management capability. They saw no warrant in the

---

[26] U.S. DEP'T OF HOUSING AND URBAN DEVELOPMENT, CIRCULAR 3-16-70, IMPLEMENTATION OF SECTIONS 212 AND 213 OF THE HOUSING AND URBAN DEVELOPMENT ACT OF 1969 [hereinafter cited as FIRST CIRCULAR].

[27] *Id.*, at § 2(b)(1). An earlier draft had been even more restrictive, and was limited to "existing operating deficit situations to the extent that there are critical emergencies in the nominal number of local housing authorities where such conditions do exist." Draft Circular, 1-14-70, Housing and Urban Development Act of 1969, at 1.

[28] *Id.*, at 33.

[29] *Id.*, at § 2(b)(2).

[30] *See especially* the National Housing and Development Law Project Memorandum *reproduced* in 116 CONG. REC. 24301-302 (1970). Actually, casual language used by Senator Brooke in floor debate tends somewhat to support the HUD interpretation. *See* 115 CONG. REC. 26722 (1969).

[31] *Ibid.* The "cover" language appears in 1969 CONF. REP., at 30. *See also* Letter from Eneas J. Kane, President, NAHRO, to the Honorable George Romney, Secretary, Dep't of Housing and Urban Development, Feb. 18, 1970.

Conference Report language on management practices which would justify linking such improvements with the subsidy, although HUD quoted this language to justify this condition. In fact, they argued that similar language authorizing HUD to impose an improved management standard as a condition to the operating deficit subsidy had actually been rejected by the Conference Committee.[32]

An even subtler problem emerged during these discussions. Brooke's bill had authorized a new subsidy to finance "improved" operating and maintenance services. This improvement requirement, while dropped from the bill as enacted, was carried forward into the Conference Report,[33] but HUD officials were concerned about an extension of the subsidy to cover improved services. They recognized that local public housing agencies could increase the amount of the subsidy simply by improving their services, and then collect the federal subsidy to fund the additional cost. To this extent, the amount of the subsidy would be open-ended, and controllable only through HUD's authority to approve or disapprove the budgets of local public housing agencies. The problem does not appear to have been extensively discussed during negotiations over the regulations, and was not resolved when the regulations were finally issued. That portion of the regulations authorizing a subsidy for existing deficits simply related the subsidy to the maintenance of "adequate" services and "adequate" reserve funds.

2. The Impact of the New Rent Limitation

The second subsidy authorized by HUD regulations was a payment to make up any deficit between operating costs and rents collected, as restricted by the new 25 percent rent/income ratio. Problems developed in the implementation of this new subsidy as well. One has already been mentioned: How was the nationally established rent ceiling imposed under the new legislation to be reconciled with the autonomy of local public housing agencies to determine their own rent schedules? HUD's response was to make the new 25 percent ceiling applicable to local public housing agencies only insofar as it affected entitlement to the

---

[32] Letter from Anthony Henry, Director, National Tenants Organization, to Assistant Secretary Lawrence Cox, Dep't of Housing and Urban Development, Jan. 19, 1970, at 5.

[33] 1969 CONF. REP., at 30.

new federal subsidy. It was not to affect the rents actually charged by local agencies, which remained their responsibility under the federal law.[34] Federal definitions of income were then provided on the basis of which the new 25 percent ceiling was to be calculated. HUD's outside advisers protested this innovation, urging that the federal definition of income for purposes of applying the Brooke Amendment should be the same as that actually established by local agencies for purposes of determining rent.[35] They felt that an independent national rent determination for purposes of calculating the new subsidy would not only detract from local autonomy but would lead to administrative confusion. HUD prevailed, but at the cost of introducing some strange distortions in the program.

For example, tenants in public housing may in some cases be allowed to stay in the project even after their incomes have gone above the maximum public housing income limits. While arguably these over-income tenants were not within the intent of the new rent ceiling, they were not specifically exempted and HUD ruled that they were covered.[36]

The regulations also repeated the statement of the Conference Report that raising all rents to the 25 percent maximum was not required by the law,[37] but HUD's advisers claimed that there would be unavoidable pressure on local public housing agencies to do so in order to qualify for the subsidy. As it happened, rent increases of this kind did not occur; tenant pressure to prevent such wholesale increases were overwhelming in most places. We should note, however, that application of the Brooke Amendment does require a disregard of local minimum rent requirements, at least in any case in which 25 percent of tenant income is less than the established minimum.

Nevertheless, under HUD's approach, the impact of the subsidy was limited. Operating deficits on units in which tenants paid less than the ceiling were not subsidized, even though the rent paid was only marginally less than the ceiling. In

---

[34] FIRST CIRCULAR, at § 4(d).

[35] Memorandum from NAHRO to Lawrence M. Cox, Assistant Secretary for HUD, Jan. 19, 1970, at 1, 2.

[36] U.S. DEP'T OF HOUSING AND URBAN DEVELOPMENT, CIRCULAR 4-24-70, RENT ADJUSTMENTS REQUIRED BY SECTION 213 OF THE HOUSING AND URBAN DEVELOPMENT ACT OF 1969, at 6. Adjustments also had to be made in minimum rent schedules so that minimum rents would not exceed the ceiling. *Ibid.*

[37] FIRST CIRCULAR, at § 4(b).

practical effect, the ceiling became a minimum, as far as distribution of the subsidy was concerned. While this approach was much criticized,[38] it was arguably consistent with the intent of the statute.

Tied in with the problem of determining the scope of the new national rent ceiling were related problems of defining tenant income for purposes of determining whether the ceiling had been exceeded. As the statute was finally enacted, tenant income for purposes of applying the ceiling was to be defined by the HUD Secretary. This open-ended authorization created an opportunity for the tenant and professional organizations advising HUD to reduce the rent burden by securing from HUD an extensive list of exemptions and deductions from income. In this way the adjusted income base against which the 25 percent rent charge was calculated would be limited as much as possible.

The importance of the income deductions and exemptions which HUD would choose led, therefore, to a period of intense negotiation over this issue between HUD officials and the tenant and professional organizations it consulted. During negotiations, these organizations pushed for as liberal a ruling as they could obtain. HUD at first responded with proposed drafts of the regulations which did contain two attempts at fairly liberalized deduction proposals. One early draft, for example, contained an extensive list of deductible items.[39] A later draft simplified this approach, and proposed a graduated flat deduction which would have been increased for each additional minor in the family.[40] Both of these deduction proposals were eventually dropped in favor of a final, even more simplified formula, in which HUD authorized only a flat ten percent deduction from family income, primarily to take care of work expenses, plus an additional $100 for each minor and dependent child.[41] To some extent, the formula that was finally adopted reflected the federal agency's desire for a regulation that would be easy to administer. This formula was also prompted by the need to accommodate differ-

---

[38] Kabaker, *Criticism Expected on HUD's Plan for Housing Rental Aid*, The Sunday [Washington] Star, Jan. 18, 1970, at A-8, col. 1.
[39] Draft Circular, 1-14-70, Appendix: Definitions of "Rent" and "Family Income" for Purposes of Implementing Statutory Limitation on Rents of Public Housing Tenants, at 3.
[40] Draft Circular, 2-11-70, Implementation of Sections 212 and 213 of the Housing and Urban Development Act of 1969, at 5, 6.
[41] FIRST CIRCULAR, at § 7(e).

ences in state public housing laws by avoiding overdetailed federal regulations that would be inconsistent with some state statutes. But the tenant and professional groups that consulted with HUD viewed this formula as unduly restrictive. In the next session of Congress they obtained corrective and liberalizing legislation.

3. The Welfare Rent Problem

Additional and very troublesome complications arose over the question of whether welfare tenants would be entitled to the Brooke Amendment rent ceiling. A proviso to the Brooke Amendment had tried to "solve" this issue. It prohibited a rent reduction under the amendment in any case in which this reduction would lead to a corresponding reduction in the amount of welfare assistance payable to the tenant. As a consequence, although supporters of the Brooke Amendment had not realized it at the time, the decision to apply the amendment to a tenant receiving welfare assistance was really left to local welfare agencies, since no rent reduction could be put into effect if it led to a reduction in the tenant's welfare assistance.

No problems were likely to arise under this statutory arrangement in states in which welfare recipients received a flat welfare grant, with no sum specifically budgeted for rent. Since expenditure items were not accounted for on an individual basis in these states, a rent reduction brought about by the Brooke Amendment would not have to be applied against the flat welfare grant that was payable. But in those states in which each expenditure item was separately budgeted, any reduction in the public housing rent would have to be applied to a reduction of the shelter allowance payable by the welfare agency. In these states, the public housing agency was prohibited from applying the Brooke Amendment to reduce the rent of the welfare recipient. To handle this problem, the National Welfare Rights Organization had proposed a change in national welfare assistance regulations. The change would have provided that any reduction in rent from the application of the Brooke Amendment would not be counted in determining the welfare recipient's budget need,[42] and the recipient would thus have been given the benefit of the rent reduction. This proposal was not accepted at this time because the national

---

[42] Untitled Memorandum and Appendix, National Welfare Rights Organization, Jan. 30, 1970.

welfare agency viewed the proposal as inconsistent with budgeting requirements in the welfare program.[43]

D. Reaction: The Welfare Crisis

These limitations on the Brooke Amendment's implementation had their impact on the benefits which the law conferred. As the Brooke Amendment went into effect, it became clear that the benefits conferred by the new rent ceiling were closely related to the tenant's source of income. Those who benefited most were tenants receiving a fixed source of income from Social Security or other government benefits,[44] other than welfare. Almost two-thirds of these tenants received rent reductions under the Brooke Amendment. Most of these tenants, as might be expected, were elderly. On the other hand, only about 15 percent of working tenants and a quarter of the public housing tenants on public welfare received reductions.

This situation is not hard to explain. Social Security and other benefits are paid out as contracted annuities, and cannot be reduced when rents are lowered. But as welfare agencies, especially in the AFDC program, learned of the provisions of the Brooke Amendment they usually refused to pass the rent reduction it required along to their welfare recipients in those states in which rent was separately budgeted on an "as paid" basis.[45] As a result of this interpretation of the Brooke Amendment by local welfare agencies, many welfare tenants in public housing were denied its benefits. Public housing tenants who received only part of

---

[43] Other curious anomalies arose. In many states, welfare payments do not meet all of the recipient's budgeted need. Even after public housing rents were reduced to the Brooke Amendment ceiling, it appeared in some cases that the money freed by the Brooke Amendment would still not bring the recipient's grant up to his need level. Some welfare agencies did not reduce the welfare grant in these cases, and HUD concurred in this practice. Letter from Ronald H. Born, General Manager, Department of Social Services, City and County of San Francisco, to Eneas J. Kane, Executive Director, Housing Authority of the City and County of San Francisco, May 29, 1970.

[44] Details for this and the following statements on the operation of the law may be found in ABELES, SCHWARTZ & ASSOCIATES, THE IMPACT OF THE BROOKE AMENDMENT ON PUBLIC HOUSING TENANTS AND LOCAL AUTHORITIES: A REPORT TO THE JOINT HEW-HUD TASK FORCE ON WELFARE RENTS IN PUBLIC HOUSING ch. V (1971).

[45] *Id.*, at VII-17. Instances in which the determination occurred on a case by case basis apparently occurred in states in which the AFDC budget was not meeting all of the recipient's need. If the Brooke Amendment decrease was less than the unmet need, it was allowed. *Id.*, at VII-19 (citing California). *See also, supra* note 43.

their support from the welfare program often found it to their advantage to give up their welfare payment and take the rent reduction instead. Other public housing tenants in the same situation preferred to quit work.

National tenant and welfare organizations and OEO legal services offices became increasingly upset as the failure of welfare tenants to benefit from the Brooke Amendment became increasingly obvious. In trying to devise a strategy to cope with this disappointment, however, these groups faced some difficult problems. They could not argue with local public housing agencies, for HUD had enforced the welfare proviso in the statute strictly, and had prohibited these agencies from making a reduction in rent if it would lead to a reduction in the welfare payment.[46] Another alternative, a change in the federal legislation, also presented difficulties. Federal housing legislation cannot bind the welfare program, especially as it is not related to the enforcement machinery which the federal welfare agency uses to police state welfare systems. To be effective as applied to local welfare agencies, any clarifying federal legislation on the welfare rent problem would have to take the form of an amendment to the federal welfare law or regulations, and not the housing law. But even then, federal enforcement of federal requirements would rest on enforcement action against a state welfare agency which refused to comply with the federal welfare directive. Enforcement action may occur only after a state has had reasonable notice and a hearing to determine whether it is in compliance with federal law.[47] The federal welfare agency has held very few such hearings, preferring to call them as a last resort after other attempts at correction have failed.[48] Finally, at the time welfare rent problems in the administration of the Brooke Amendment surfaced, Congress was considering substantial reforms in the entire welfare program. Its attention to the more limited welfare rent problem was not to be expected until the larger reform issue was settled. This reform would have enacted a flat family income allowance which would largely have eliminated existing budgeting procedures under which rents are budgeted on an "as paid" basis.

---

[46] *See* RENT ADJUSTMENT CIRCULAR, *supra* note 36, at 5.

[47] 42 U.S.C. §§ 304, 604, 1204, 1354 (1970).

[48] Letter from Robert Finch, Secretary, U.S. Dep't of Health, Education, and Welfare, Feb. 27, 1969, *In re* Barbara Stanton, as *reproduced in* 2 CCH POV. LAW REP. NEW DEV. par. 9518.

Welfare assistance reductions following public housing rent reductions would not have been possible under a flat family allowance system. As of this writing, congressional action on the family allowance plan has still been deferred.

Faced with these dilemmas, welfare and tenant organizations took the only other course open to them. They began to pressure local welfare agencies to let welfare tenants have the Brooke Amendment rent reduction even though such a course of action arguably violated state welfare statutes and regulations. Massachusetts—Senator Brooke's home state—handled the welfare tenant problem by legislation, first applied to the elderly in 1970 and then extended to all public housing tenants in 1971. This legislation requires as a matter of state law that no tenant pay more than 25 percent of his income for public housing.[49] Since the welfare shelter allowance in Massachusetts is on an "as paid" basis, this state statutory limitation on rents to be charged in public housing benefits welfare tenants in public housing to the extent that their rents are held to the 25 percent federal rent ceiling. However, the welfare allowance for shelter must be reduced proportionately. On balance, this solution to the problem seems as fair as any.

Tenant organizations in Maryland and Rhode Island sought an administrative resolution of the welfare issue under which welfare tenants in public housing would gain in both programs. The Brooke rent ceiling would be imposed, but no reduction would be made in the welfare payment to reflect this rent decrease. In Maryland, this interpretation was implemented through an administrative ruling of the state's attorney general,[50] although the regional office of the federal welfare agency refused to acquiesce[51] and the state technically faced federal noncompliance hearings and a cutoff of federal welfare aid. Welfare rights attorneys, who usually campaign vigorously for stricter federal use of the noncompliance remedy, now took welcome refuge in the fact that federal action against Maryland would be slow, even

---

[49] *See* MASS. GEN. LAWS ANN. ch. 121B, § 32 (1972).

[50] Letter from Francis B. Burch, Attorney General, State of Maryland, to Rita C. Davidson, Secretary, Maryland Dep't of Employment and Social Services, Jan. 5, 1971.

[51] Letter from Z.Z. Larimer, Chief, Assistance Payments, Region III, U.S. Dep't of Health, Education, and Welfare, to Rita Davidson, Secretary, Maryland Dep't of Employment and Social Services, May 18, 1971.

if forthcoming, and in any event would not be retroactive.[52] The situation in Rhode Island was not so easily mastered. Initial resistance by state welfare officials to a ruling favorable to tenant demands led to a successful rent strike in Providence public housing to which state officials finally capitulated.[53] Again, a favorable ruling by the state's attorney general won the day.[54]

Both the Maryland and Rhode Island rulings were taken in the face of seemingly contrary state and federal welfare requirements. For example, the federal AFDC statute requires welfare agencies, in determining the amount of the welfare grant, to take into account "any other income or resources" of the person claiming the grant.[55] The Rhode Island attorney general interpreted this provision to exclude an "indirect benefit" such as that resulting from the Brooke Amendment.[56] Maryland ruled that the federal "income or resources" provision was not intended to "convert a federal subsidy payable to a housing authority" into income.[57] Similar state statutory requirements in Rhode Island were waived aside on the ground that giving the Brooke reduction to welfare public housing tenants would not "increase the cost of shelter" provided under the state welfare law.[58]

A new constitutional problem was now presented. Could a more favorable treatment of welfare tenants in public housing be challenged as a classification which improperly discriminates

---

[52] See Letter from Mark K. Joseph, Deputy Comm'r, Baltimore Dep't of Housing and Community Development, to Mr. Frederick Oken, Assistant Attorney General, State of Maryland, Dec. 28, 1970. The Maryland strategy was fully supported by the National Tenants Organization and by the National Welfare Rights Organization. See Letters to Rita C. Davidson, Secretary, Maryland Dep't of Employment and Social Services, from Anthony R. Henry, Director, NTO, Dec. 14, 1970, and Jim Evans, NWRO, Nov. 30, 1970.

[53] See Smith, *Fair Welfare and the Brooke Amendment,* The Providence Sunday Journal, Oct. 24, 1971, at E-5, col. 1. See also Rhode Island Fair Welfare, How to Organize a Brooke Amendment Campaign and Win Lower Rents in Public Housing (mimeo, n.d.).

[54] Letter from Richard J. Israel, Attorney General, State of Rhode Island, to John J. Affleck, Director, Rhode Island Dep't of Social and Rehabilitative Services, July 16, 1971.

[55] 42 U.S.C. § 602 (1970).

[56] Israel Letter, *supra* note 54, at 5.

[57] Burch Letter, *supra* note 50, at 2. A memorandum of law submitted to the state welfare department also made the point that United States Supreme Court interpretations of the federal welfare law had given the states considerable latitude in setting need standards and benefit levels. Memorandum from Baltimore Dep't of Housing and Community Development to Maryland Dep't of Employment and Social Services, Nov. 5, 1970, at 9, citing King v. Smith, 392 U.S. 309, 318-19 (1968). This argument was also made in the Burch Letter, *ibid.*

[58] Israel Letter, *supra* note 54, at 8.

against welfare tenants not living in public housing, and thus violates the Equal Protection clause? This argument was largely dismissed by a citation of *Dandridge v. Williams*.[59] Under *Dandridge,* classifications of this kind in welfare programs will be held constitutional if any "imaginable" justification can be found for them. Rhode Island thus argued that giving the Brooke Amendment rent reduction to welfare tenants in public housing, with no corresponding reduction in the welfare grant, could be justified because it put welfare tenants in public housing on a par with working tenants in public housing, who receive the benefit of the rent reduction.[60] This argument forgets that welfare tenants not living in public housing get no rent reduction at all.[61] Nor is there much substance in another Rhode Island argument, that increasing the welfare grants of welfare tenants in public housing "encourages" increased occupancy of public housing by welfare tenants.[62] This argument assumes that a marginal increase in the welfare grant will be sufficient to attract welfare recipients into public housing, and that enough public housing units will be available for those welfare recipients who want to enter the public housing program. Nevertheless, the willingness of the United States Supreme Court in *Dandridge* to be lenient in its interpretation of the Equal Protection provision as a limitation on state welfare programs suggests that the Maryland and Rhode Island rulings would stand. The irony is that Maryland was the state in which welfare organizations brought the *Dandridge* case in an attempt to overrule what they saw as an overly restrictive practice of the state welfare department. They used the case to their advantage when they wanted to sustain a departmental practice which they viewed as more favorable.

---

[59] *E.g.,* Burch Letter, *supra* note 50.
[60] Israel Letter, *supra* note 54, at 10.
[61] Memorandum, *supra* note 57, at 21-22. This situation is produced by the structure of the federal housing subsidy programs, which make subsidies available to public housing without making comparable subsidies available to all privately owned housing. As a result, rents in the public housing program are necessarily lower. Whether federal legislative choices of this type can serve as a defense to an Equal Protection challenge to state practices which attempt to adjust federal program disparities is not altogether clear.
[62] Israel Letter, *supra* note 54, at 10.

E. Congress Responds: The Brooke Amendment—Second Round

HUD's approach to the content of the Brooke Amendment regulations had often appeared intransigent. NTO and NAHRO delegates to a meeting with HUD while the regulations were being drafted reported, for example, a conference at which HUD insisted that major changes demanded by NTO and NAHRO were nonnegotiable. HUD also delayed its implementation of the new rent ceiling provision, thus provoking an NTO lawsuit which led to a court order mandating HUD compliance within the time period specified by the 1969 law.[63] NTO is the National Tenants Organization, one of the organizations from which HUD had sought advice on the drafting of the regulations.

Brooke and his supporters, therefore, approached the 1970 session of Congress determined to rectify the inadequacies of the 1969 legislation, and to overturn HUD's restrictive interpretation of the 1969 law. There were three items on their legislative agenda: enactment of a provision requiring pass-through of the Brooke reduction to welfare tenants; a more liberal definition of the income deductions to be allowed in computing the 25 percent rent limitation; and a statutory definition of the new operating subsidy to carry out the original congressional intent. They were moderately successful in their effort to secure congressional acceptance of their proposals.

In order to bring about the welfare change Brooke introduced[64] an amendment to the 1970 National Housing Act which would have barred welfare agencies from reducing welfare benefits if a tenant received a rent reduction under the 25 percent limitation.[65] This amendment was known as the welfare "pass-through," because its effect was to pass through to the welfare recipient the extra amount of the welfare payment represented by the rent reduction. This pass-through was opposed by HUD because it would have given a windfall to welfare tenants who happened to live in public housing.[66] But HUD's opposition

---

[63] National Tenants Organization, Inc. v. Department of Housing and Urban Development, Civil No. 974-70 (D.C. Cir., Order of Court, filed Apr. 27, 1970.)

[64] *Hearings on Housing and Urban Development Legislation of 1970 Before the Subcomm. on Housing and Urban Affairs of the Senate Comm. on Banking and Currency,* 91st Cong., 2nd Sess., at 956-57 (1970).

[65] S. 4086, 91st Cong., 2nd Sess. § 1 (1970).

[66] 1970 *Senate Hearings, supra* note 64, at 1824-25.

did not play a major role in the decision which was finally made in Conference Committee to remove this amendment from the law.[67] Rather, its removal was the result of a political compromise. Members of the House committee charged with housing legislation had proposed that welfare payments for housing be made directly to public housing agencies, a change that would have effectively prevented any rent strikes by public housing tenants. Supporters of Brooke's proposal to prohibit a reduction in welfare assistance to tenants receiving a rent reduction gave up this amendment in return for a promise that the direct payment provision would not be pressed.[68] But the welfare reduction prohibition was finally enacted in 1971, in the form that Brooke originally wanted it.[69]

Action in 1970 on the restrictive HUD definition of income for purposes of applying the 25 percent rent limitation, as well as action on the restrictive interpretation of the operating subsidy provision, were caught in a controversy over the local autonomy issue in public housing administration which surfaced again at this time. Brooke finally responded to local autonomy proponents by introducing legislation which would have withdrawn from the HUD Secretary the right to define income for purposes of applying the 25 percent rent limitation.[70] The Senate did not follow Brooke on this point, however. Its version of the 1970 housing bill retained the authority of the HUD Secretary to define income, but mandated a more expansive definition of the income exclusions. This change benefited public housing tenants, because it had the effect of reducing the adjusted income base on

---

[67] S. 4368, 91st Cong., 2nd Sess. § 202(2) (1970), as explained in S. REP. NO. 91-1216, 91st Cong., 2nd Sess. 14 (1970).

[68] NTO reported an unsuccessful attempt to persuade Congressman Barrett of the House housing subcommittee to keep the welfare pass-through amendment in the law. Memorandum of Conversation Between Jeffrey Schwartz, NTO, and Tim Naegele, Administrative Assistant to Senator Brooke, Dec. 30, 1970. Barrett had introduced the direct payment provision at the request of the Philadelphia Housing Authority. *Id.*, at 2. State welfare departments may now make direct rental payments to public housing agencies on behalf of aged, blind, and disabled welfare recipients. Pub. L. No. 92-603, § 409 (Oct. 30, 1972).

[69] *See* Pub. L. No. 92-213, § 9 (Dec. 22, 1971), amending 42 U.S.C. § 1402 (1) (1970). For the implementing Federal Circular see U.S. DEP'T OF HOUSING AND URBAN DEVELOPMENT, CIRCULAR 1-18-72, IMPLEMENTATION OF SECTION 9, PUBLIC LAW 92-213; PUBLIC HOUSING RENT REDUCTIONS, WELFARE FAMILIES. Corresponding regulations by the Department of Health, Education, and Welfare are in 37 FED. REG. 15866 (Aug. 5, 1972).

[70] 1970 *Senate Hearings, supra* note 64, at 957-58; S. 4086, *supra* note 65, § 2.

which the 25 percent rent charge is calculated.[71] With some revision, this part of the Senate bill was finally passed.[72] It has excluded nonrecurring income and the income of full-time students from gross income for purposes of calculating the rent limitation, and has required the following deductions: $300 for each dependent and secondary wage earner, extraordinary medical expenses, and a flat five percent of the family's gross income (ten percent in the case of elderly families). In addition, the housing Secretary "may allow further deductions in recognition of unusual circumstances."

Brooke and his Senate colleagues also pushed for congressional reaffirmation of the original intent of the 1969 amendment concerning operating subsidies. Recall that concern over the restrictive HUD interpretation of the 1969 legislation had revolved around three major problems: the operating subsidy was not permanent, it was conditioned on improved project management, and was not specifically authorized to be paid for an improvement in operating and maintenance services. To overturn this interpretation, Brooke sought a provision which, as finally enacted, authorized the amendment of annual contributions contracts to provide for payments "to achieve and maintain adequate operating and maintenance services and reserve funds including payment of outstanding debts."[73] In addition to this provision, the statutory definition of housing "administration" was amended to expand the range of "tenant programs and services" for which, by implication, the new subsidy could be provided.[74]

Unfortunately, Brooke's explanations during congressional hearings on the 1970 amendment did not entirely overcome the restrictive interpretations which had been placed on the 1969 legislation by HUD. "Bureaucratic machinations" which under-

---

[71] S. 4368, *supra* note 67, § 202(1).

[72] Pub. L. No. 91-609, § 208(a) (1970), as codified in 42 U.S.C. § 1402(1) (1970).

[73] S. 4368, *supra* note 67, § 204, as enacted in Pub. L. No. 91-609, § 210 (1970). The bill as enacted was changed slightly from Brooke's original version, S. 4086, *supra* note 65, § 3. Brooke's bill had specifically authorized payments "to cover any public housing agency's operating deficit . . . for the fiscal year which includes December 24, 1969." The bill as enacted deleted this clause, and added the reference to outstanding debts at the end of the sentence quoted in the text. This reference was apparently intended to incorporate the deleted Brooke clause.

[74] Pub. L. No. 91-609, § 903(c) (1970), as codified in § 2(6), public housing law.

mined his 1969 amendment were scored, and Brooke made the point that the new amendment was intended to provide "a sound physical and social environment" in the projects.[75] Comments were also made in floor debate which were intended to prevent the subsidy from being conditioned on "satisfactory standards of management and tenant responsibility,"[76] and an intent that the subsidies should "improve" the maintenance and operation of the projects was specified in the Senate report on the bill.[77] Nevertheless, the statute still did not spell out explicitly the relationship of the subsidies to the 25 percent rent limitation. Even though Brooke stated that the operating subsidy was not to be limited to making up deficits arising from the 25 percent rent limitation,[78] no such language appears in the act. Matters were not helped either by the fact that the floor debate on the purposes of the new operating subsidy was casual.[79]

Under the circumstances, it remained for the Senate report on the bill to introduce additional confusion.[80] The question at stake was whether the new operating subsidies were mandatory or whether their nature and amount was still to be determined at HUD's discretion. On both points the Senate report was ambiguous. While it spoke of the amendment as *requiring* the Secretary to amend annual contribution contracts to make the payments for operating subsidies, it listed the operating and maintenance services that *may* be funded by the Secretary. Among these services were items such as tenant counselling, improved security services, and "adequate and timely repairs to structures." Tenant organizations complained that the language of the report made the Secretary's funding decision discretionary and uncontrollable by the courts. But no attention was paid to their de-

---

[75] 1970 *Senate Hearings, supra* note 64, at 956-57.

[76] 116 CONG. REC. 33460 (1970).

[77] S. REP., *supra* note 67, at 16.

[78] 116 CONG. REC. 33460 (1970); 1970 *Senate Hearings, supra* note 64, at 955. This was one of the three "purposes" of the bill to which Senator Brooke continually referred during the congressional debate. The other two were to improve operating and maintenance services, and to eliminate outstanding deficits. *See* 116 CONG. REC. 42440 (1970) (statement on Conference Report). *See also, supra* note 73.

[79] The bill's intent was not elaborated to any extent during debate. *See* 116 CONG. REC. 33491-33493 (1970).

[80] S. REP., *supra* note 67, at 16.

mands that Congress set a mandatory and basic operating and maintenance standard.[81]

F. Postscript: Congressional and Administrative Action Since the 1970 Changes

These most recent changes in the Brooke Amendment have led to even more deterioration in the financial condition of local public housing agencies. The Brooke rent limitation has been more widely applicable since enactment of the welfare pass-through, which guarantees the rent limitation to welfare recipients. At the same time, the more generous income exclusions mandated by the 1970 Act have lowered the rents payable by all tenants. In many cases the application of the 25 percent rent/income ratio has lowered the rents of many tenants below previously established minimum rent schedules, and in some instances the local public housing agency has even had to pay tenant utilities.

These developments have not escaped HUD officials, who have sought to place limits on the potentially unlimited financial burden which the operating subsidy imposes.[82] They have expressed their concern to congressional appropriations committees,[83] which have concurred with HUD[84] and have limited appropriations for the operating subsidy below what is needed to meet local requirements in full. Having taken its cue from this cautious congressional approach, HUD administrative policy has so far restricted operating subsidy payments to meeting operating deficits, allowing some maintenance of financial reserves. But it has not provided for an expansion of services to public housing tenants.[85]

---

[81] *See* National Tenants Organization, 1970 Public Housing Amendments, Recommended Changes in the Senate-passed Bill 3, 4 (n.d.); Memorandum to Jeff Schwartz, General Counsel, National Tenants Organization, from Sam Abbott, Staff Attorney, Law Reform Unit 3 (Sept. 29, 1970).

[82] See the staff report in *Hearings Before the Subcomm. on HUD-Space-Science-Veterans Appropriations, House Comm. on Appropriations*, 92nd Cong., 2nd Sess. 1302-04 (1972).

[83] *E.g., Hearings Before the Subcomm. on HUD, Space and Science Appropriations, House Comm. on Appropriations,* 92nd Cong., 1st Sess. 70-71 (1971).

[84] S. REP. NO. 92-264, 92nd Cong., 1st Sess. 9 (1971).

[85] *E.g.,* U.S. DEP'T OF HOUSING AND URBAN DEVELOPMENT, CIRCULAR 11-28-72, SUBSIDIES FOR OPERATIONS: LOW-RENT PUBLIC HOUSING PROGRAM. The special family subsidies for the elderly and the like have been available only to meet operating deficits not covered by the operating subsidy.

Several lawsuits are pending which challenge HUD's administration of the operating subsidy provision. *See also* Barber v. White, Civil No. 15,235 (D. Conn., filed Nov. 28, 1972), holding that the loss in revenue resulting from the Brooke Amendment rent ceiling does not deny Due Process to a local public housing agency.

In the meantime, all of these issues have become embroiled in a more comprehensive proposal by the Republican administration, which in 1970 introduced a total revision of federal housing legislation simplifying all of the federal housing subsidies. While action on this proposal has been continually deferred by the Democratic Congress, the Senate did pass[86] one version of the bill in 1972. But the House Banking and Currency Committee refused, in the same session, to consider similar legislation which had been reported by its subcommittee on housing.[87] Generally, the Senate bill was more favorable to the public housing program, but both would have preserved the major features of the Brooke Amendment while moderating its financial impact on local public housing agencies. As these two bills represent a legislative compromise which may finally be adopted, a brief summary of their provisions appears to be in order.

The major change which would have been legislated by both bills separated the operating subsidy introduced by Senator Brooke from the traditional federal subsidy for debt service, reflecting Brooke's own original legislative proposal. With reference to the scope of the subsidy, the Senate version was the more generous, as the subsidy was authorized to "achieve *and maintain* adequate operating services *and reserve funds.*" In the House version, the italicized words in the statutory language just quoted were omitted, so that (for example) there would have been no statutory commitment to achieving adequate operating reserves.

Another limitation on the operating subsidy contained in both bills would have required public housing agencies receiving the subsidy to charge rents which would have produced an aggregate minimum rental of 20 percent of tenant income on all of its dwelling units. Additional limitations on the operating subsidy were imposed by the House bill, which conditioned payment of the subsidy on "sound management practices" including "tenant eligibility criteria which . . . will assure that the project will include families with a broad range of incomes and will avoid concentrations of very low-income and socially deprived problem

---

[86] The bill is reproduced in 118 CONG. REC. S3152, 3163-68 (daily ed. Mar. 2, 1972).

[87] This bill is reproduced in *Hearings on Housing and Urban Development Act of 1972 Before the House Comm. on Banking and Currency,* 92nd Cong., 2nd Sess. 2, 112-48 (1972). For a summary of the original administration and other proposed housing bills see *Comparative Summary of Pending Legislation on Federally-Assisted Housing,* 28 J. HOUSING 476-81 (1971).

families."[88] Both bills would then have eliminated the special annual subsidies, such as those payable for elderly families. Finally, unlike the Senate bill, the House bill would have required annual independent congressional appropriations for the operating subsidy. The Senate bill would have allowed the operating subsidies to be covered by sums available to meet the annual contribution payments for public housing.[89]

Both bills retained the Brooke Amendment rent ceiling as a federal rent limitation to be imposed independently of local rent schedules, and both bills retained substantially the same deductions from income which are presently authorized. However, the House bill contained the welfare pass-through provision adopted in 1971, while the Senate bill did not. Both bills also attempted to limit housing subsidies by legislating a statutory minimum rent even for those local public housing agencies not receiving an operating subsidy. The House bill provided for a minimum rent no "less than a minimum amount established by the [local] public housing agency and approved" by the national housing secretary. The Senate bill provided that the minimum rent would have been "equal to the utility costs attributable to the dwelling," but the Secretary was authorized to waive this provision in any area in which unusually high utility costs would cause "undue hardship." The Senate bill also sought to broaden the tenant base of the public housing program by requiring a "reasonable cross-section of income levels of tenants within the low-income ranges," and by allowing only 20 percent of the dwelling units in a public housing project to be occupied by the "very lowest income group."[90]

G. Summary

Congressional impasse over the revision of federal public housing legislation reflects growing congressional concern with the scope and proper role of American housing subsidies. If we return to the series of issues in the development of housing subsidy programs that were raised in Chapter I, we can conclude that the initial federal subsidy for public housing was changed because of conditions that were produced by the structure of the program that Congress initially legislated. Limiting public housing to lower

---

[88] § 9(c)(1). Enforcement of "satisfactory standards of [tenant] behavior" were also required. § 9(c)(2).

[89] See § 9(d) (House bill); § 9(c) (Senate bill).

[90] §§ 3(1), 3(2). Both bills repealed the so-called 20% gap provision.

income groups and placing an income ceiling on admission to the program led to financial difficulties which finally upset the federal subsidy formula. Senator Brooke's initial amendment to the federal law was conceived as a remedy which would limit the rents to be paid by public housing tenants within reasonable bounds, while at the same time providing financial relief to hard-pressed local public housing agencies. But the amendment has had consequences not foreseen by Senator Brooke and his supporters. Public housing project revenues have been diminished even further by the rent ceiling, while Congress has proved reluctant to meet in full the subsidy burden that the application of the new rent ceiling has imposed. What was intended as a marginal change to provide financial relief to tenants and local authorities eventually opened up for review the conceptual basis on which the entire program is founded. Conflicts over legislative language and administrative regulation reflect these pressures. The absence of full legislative and administrative consensus on the character and future role of public housing has led to an impasse in which Congress has authorized but refused to financially support the new operating subsidy to the extent that it is required.

Predictably, the legislative struggle centers on the relationship between the federal public housing subsidy and public housing rents, since any operating costs not covered by rents will have to be met by the federal government. None of the solutions to this problem are comforting. Federal subsidies can be reduced only by raising rents for tenants presently in the projects, thus causing financial hardship; by changing the present composition of the projects through admitting more affluent tenants; or by a combination of both measures. All of these strategies would be socially and economically disruptive, and would to some extent change the initial objective of the program, which was intended as a method to provide housing for low-income families within their means. Ghetto concentrations of public housing projects in some large cities would also make these projects unattractive to any who have the means to live elsewhere. Changing tenant composition in the public housing program may thus require new locations for new projects, away from the inner cities. If so, the contribution of public housing to meeting the problems of inner city neighborhoods will be diminished.

In the American context, in which legislative and administrative consensus is difficult to achieve, we may expect for some time to live with the kind of policy compromise that has prevailed in the public housing program since the Brooke Amendment was first enacted. If housing standards continue high at the same time that inflationary pressures increase housing costs, and large segments of the population remain at poverty or near-poverty levels, the federal government may react by withdrawing even more from meeting its full financial responsibility for housing need. We will find similar pressures at work as we turn to an examination of the English program of publicly owned housing accommodation.

New York City Housing Authority, Grant Project.

New York City Housing Authority, Mitchell Houses Project.

SUBSIDIZED HOUSING IN UNITED STATES 115

Santa Venetia Oaks, Marin County, California.

English Council Housing at Barker Road, Bradford, England.

Alton Estate, Roehampton, England. Greater London Council Photo-Unit.

Crossways Estate, Tower Hamlets, England. Greater London Council Photo-Unit.

Chapter V

COUNCIL HOUSING IN ENGLAND

A. An Overview of the Program

1. The Economic and Political Background

In comparison with the United States, England presents a very different economic, political, racial, and legal background for the examination of housing subsidy policy. This chapter will begin with a review of this background, and will especially consider the income redistribution issues which the more extensive English housing subsidy has raised. In the remainder of the chapter, a more detailed account of the English public housing program will be given. English public housing is referred to as "council housing," because it is built and managed by the councils of local government authorities, and the English term will be used here.

We noted in the first chapter that, generally, all economic segments of the English population are equally served by the different types of available housing, both rented and owner-occupied, and privately and publicly owned. This statement needs further clarification, however, because close analysis of the English housing situation indicates that this impression is not entirely correct, and English housing patterns are beginning to resemble the American. As in America, homeowners in England tend to earn higher incomes[1] and to live in the suburbs, while council housing tenants earn less and tend to live in the inner cities.[2] Even so, except at the highest income levels the difference in the percentage of families living in council rather than privately owned housing is not that great.[3]

It is in the differences between the owner-occupied and rental housing supply that the English housing situation varies most from the American. While owner-occupied housing in England is privately owned and not subject to price control, most rental housing is publicly owned and all rental housing is subject to rent control. To understand this distinctive character of the rental housing market in England one dominant fact must be kept in mind. Practically all privately owned rented dwellings were built before 1919, while no national subsidies for council housing were available until 1919.

This spread in the average age of private as compared with publicly owned rental dwellings explains most of the difference between private and publicly owned rental housing. Rents for council housing, for example, average about 25 percent higher than rents in private accommodation,[4] and this relationship correlates with the finding that a higher proportion of families in the lowest income category are in private housing.[5] This correlation seems inconsistent with another finding, that skilled manual

---

[1] Nationally, the incomes of homeowners are 50 percent higher. Parl. Deb., Standing Comm. E, Housing Finance Bill 725 (1972).

[2] As in Greater London. *Ibid.*

[3] MINUTES OF EVIDENCE TAKEN BEFORE SUBCOMM. B. OF THE HOUSE OF COMMONS ESTIMATES COMM., Sess. 1968-69, Vol. III, at 960 [hereinafter cited as EVIDENCE]. This Parliamentary inquiry into housing subsidies provides the most thorough recent survey of housing subsidy problems available in England. Testimony was submitted covering every detail of housing subsidy policy by national departments, local authorities and their associations, and private organizations.

Note, however, that tenants in publicly owned housing were found to have more dependents than families not living in such housing. D.V. DENNISON, THE GOVERNMENT OF HOUSING 191-93 (1967). As a result, they have less income actually available to meet housing expenditure.

[4] DEP'T OF EMPLOYMENT, FAMILY EXPENDITURE SURVEY REPORT FOR 1971, at 11 (1972).

[5] *See* Berry, *Families on Low Incomes,* 27 HOUSING & PLANNING REV., No. 1, at 8 (1971). One-half of all welfare recipients are in council housing, a proportion which has more than doubled in the last 15 years. Lynes, *Social Security,* 20 NEW SOCIETY 678 (1972).

laborers are over-represented in council housing,[6] but this occupational distribution can probably be explained by the fact that local admission policies for council housing favor the more stable skilled workers, who are likely to have a longer residence in the locality.

Another segment of the housing market which has received little explicit public attention in America but which is an important component of English rental housing is furnished accommodation, which supplies about one-sixth[7] of all private tenancies. Furnished dwellings tend to be inferior in quality and more overcrowded than unfurnished rental housing,[8] as many of the tenants who live in furnished housing are either poorer than average or are recent and often colored immigrants who cannot find housing elsewhere. A separate legal code applies to furnished dwellings; they are subject to their own system of rent control, and they present some very special problems of housing policy. However, in order to clarify and simplify the presentation of the issues in housing subsidy programs that have arisen in unfurnished housing in England, especially as some of the same issues that have arisen in furnished housing have also arisen in the unfurnished sector, we will put aside a discussion of the furnished housing problem in this book.

Having discussed some of the characteristics of the English housing market, we can look next at regional and intergovernmental differences in the distribution of the housing subsidy burden. These differences are very much affected by the pattern of regional variations in housing costs and rents, and by the fact that English local governments assume a share of the housing subsidy through local property tax contributions. These

---

[6] Detailed figures are available for the inner London borough of Camden. Almost one-half of all tenants in council housing are in skilled manual trades, while only about one-fourth of tenants in the private sector are in this category. Moreover, in this borough virtually no professional and managerial groups are in council housing, while about one-fourth of those in private rental housing are in this category. Centre for Urban Studies, *Report on the Housing Rents Study*, in HOUSING IN CAMDEN, Vol. II, at 27 (1968). These figures are alleged to be typical for the country as a whole, but the figures for the professional and managerial group may reflect the high status character of Hampstead, which is now part of Camden. Tenants within this group are more likely to find private rental accommodation in this area.

[7] REPORT OF THE COMMITTEE ON THE RENT ACTS, CMND. NO. 4609, at 127 (1971) (Francis Report).

[8] *Id.*, at 130-34. The new housing subsidy system is to be extended to furnished housing.

contributions were optional under the law as it existed prior to 1972, but have now been made mandatory.

Taking the cost problem first, we find the greatest regional variation between London and the rest of the country, with both public and private rents in London almost twice as high.[9] These rent differences are reflected in the fact that the subsidy contribution to council housing in the London area also runs almost twice as high as it does elsewhere.[10] As a result, to the extent that the housing subsidy is met from national revenues, there is a regional redistribution of income to the London region. We will see later that this tendency in the subsidy system has been reinforced by recent legislative changes. These regional variations in housing costs play an important role in English housing subsidy policy, for the dominance of the Greater London area nationally, and the sharp polarization between housing costs in London and in the rest of the country, have highlighted regional differences as a political problem. In the United States, regional differences in housing costs may be as great or greater, but the size of the country and the absence of one dominant urban center tend to eliminate the problem of regional impact from political discussions over housing subsidy issues.

Differences in the distribution of the housing subsidy in England also occur within regions. Here the differences depend on the extent to which the housing subsidy is met from local property taxes. We have already noted that local governments in the inner areas of English urban regions have more council housing, and also contain wage earners with lower per capita incomes, than local governments on the outer fringes of those regions.[11] The same local governments that build council housing are also responsible for collecting local property taxes.[12] To the extent that council housing costs must be met from property taxes, therefore, the council housing program has a regressive effect in those local government areas that have lower than average incomes.

Other differences between the English and American housing subsidy programs may stem from subtleties in national character.

---

[9] DEP'T OF EMPLOYMENT, FAMILY EXPENDITURE SURVEY REPORT FOR 1970, at 104-05 (1971).

[10] MINUTES OF EVIDENCE, *supra* note 3, Vol. II, at 137.

[11] Standing Comm., *supra* note 1, at 726.

[12] For general discussion of local government finance problems see THE FUTURE SHAPE OF LOCAL GOVERNMENT FINANCE, CMND. NO. 4741 (1971).

While it may not entirely be true that English society has a more highly developed social and political conscience, its welfare system is more advanced in that it provides greater coverage for social and economic risks and needs. As a consequence, the English are more sensitive to whatever gaps and disparities still exist in their social and economic benefit system, as illustrated by the following example: Homeowners in both countries are allowed to deduct mortgage interest payments incurred in the purchase of a home from their national income taxes. Policy-makers in both countries are increasingly aware that the benefits conferred by this deduction provide an indirect national subsidy to homeowners in the form of taxes foregone, but the English show a greater awareness of the impact of this tax deduction on the equities in their housing subsidy program. Parity of subsidy between renters and homeowners has constantly been stressed by Labor Party spokesmen in recent housing debates, and the tax benefits of the mortgage interest deduction have increasingly been treated as a subsidy payment.

The wider availability of English council housing, the greater responsibility of local governments for part of the financial cost of that housing, and a greater public awareness of the policy issues that are involved in subsidy programs have all contributed to making housing subsidies much more of a political issue than they are in the United States. Parliamentary consideration of a change in program as momentous as the Brooke Amendment would not go practically unnoticed by the English public. The political character of decision-making on housing subsidy policies carries a political cost, however, for housing legislation enjoys both the advantages and disadvantages of the English parliamentary system. In England, the parliamentary system and the discipline of the English political parties has meant that legislation proposed by a government in power is invariably enacted, usually with few amendments. This system permits legislative change which is often dramatic and radical, provoking a political response which may lead to a reversal in policy when a new government is elected. In America, on the other hand, congressional legislation in sensitive fields like housing tends to be the product of a developed consensus not always quickly reached, as the experience with the Brooke Amendment shows. Nevertheless, relatively speaking, once a consensus has been achieved American legislation tends to be comparatively stable.

As a result of England's more volatile political situation, its housing subsidy program, though established since the First World War, has not exhibited the continuity of the American public housing program, and the basis of the English housing subsidy has been changed several times.[13] The housing reform of 1972, enacted two years after the election of a Conservative government, is perhaps the most radical example of this change in recent history. Whether or not the election of a Labor Party government will bring a change in the legislation is open to question. Just before its defeat in 1970, the Labor government commissioned an internal study of the housing subsidy system, which proposed reforms very similar to those enacted in the housing act of 1972. These reforms would apparently have been put forward by the Labor government had it stayed in power. Nevertheless, the 1972 act aroused considerable Labor opposition, primarily because of the inflationary impact it is expected to have on rent levels in council housing. The Conservative government legislated rent increases as part of the new legislation which the Labor Party apparently was not prepared to make.

Many knowledgeable observers in England contend that the reforms legislated by the 1972 law are fundamental enough to withstand any change in political fortune. Their comment appears true to the extent that the changes made by the act have brought increases in council housing rents. These will tend to become embedded in the system, and will be resistant to change or modification by new legislation. Other aspects of the subsidy system are more subject to alteration and repeal by a new government. For this reason, our discussion of the English subsidy program will concentrate on general policy issues and, as in the case of the American subsidies, isolate those aspects of the law which appear most central to the system, and most enduring as a policy problem.

2. The Legal and Administrative Background

While the economic and political climate under which English housing policy is made differs from the American, we should now note that the legal and administrative background differs as well. These differences may stem from the fact that while the English

---

[13] For a summary of housing subsidy legislation through 1967, see EVIDENCE, at 750-56. For the legislation up to 1965 see REPORT OF THE COMM. ON HOUSING IN GREATER LONDON, CMND. NO. 2605, at 233-50 (1965) (Milner Holland Report).

housing statutes go into more detail than their American counterparts, their legislation is also more broadly formulated and leaves many policy questions to be worked out through administrative orders or circulars issued by the national housing department.

Moreover, as there is no written English constitution, there are no substantive constitutional restraints on English legislation and administrative practices. These practices may be loose and varied, but it simply is not possible to identify, as a matter of constitutional concern, the legal tension points that arise within the system. Neither are the English courts able to exercise much restraint on administrative interpretations by national departments and local governments. Questions of government policy are not reviewable in the English judicial system, and the courts are reluctant to intrude policy issues into their decisions interpreting national statutes. As much of the substantive policy in the housing subsidy program has been explicitly left to administrative discretion, no opportunity is presented to review this policy by way of a court test. The substantive basis for admission to and eviction from council housing provides one example of this situation, as the substantive grounds for making decisions on evictions and admissions have been left to the local governments which manage council housing, and the courts are in no position to review their decisions.

Other important differences in the two programs arise out of the unitary nature of English government. As there are no state governments intervening between the national housing department and the local housing authority, the latter operate their programs solely on the basis of the national statute. The fact that local authorities also act as administrative agencies of the national government for purposes of program administration provides even more potential for national control of the local housing program. In practice, however, as we suggested in Chapter II, this control has not been fully exercised, and the division of program responsibility in England is about as divided as it is in the United States.[14]

The greater involvement of the English political system in housing issues has led to a situation, however, in which national

---

[14] The most intensive study, which includes housing, is J.A.G. GRIFFITH, CENTRAL DEPARTMENTS AND LOCAL AUTHORITIES (1966).

decisions on housing policy carry more importance than they do in the United States. This policy role of the national government is undoubtedly enhanced both by the absence of a state government structure and the historically more dependent position of English local authorities on the national government. The recent shift to a greater emphasis on programs of housing improvement will illustrate our point about the importance of national leadership on housing policy issues. When the Labor Party last formed a government in 1964, national housing shortages still existed and the national emphasis was on new construction.[15] Within the next few years, however, career officials in the national housing department convinced the government that the housing shortage would be over by 1973,[16] and urged the housing minister toward greater emphasis on housing improvement. Legislation followed in 1969[17] which contained new and expanded techniques for housing improvement programs. The Conservative government which took office in 1970 continued this emphasis on housing improvement programs, and we shall see that housing improvement criteria have been directly linked to the rent control legislation, and through it to the level of subsidy authorized by the housing subsidy law.

B. Basic Features of the English Program

1. Subsidies, Rents and Rebates

As in the United States, national subsidies have always been provided for locally owned council housing, and likewise as in America, these subsidies have taken the form of annual payments for each dwelling unit. While the size and basis of this payment have varied, the important fact is that the subsidy, until recently, was never related to the capital cost of the housing. It usually provided for fixed annual payments for each dwelling, and was far from sufficient to cover the principal and interest on the debt which was incurred to build housing projects. Legislation in 1967[18] changed this subsidy formula to provide a debt service subsidy for the first time. An annual subsidy for each dwelling was authorized, payable for 60 years, in an amount equal to the

---

[15] The following discussion is based in part on Des Wilson, *How Labour Lost Its Grip (Housing)*, 81 NEW STATESMAN 799 (1971).
[16] EVIDENCE, at 160-62.
[17] Housing Act 1969, ch. 33.
[18] Housing Subsidies Act 1967, ch. 29, § 2(2).

difference between the interest on the debt at the rate prevailing at the time the dwelling was built, and the interest that would have been payable at an interest rate of four percent. Subsidies were also available which provided for supplementary annual payments for dwellings in certain special circumstances. The most important of these supplementary subsidies were payable for high-rise housing, for expensive sites, and to councils with unduly burdensome housing costs.[19] To a large extent, these supplementary subsidies were used by local authorities in areas such as Greater London, where land prices and housing costs are high, and where local authorities often built high-rise buildings in order to absorb some of this additional land cost burden.

The most recent housing subsidy legislation, as we have indicated, was enacted in 1972. This act abolishes the principal annual subsidy payable under the 1967 law, establishes a new rent standard for council housing units, requires rent rebates for those who need them, and provides for a subsidy to help meet the cost of these rebates. Supplementary subsidies similar to those contained in the 1967 law have also been enacted, and the special supplementary subsidies contained in that law have been repealed.

Other important elements of the national subsidy as it existed before 1967 have remained unchanged. Like previous subsidies, the 1972 subsidies are not related to capital costs, and do not cover in full the annual payments needed to meet principal and interest on the debt incurred to pay for construction. The failure of the English housing subsidy program to meet construction costs in full has led to some special rent-setting problems in council housing, and these have been aggravated by the way in which English local authorities enter into long-term debt obligations in order to finance their housing projects. While bonds issued to cover public housing construction usually remain outstanding until maturity in America, English local authorities usually refinance outstanding debt during the life of the project for which it was incurred.[20] The failure of the English subsidy to meet construction costs in full, and the practice of local authorities to refinance outstanding debt, injects an historic capital cost factor into the determination of rents in the council housing program which is absent in America. Some of the annual expense associated

---

[19] EVIDENCE, at 1, 2 (memorandum of housing ministry).
[20] *See* EVIDENCE, at 335, 683, 955.

with the capital cost of the housing must be met out of tenant rents and the local tax contribution because this expense is not covered by the national subsidy payment. As land and building costs have been rising rapidly, construction costs and rents are higher on newer dwellings, and these cost differences have led to rent differentials which are based on the time of construction. Most local authorities had managed to avoid the extreme rent differentials that the cost of newer and older buildings would require, however, because the national government allowed them to pool all of their subsidies for accounting purposes. Once subsidies were pooled, they were redistributed in order to balance the rents on newer and older accommodations. That is, higher rents than needed were charged on older dwellings in order to hold down rents on newer dwellings which had higher construction costs. In some authorities, this policy was accompanied by a dwelling assignment policy under which supposedly less desirable tenants, such as colored immigrants,[21] were assigned to the older and less attractive dwellings.

These subsidy pooling and dwelling assignment practices were complicated by the historic tendency of English local authorities to utilize space rent rather than graded rent systems. Rents were based on the size and quality of the dwelling, and no adjustment was made for income except in those authorities which adopted a rent rebate system. In these authorities, a portion of the rent was rebated back to the tenant, depending on the extent to which he was unable to meet what was considered a fair rent charge on his income. This approach to rent-setting has now been mandated for all authorities by the national legislation, and is a critical feature of the council housing program. Since it appears to Americans as a somewhat backhanded way of setting rents, we will indicate the origins of and reasons for this system.

One reason for the use of this two-tier rent structure lies in the statutory nature of the program. Since there are no income limits for admission to council housing, some of the tenants in the projects are not able to pay the full rent. This feature of the program forced local authorities into a two-tier rent system, under which tenants who could not pay the rent set for their

---

[21] MINISTRY OF HOUSING AND LOCAL GOVERNMENT, NINTH REPORT OF THE HOUSING MANAGEMENT SUBCOMM. OF THE CENTRAL HOUSING ADVISORY COMM., COUNCIL HOUSING: PURPOSES, PROCEDURES AND PRIORITIES 125 (1969) [hereinafter cited as CULLINGWORTH REPORT].

dwelling would have that rent moderated through a rent rebate. The result was to introduce considerable ambiguity into the subsidy program. It was not clear just how rents were to be determined, nor was much guidance provided on whether the national subsidy was to be applied only to rent rebates or whether it could also be applied to the general reduction of rent levels. Until the 1972 legislation, local authority rent determinations were little circumscribed by national legislation,[22] as this statute allowed local authorities to make "such reasonable charges . . . as they may determine." While judicial interpretation added some gloss to these words, the net effect was to leave most of the authority over rents to the local authorities.[23]

Two-tier rent systems were also encouraged in council housing by legislative developments which led to the practice of local tax contributions to the council housing program. These contributions were legislatively required up until the mid-1950's, when they were made legislatively optional unless a deficit appeared in the council's annual Housing Revenue Account, or HRA. This account is required by statute,[24] and must show that income and expenditure is in balance at the end of each year. Only the accumulation of a surplus sufficient to meet contingencies and pay for repairs has been allowed.

The legislative decision to make the local tax contribution optional came at a time when housing costs were beginning to increase. Local authorities were often reluctant to meet all of these increased costs out of taxes, and only about one-half of them did so, although the proportion of local authorities making tax contributions was higher in Greater London than it was in the rest of the country.[25] The only alternative to this method of financing was an increase in rents. But as general rent increases for all dwellings would create hardship for lower-income tenants, many authorities also introduced a system of rent rebates in order to reduce rents to appropriate levels for these lower-income groups.[26] What resulted was a compromise under which the cost

---

[22] Housing Act, 1957, 5 & 6 Eliz. 2, c. 56, § 111.
[23] The cases are discussed in Jewell, *Local Authority Housing: Differential Rent Schemes*, 1961 J. PLAN. & PROP. L. 75.
[24] Housing (Financial Provisions) Act, 1958, 6 & 7 Eliz. 2, c. 42, Sch. 5, § 5(5).
[25] *See* EVIDENCE, at 881-82 (memorandum by national housing ministry).
[26] This history is discussed in R.A. PARKER, THE RENTS OF COUNCIL HOUSES ch. 4 (1967).

of the rebates was met both from higher rents charged to the more affluent tenants, and from local taxes.

Not all local authorities introduced a rent rebate plan, however. The introduction of rent rebates requires a means test of tenant income in order to determine who is entitled to the rebate payment, and critics of the rent rebate approach objected to a means-tested housing subsidy. Some local authorities therefore endeavored to keep their rents low as an alternative to introducing means-tested rent rebates. In other authorities, low council housing rents were adopted in response to local political pressures for low-cost council housing.

Contrary advice was soon to come from the national level, however, and beginning with a White Paper in 1965[27] the Labor government sought to encourage local authorities to use their national subsidies only to meet the cost of rent rebate plans. National departmental advice on rent rebates followed, and these were encouraged in a policy statement which in other ways only added to the confusion.[28] For example, the statement recognized that the need for and amount of rebates would depend on whether and to what extent the local authority made a contribution to its housing program from local taxes. But no amendment to the statute was proposed which would have made the tax contribution mandatory and which would have explicitly linked that contribution to rent rebate plans.

In addition, the national department's statement temporized in its endorsement of the rent rebate approach. Local authorities were advised that rents and rebates should be structured so that "the great majority of tenants" will not find it necessary to apply for a rebate on rent.[29] While the department recognized that this last advice would compromise somewhat the national policy of limiting the use of national subsidies to rent rebate plans, there was concern that too many tenants would be subjected to a means test of income if the rebate plan were extended too widely.

---

[27] THE HOUSING PROGRAMME 1965 TO 1970, CMND. NO. 2838, at par. 41 (1965).

[28] CIRCULAR 46/67. References throughout these chapters are to Circulars issued by the Ministry of Housing and Local Government, or by its successor Department of the Environment. The second number refers to the year of issuance and the first to the number of the circular in the year issued.

[29] *Id.,* at par. 6. For a description of the rent rebate systems in effect in an inner London area see Centre for Urban Studies, *Report on the Housing Rents Study,* in HOUSING IN CAMDEN, Vol. II, ch. 6 (1968).

These difficulties in finding a way to resolve the ambiguities in the housing subsidy legislation finally led to the 1972 law,[30] which mandates a national rent rebate system. It would have been possible, of course, to establish a rent ceiling based on income, as the Brooke Amendment now requires in American public housing, but this alternative apparently was never seriously considered. Perhaps the long history of rent control in England has led to a situation in which an independent decision on rent levels without regard to ability to pay is assumed to be a necessary initial decision in the housing program. An unwillingness to apply a means test to everybody who lives in council housing is probably another factor arguing against the use of rents based on income for all council housing tenants. In any event, a two-tiered system of rents, with rents rebated from an independently determined rent standard, remains an essential part of the English system. As we shall see, this system has produced many anomalies in the adjustment of rental policies to housing need, and these anomalies have continued to prove troublesome.

2. Scope of Program, Tenant Admissions, and Restrictions

As in the United States, additional national controls are imposed on local council housing, but English local housing authorities generally have more control over important substantive decisions in their programs than their American counterparts. While housing costs and program size are limited by national criteria in England, the location of projects is entirely a matter for local authority decision, and recent legislative changes have not affected the almost total control which local authorities exercise over tenant selection and admission.

Let us look first at the way in which national controls are exercised over the size of the subsidized housing supply. The national government has always determined the number of subsidized housing units to be built in any one year, and has then allocated these units between high priority and low priority housing authorities.[31] Production targets set by high priority local authorities are usually accepted as presented to the national housing department, and the remaining units in the annual pro-

---

[30] For a discussion of rent rebate practices on the eve of the 1972 legislation see FOURTH REPORT FROM THE ESTIMATES COMM., House of Commons Sess. 1968-69, Vol. I, at 13.

[31] This discussion is based on GRIFFITH, *supra* note 14, at 221-57, and EVIDENCE, at 112, 150.

gram are then allocated to the housing authorities with a lower priority. This system leaves most of the initiative in establishing housing programs to local authorities. Their housing efforts vary,[32] although a recent survey of middle-sized authorities showed that council housing per capita in larger as compared with smaller communities is about the same.[33]

Within each local authority, the national housing department leaves the selection of housing project locations to local determination.[34] While housing authorities in the larger cities are more likely to build high-rise structures, the typical English council housing project is most similar to what Americans would call a garden apartment or townhouse development. Most English council housing projects are not the public housing ghettos so typical of larger American cities but, especially in the larger cities, council housing is concentrated in fairly large individual developments, usually built all at one time. These physical characteristics of the council housing supply have a very distinct bearing on the rent-setting problem, as we shall see.

Cost limitations are also imposed nationally in the council housing program. These controls were first authorized by the 1967 legislation, when a shift to an interest rate subsidy made it necessary to control the size of the subsidy by controlling the capital cost of the dwelling.[35] This legislation was implemented through nationally adopted cost controls, and imposed under what is known as a "cost yardstick."[36] As the cost yardstick has been drafted, costs are calculated with reference to housing densities, certain building types such as high-rise accommodations are discouraged, and the details of new housing developments are then left to be negotiated between the national department and local authorities,[37] subject to the cost limitation. Regional variations are built into the formula, and there is also a ten percent

---

[32] On London see Dear, *The Growth of London's Housing Stock*, GREATER LONDON COUNCIL INTELL. UNIT QTLY. BULL. NO. 14, Mar. 1971, at 3. On the interwar period generally see Jennings, *Geographical Implications of the Municipal Housing Programme in England and Wales*, 1919-39, 8 URBAN STUDIES 121 (1971).

[33] EVIDENCE, at 903.

[34] MINISTRY OF HOUSING AND LOCAL GOVERNMENT, HOUSING SUBSIDIES MANUAL 48 (1967).

[35] Housing Subsidies Act, 1967, ch. 29, § 3. This part of the 1967 act was repealed by the 1972 law, but cost controls are authorized under § 4(11) of the 1972 law.

[36] CIRCULARS 36/67, 31/69.

[37] EVIDENCE, at 123-25 (memorandum submitted by Greater London Council).

tolerance to take care of local variations in building costs. However, the yardstick has not been accepted without complaint at the local level. Some authorities have complained that the tolerance is not enough, and as the yardstick is related to housing densities there are also complaints that it has forced local authorities to build more multi-bedroom dwellings at a time when the greatest demand on the English scene is for smaller units.[38]

National regulations also impose minimum space and amenity standards on council house dwellings, which are substantially detailed, and are based on a set of standards recommended by a national housing advisory committee which reported in the early 1960's.[39] These standards are generally admitted to be higher than those to which housing is built on the private market,[40] an important fact to be kept in mind when assessing the competitive impact of local authority housing. We shall see that the fair rent system which has now been legislated for the council housing program will translate these higher council housing standards into higher rents, and this rent increase will not entirely be offset by the rent rebate plan.

While rising operating costs and higher standards have led to increases in council housing expenditures, English local authorities have not suffered the financial crisis that overtook many American public housing agencies in the postwar years. A wider range of income groups lives in English public housing, and they were better able to absorb the rent increases that became necessary. Moreover, until the 1972 legislation, many English local housing authorities were able to shift the entire unsubsidized rent for council housing occupied by welfare tenants to the welfare program,[41] partly through the practice of excluding welfare tenants from the rebate system.

English local housing authorities have also enjoyed an almost unfettered discretion in the selection and retention of their tenants, a legal situation which remains unchanged.[42] Little

---

[38] EVIDENCE, at 111. The reason is that the yardstick is based on the number of bed spaces per acre. It is obviously easier to get more bed spaces per acre at lower cost by building more multi-bedroom dwellings.
[39] CENTRAL HOUSING ADVISORY COMM., HOMES FOR TODAY AND TOMORROW (1961) (Parker Morris Report).
[40] EVIDENCE, at 108.
[41] EVIDENCE, at 867.
[42] The discussion that follows is largely based on CULLINGWORTH REPORT chs. 2 and 3.

explicit direction on tenant selection is provided in the housing law, which only states that "reasonable preference . . . [be] given to persons who are occupying unsanitary or overcrowded houses, have large families or are living under unsatisfactory housing conditions."[43] Tenant selection is also affected by the slum clearance statute, which contains a provision that local authorities "shall satisfy themselves:

"(i) that insofar as suitable accommodations available for the persons who will be displaced by the clearance of the area does not already exist, the authority can provide, or secure the provision of, such accommodation in advance of the displacements."[44] While the statute just cited does not explicitly require the rehousing of these displaced families in council housing, English local authorities usually do so if these families cannot find housing in the private market.

Tenant selection practices by local authorities are not substantially restricted by both statutes, partly because the tenant selection provision only requires that a "reasonable" preference be given to persons in housing need. In addition, the replacement housing provision has been limited in local practice by a residence restriction, and rehousing may be denied to families who have not lived in the clearance area for a stipulated period of time, which may be as much as one year.[45] As one recent study concluded after a review of these two statutes and local authority practices, the policies for the allocation of local authority housing are not sufficiently clear.[46]

These two statutes have also been qualified by widespread adoption of residential requirements for admission to council housing, a practice which has been invalidated in some American states. No explicit statutory provision deals with residential requirements, there have been no court cases on the subject, and the most recent national departmental advice has recommended their reduction or abolition.[47] Nevertheless, while prior residence

---

[43] Housing Act, 1957, § 113(2).

[44] Housing Act, 1957, § 42(1) (proviso).

[45] *See* Mandelker, *Strategies in English Slum Clearance and Housing Policies,* 1969 WIS. L. REV. 800, 810, n. 35.

[46] *See* CULLINGWORTH REPORT, at 18-23.

[47] CIRCULAR 21/67, par. 4. However, the circular does not suggest that recently arrived families should "take priority" over those already on the waiting list, and also accepts that residential requirements may still be needed in areas of severe housing pressure.

is ordinarily not a condition to placement on a waiting list for council housing, many local authorities take length of residence into account when deciding whether or not to admit an applicant once he has been placed on a list.[48] The result is that newcomers to the community, such as colored immigrants or unskilled workers with unstable employment patterns, may be excluded from council housing altogether.

Neither are any controls placed on local authority eviction of tenants they consider undesirable, even though English law largely protects private tenants from eviction. Private tenants, in addition, are entitled to tenure for life, and for two further lives within the family.[49] This lack of effective control in English law over local authority tenant selection and eviction has allowed local authorities to select and keep only the most desirable and trouble-free tenants,[50] thus avoiding the problem of housing the more difficult families. Some control over local authority practices that restrict the entry of disadvantaged groups has now been provided by the Race Relations Act of 1968,[51] however. As it relates to council housing, this act primarily helps colored applicants, a group which has been under-represented in council housing accommodation.[52] This statute makes it unlawful to "discriminate against any person" on the ground of color, race, or ethnic or national origin by refusing accommodation to him except "on the like terms and in the like circumstances as in the case of other persons."[53] The major interpretive problem under this law is to determine what practices of local housing authorities are illegal. Many admission practices which are plausibly fair on their face are argued to be discriminatory as applied to colored applicants, and therefore in violation of the statute.

Admission requirements based on length of residence are one example of a requirement which technically complies with the provisions of Race Relations Act, as they apply to all applicants equally. But colored immigrants are usually the most recent arrivals in any local authority area, and are most likely to be excluded by a residence limitation. The question is whether a

---

[48] CULLINGWORTH REPORT, ch. 4.
[49] FRANCIS REPORT, *supra* note 7, at 4.
[50] EVIDENCE, at 744-46 (memorandum submitted by National Housing and Town Planning Council).
[51] Race Relations Act, 1968, ch. 71.
[52] CULLINGWORTH REPORT, at 120-22.
[53] Race Relations Act, 1968, ch. 71, §§ 1, 5(a).

residential requirement in this case is an illegal discrimination. The national housing department has recognized the problem but its advice has been ambivalent.[54] There has been no judicial determination that a residence requirement violates the Race Relations Act, and a recent case adopting a narrow construction of the statute casts doubt on whether a residence requirement would be found illegal. This case held that a local regulation which limits entry to British nationals does not violate the statute because discrimination on this basis is not explicitly outlawed.[55] Many colored immigrants are recent arrivals, and do not have British nationality.

C. Summary

This overview of English council housing has revealed both striking similarities to and striking differences from the American system. Like American public housing, English council housing is subsidized by a national subsidy, but while the subsidy has never covered debt service in full, it has provided relief for local authorities with higher than average housing costs, a monetary supplement which has not been available in America until very recently. As in America, national control of the program is also limited, and national directives have most affected cost controls, and the size of the local authority building program. Decisions on tenant admission, and on the allocation of housing units, have largely been left to local authorities. National guidance on these aspects of local housing administration has not been decisive, and even the effect of the English Race Relations Act on tenant selection is in doubt.

As a result, some long-standing ambiguities can be found in the English program.[56] No income limits are placed on admission, and most income categories in the English population are represented in council housing projects. Nevertheless, council housing does carry a subsidy, and even affluent tenants in the projects will receive the benefits of that subsidy unless some way can be found to limit those benefits to tenants who really need it. Local authorities have historically attempted to remedy this problem through the adoption of rent rebate systems, under which a

---

[54] CIRCULAR 63/68, par. 7.
[55] London Borough of Ealing v. Race Relations Bd., [1972] 1 All E.R. 105 (H.L.).
[56] *See* CULLINGWORTH REPORT, at 21-22.

standard space rent for a dwelling is first determined, and a rent rebate paid to tenants who cannot afford the predetermined rent. But this system was optional with local authorities for a long period, many authorities did not give rent rebates, and in those that did the extent of the rebate varied.

These problems have now been remedied by the 1972 Housing Act, to the extent that this legislation both enacts a national rent standard for English council housing and requires a nationally determined rent rebate system for all council housing tenants. We need to look at both elements of this housing subsidy system, and we will direct our attention in the next chapter to the impact of the 1972 legislation on council housing rents. The new subsidy system will be discussed next.

Chapter VI

RENT REGULATION IN ENGLAND

Until the housing subsidy reform legislated by the 1972 housing law, rents in council housing and in the private sector had differed. Rents for council housing were determined by local authorities under a statutory test which conferred considerable discretion on the local authority and which provided little judicial review or other form of supervision. Rents in the unfurnished private sector, on the other hand, had been subject to two forms of rent control, an older "controlled" rent system which related rents to tax assessment values, and a newer system of rent regulation which is based on the independent determination of a "fair rent" for each dwelling.

With the enactment of the 1972 housing law, this system of differing rent standards has been eliminated. Statutory provisions allowing for the determination of council housing rents by local authorities have been repealed, and the fair rent standard has been extended to the council housing sector. In the private sector, the older system of rent control will gradually be replaced with the fair rent system. Parity will then be achieved between public and private rental housing, except for private furnished accommodation, and the law will also have mandated a national rent standard for the entire council housing program. Whether the fair rent standard that has been adopted actually achieves uniformity throughout the country and parity between the public and private sectors will be considered in more detail at a later point.

The 1972 legislation also mandates nationally the rent rebate system of rebating council housing rents which previously had been adopted on a voluntary basis by some local authorities, and extends the rebate plan to tenants in private rental housing, also on a mandatory basis. These rebates are in turn based largely on the fair rents which are chargeable for council housing dwelling units. The place to begin our discussion of English housing subsidies, then, is with the fair rent concept and the operation of the fair rent system, and these are the topics which will be discussed in this chapter.

A. The Nature of the System

1. An Overview of the Problem

Much misinformation exists about the nature of rent controlling legislation in England, some of which arises out of misunderstandings about the character and nature of the privately rented housing stock. Out of 8,000,000 dwellings in England and Wales as of this writing, private rental housing contributes slightly more than 3,000,000—an ever diminishing portion of the housing supply. About 1,000,000 of these privately rented tenancies are in two special categories—either furnished accommodation, or service dwellings let in connection with the tenant's occupation. Of the remaining private tenancies, about 1.2 million fall (as of 1971) within the "controlled" rent sector, and another 1.3 million fall within the "regulated" rent sector. "Controlled" rents in England were first established after the First World War, and have been pegged at historic price levels under a series of different national rent acts. Many of these controlled tenancies were decontrolled under Conservative legislation in 1957, but a Labor government reestablished rent control in 1965 for those tenancies in the lowest sector of the rental scale,[1] and their rents were set in relation to the Gross Value of the tenancy. Gross Value is what Americans would call the "assessed" value of the property, as it is determined for property tax purposes. Property

---

[1] However, rents at the very bottom of the rental scale were decontrolled under the 1957 law only when possession was obtained by the landlord. Rent Act of 1957, 5 & 6 Eliz. 2, c. 25, § 11.

in England is not assessed for property tax purposes as it is in the United States, on the basis of its capital value. Instead, an annual rental value is determined for each property, including owner-occupied property, and the local tax, or "rate" as it is called in England, is based on this rental valuation. These valuations are carried out nationally, and are periodically revised. As in America, values for property tax purposes are set at a level which is below the actual market value of the property.

Rentals for controlled tenancies are currently set at twice the annual gross value, and are presently estimated to be at levels which are about one-third of the rents which would be set under the "regulated" tenancy system. The controlled tenancy system has become transitional, however. As controlled tenancies are usually older than other tenancies—estimates indicate that less than one-half are in standard condition, or capable of being placed in that condition—they are expected to disappear as demolition and slum clearance programs are executed. In addition, the legislation now provides for the gradual phasing of controlled tenancies into the regulated tenancy system, the second type of rent control, and the system of rent control which will eventually become the only system of rent control for unfurnished property in England.

Some of the history behind the enactment of the regulated tenancy system in 1965 will help to explain its major characteristics. As indicated earlier, the Conservatives had severely curtailed rent control in 1957, and a new Labor government elected in 1964 was determined to change this legislation. They were given support in this effort by a 1965 report of a national inquiry committee on the condition of housing in Greater London, which attracted considerable public attention.[2] This report pointed out the generally higher levels of rent in the London area, and the extent to which they were based on scarcity—an excessive demand for housing in relation to the supply. High rents and housing scarcity in London, and in other crowded urban centers, led to the Labor government initiative which produced a new rent act in 1965, and a system of rent regulation based on a statutory "fair rent" formula.[3]

---

[2] REPORT OF THE COMM. ON HOUSING IN GREATER LONDON, CMND. NO. 2605 (1965) (Milner Holland Report).

[3] 710 PARL. DEB., H.C. (5th ser.) 40-46 (1965) (statement of minister of housing on second reading).

This formula has eliminated scarcity value from the rents to be charged under the rent regulation system, but the statutory fair rent formula was not made automatically applicable to regulated tenancies by virtue of the statute. Instead, rents were frozen by the statute at the amount payable when the act went into effect, subject to an application by either landlord or tenant to have the rent registered. An application to have the rent registered may be filed with one of a new group of officials known as Rent Officers, and this officer's decision is subject to a further appeal to one of the Rent Assessment Committees which have been set up on a regional basis for all of England. As is conventional in English administrative practice, there is a further appeal from rent assessment committee decisions to the courts on points of law. Once registered, a rent is effective for three years, or until there has been a change in circumstances, at which time it may again be reviewed. The 1972 legislation continues this system for the private sector and extends it to council housing, with the exception that the rent freeze has been eliminated on the grounds that it proved to be ineffective.

From this brief review, the rent regulation system can be seen as a regulatory administrative control, triggered by an application for a fair rent determination from either the landlord or the tenant. The system is voluntary rather than mandatory; the decision to rely on a voluntary procedure was based on findings in the London housing study that a majority of tenants were satisfied with their rents.[4] In any event, a heavy load of applications to the Rent Officers would have overwhelmed the machinery, and the government at that time relied on the findings of the London study that most tenants were satisfied with their rents, and did not anticipate vast numbers of applications. That their gamble was a reasonable one is indicated by the fact that only 14 percent of the tenancies subject to the statute had their rents registered as of mid-1970.[5] Moreover, rents had been increased rather than decreased in two-thirds of the cases. Whether or not the low level of rent registrations reflects satisfaction with existing rents or simply ignorance or fear of using the system is problematic, however. A few studies would indicate, either that tenants

---

[4] *Ibid.*

[5] *See* REPORT OF THE COMMITTEE ON THE RENT ACTS, CMND. NO. 4609, at 11 (1971) [hereinafter cited as FRANCIS REPORT]. About 25% are estimated to be registered as of mid-1972.

do not know of or are afraid to use the system, or that many tenants in regulated tenancies are more concerned about repairs rather than about the rents they are charged.[6]

These observations require some additional comment. Even though controlled and regulated tenants both enjoy security of tenure under the rent acts, housing shortages in areas like London have prompted landlords to use harassment techniques to remove their tenants in order to secure possession of their property, often in order to sell it free of the tenant's statutory right to possession. The law provides no really effective remedy against such methods, and some observers believe that tenants have been reluctant to use the rent registration machinery because of their fear of this harassment. With reference to the repair problem, the rent act permits a downward adjustment of rent to take account of disrepair, but does not give rent officers the authority to order new repairs where they are needed. Tenants are allegedly dissatisfied with the rent regulation machinery because it can do nothing about dwelling repairs. Whatever the reason for the restricted use of the rent regulation machinery in the private rental sector, the statute has now adopted a different system for council housing, as fair rents are required to be determined for all dwellings in the council housing program. An analysis of how fair rents are applied to council housing will have to be deferred, however, until we have considered the fair rent standard in more detail.

2. The Fair Rent Standard

In view of the explicit purpose of the fair rent system,[7] to protect tenants from scarcity in the market, the way in which rents are determined under usual conditions of supply and demand should be explained first. These relationships are portrayed in Figure 1, a conventional supply and demand diagram. Housing rents in a housing market are a function of the level of demand for housing and of the supply against which that demand presses. As Figure 1 indicates, rents fall as quantity increases, and they

---

[6] Notting Hill Housing Service & Research Group, The Rent Acts and the Housing Market in North Kensington (1970) (Memorandum of Evidence to the Francis Committee); Zander, *The Unused Rent Acts,* 12 NEW SOCIETY 366 (1968). Both of these studies were carried out in London, but their findings are confirmed in Interim Rep. by the Rent Registration Group, Brighton Rent Project, Rents in Brighton (Oct. 1969).

[7] *See* the Second Reading speech by the then minister of housing, PARL. DEB., *supra* note 3, at 46. It should be noted that parliamentary debate is not considered by English courts of law when they interpret statutes.

FIGURE 1. – SUPPLY AND DEMAND CURVES IN HOUSING MARKETS

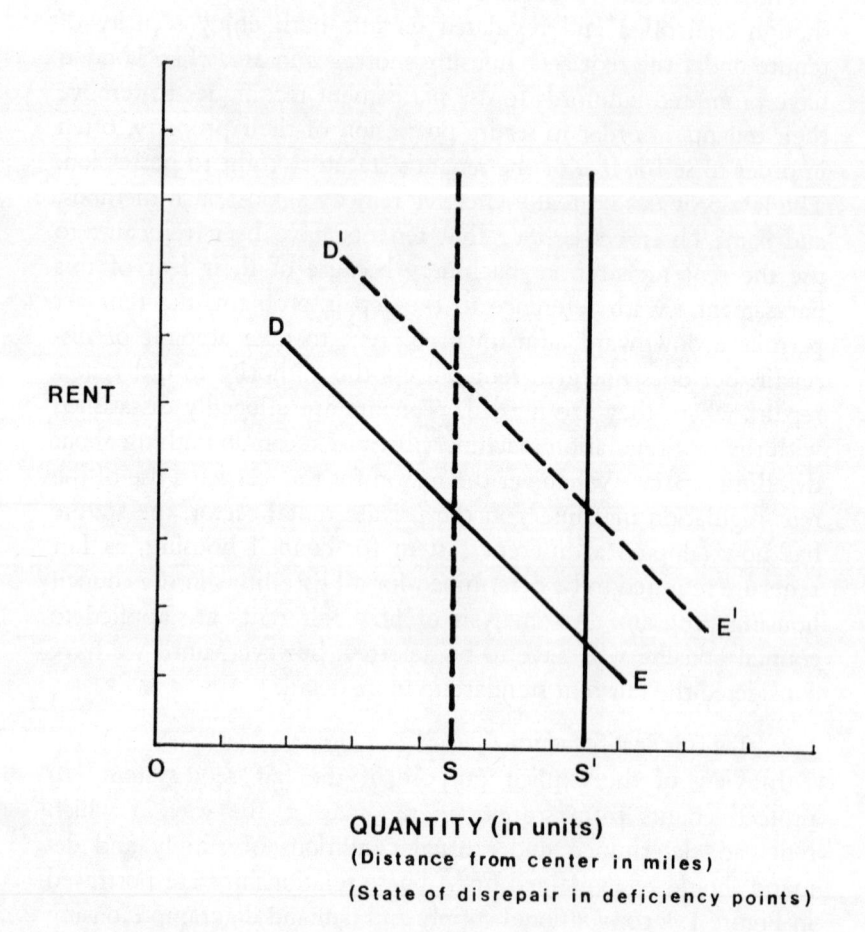

QUANTITY (in units)
(Distance from center in miles)
(State of disrepair in deficiency points)

rise as quantity diminishes; they are set at the point at which the demand for housing is in equilibrium with the available supply. In the diagram, the supply curve is vertical, suggesting that it is inelastic. That is, at any given point in time, at any place, the supply of housing is fixed. It is true, of course, that new increments to the housing supply occur through new construction (and conversions), but these additions to the supply are nominal at any given point of time, and the usual tendency is to disregard them.

Some other analytic difficulties which creep into this representation of the housing supply need to be discussed. One is that housing markets are spatial, so that spatially differentiated markets are noncompetitive. Housing in Hampstead, a very desirable section of London, does not compete with housing in a South London slum. Several ingredients make up the spatial dimensions of the housing market. One is distance; housing rents tend to vary inversely with distance from the center, and this relationship has been indicated on the horizontal axis in Figure 1. Rents are higher for housing closer to the center of London, partly because of the distance factor but also because the more one narrows the spatial circumference of the housing market the more that supply is constricted. For this reason, housing at point S' is more expensive than housing at point S.

State of repair is another factor influencing the character of the supply. By and large, any dwelling is only competitive with other dwellings that are in the same or similar condition, and the rent for housing will tend to vary inversely with the state of disrepair. This relationship is also represented on the horizontal axis in Figure 1. From this perspective, the supply of housing as represented in Figure 1 is simply a series of index points representing the product of the various factors influencing its availability and desirability, all of which determine rent levels. Indeed, a fourth factor, "amenity," or the desirability of a particular locality as a place to live, also affects supply. Hampstead, for example, is not as close to the center as other residential areas in London, but its high amenity results in higher prices for housing which in other areas would bring less. An amenity scale could be added to our diagram. The several factors which affect the housing supply could also be disaggregated and portrayed on a series of supply and demand charts. They have been aggregated here for simplicity of presentation, and in Figure

1 the supply curve simply represents an aggregated and averaged index of the quality of the housing supply.

Comments are also in order on the demand curve. What this curve represents is the amount of rent which housing consumers, as an aggregate, are willing to spend for increasing or decreasing units of the housing supply at a series of different quality levels. The *slope* of the demand curve expresses the responsiveness of rents to variations in the number of units in the supply. On this diagram, the demand curve is drawn to represent a price elasticity of 1.0; that is, for each decrease in the unit of supply, there is a corresponding increase in the amount of rent paid. Price elasticities of this order have been verified empirically, and will be accepted here as a constant for purposes of our presentation.

The *height* of the demand curve indicates how much of his income the consumer is willing to spend on housing. A rise in the height of the curve, to line D'-E', for example, indicates either that consumers have more income, and that they are willing to spend some of that additional income on housing, or that consumers do not have extra income but have shifted more of their present income to their housing expenditure. Most probably, there will be consumers in the housing market who fit both cases. What should also be clear on the basis of our previous discussion is that the height of the demand curve varies with different population and income groups. Poorer families for example, who have less income, spend proportionately more of it for housing. The demand curve, again, is an aggregated representation of the demand for housing in any one housing market.

In view of these complexities, just how to proceed to define a "fair" rent which will have the effect of discounting scarcity value is not altogether clear. Initially, the disaggregation problem seems paramount. A way must be found to adjust market rents for different consumer groups, and in different housing markets enjoying different conditions of supply. For example, very poor families do not compete for housing in Hampstead; they shift to other markets where enough of the supply may be bid away to satisfy their housing needs. On the other hand, very wealthy families will ignore standard housing, and housing available in areas that are not attractive to them.

Subject to this initial difficulty, the rent act of 1965 attempted to adjust rents, given certain assumptions about supply and demand which were not present in the market, but which the draftsmen thought were "fair" to consider in determining a proper rent. In this sense, the statute called for the determination of a "fair rent." Rent was to be the dependent variable, and supply and demand the independent variables affecting rents. But certain assumptions were to be made about supply and demand which would result in a rent other than what the market might have produced. This much seems clear in comments by the then minister of housing in the House of Commons, who made it clear that rate of return was not a factor to be considered in making fair rent determinations.[8] Under market conditions, the supply price for housing would have reflected a rate of return on capital which would have been considered sufficient to compensate for the investment risk. By indicating that rate of return was not to be considered in the determination of a fair rent, the minister appears to be suggesting that fair rents are to be lower than market rents.

With that background in mind, it will be helpful to proceed to the language of the statute next. The applicable section states:[9]

(1) "In determining . . . a fair rent . . . regard shall be had, subject to the following provisions of this section, to all the circumstances (other than personal circumstances) and in particular to the age, character and locality of the dwelling-house and to its state of repair.

(2) "For the purposes of the determination it shall be assumed that the number of persons seeking to become tenants of similar dwelling-houses in the locality on the terms (other than those relating to rent) of the regulated tenancy is not substantially greater than the number of such dwelling-houses in the locality which are available for letting on such terms."[10]

With the statute before us, we can now look at some of the major problems that have arisen in its interpretation. These

---

[8] *See* note 3, *supra*.

[9] Rent Act, 1968, ch. 23, § 46. The 1968 statute was a consolidation which incorporated the earlier 1965 law.

[10] A third subsection provides that any defect or disrepair attributable to the tenant's failure to repair under the terms of his agreement is to be disregarded, as well as any improvement carried out by the tenant. The tenant is held accountable by the statute for any defect, disrepair, or improvement attributable to his predecessor in title. *See* Metropolitan Properties Co., Ltd. v. Woolridge, [1968] 112 SOL. J. 862 (Q.B.).

problems have revolved around the disaggregation problem to which reference has already been made, and difficulties with statutory concept which arise from a failure to understand the role of supply and demand in determining rent levels.

a. *Disaggregation of market areas.* Clause (1) of the statute would apparently require that fair rents be fixed for housing sub-markets differentiated, in the words of the statute, according to the "age, character and locality of the dwelling-house and its state of repair." Problems of defining the appropriate "locality" within which fair rents are to be determined present some special problems, however, especially since clause (2) also requires the rent officer to disregard any scarcity in the "locality" in which the dwelling is located. The result is a statutory ambiguity[11] which appears insurmountable on its face, but which can best be discussed below in connection with other problems that the use of the word "locality" raises.

The statute does seem to mean that the fair rent of any dwelling should be set only with reference to dwellings of a similar character, having regard to the circumstances enumerated in the statute.[12] There is a problem even with this interpretation, however, since our earlier analysis indicated that different housing sub-markets are in competition. As a result, would-be tenants with insufficient income might shift their search from a market of three-bedroom homes in good repair to a market of two-bedroom dwellings in worse condition in order to find accommodation which they can afford. Some method would appear to be needed to consider this shift in demand, especially in view of the definition of "scarcity" which was given in debate by the government spokesman for the legislation. He indicated that by scarcity he meant a situation in which "there is not a freedom of choice, and in which a person may be forced to take something which he would not otherwise choose."[13] In our example above, a fair rent determination for dwellings in the better three-bedroom market would seem to be needed which would not preclude tenants from obtaining accommodation in that market which is within their means.

---

[11] The point was made in debate by a former Conservative minister of housing. PARL. DEB., *supra* note 3, at 74.

[12] *See* FRANCIS REPORT, at 60.

[13] PARL. DEB., *supra* note 3, at 47.

There is also a problem in deciding whether to consider other tenures. What, for example, should be the impact on regulated rents of the availability of council dwelling? The statute does not explicitly take account of rents in different tenures, but long waiting lists for council housing may be evidence of scarcity of accommodation in the private rental market.[14]

b. *Misconceptions in the statutory formula.* Other problems have arisen because the statute has not been entirely successful in making explicit its intent, to eliminate scarcity value through the fair rent determinations. The statute talks about an imbalance between the number of persons seeking accommodation, and the supply of accommodation available, obviously in an attempt to describe a scarcity situation. But the term "scarcity value" is nowhere defined in the statute.

This statutory approach to the scarcity problem does not provide enough guidance for the adjustment in rent which a scarcity situation would appear to demand. If supply is not in balance with demand—the situation described in the statute—then supply can be increased by assuming that there are enough units in the relevant market to house all of the families who are seeking shelter. In Figure 1, that is, the supply curve would be moved to the right, from S′ to S. But knowing that the number of persons seeking shelter is in excess of the supply does not provide us with enough of a basis with which to make the necessary corrections in housing demand. We also need to have additional information about the height of the demand curve. That is, we need to make some assumptions about the incomes of those seeking shelter and the rents they are willing to pay before we can determine what fair rents ought to be under conditions of scarce supply.

Discussions with those associated with the rent regulation machinery suggest that the income factor is taken into account in practice. For example, if the dwelling under consideration is an apartment built specifically for the elderly, the rent officer takes into account the demand for housing among the elderly, having regard to their generally lower incomes. But considerations

---

[14] FRANCIS REPORT, at 59-60. This inference assumes that the amount of council housing in a local authority is responsive to the supply of and demand for housing in the market at various income levels. Such an inference is not necessarily correct, since the council housing program is not required to be responsive to housing shortages in the market.

of this kind appear precluded by the parenthetical statutory proviso which does not permit a consideration of personal circumstances when fair rents are determined. This language was added to the legislation after its introduction, on Conservative party insistence, but the intent of the amendment is not altogether clear.[15] Under one interpretation, the amendment excludes all consideration of the personal financial means and other characteristics of the tenant for whom the fair rent is being fixed. Even so, the amendment might still permit consideration of the market demand of the *class* of tenants to which the tenant in question belongs. There was reference in debate, however, to the need to set fair rents only in relation to the property, and not the person, and so even this modified consideration of personal circumstances appears to be precluded.

c. *Role of locality and amenity in the determination.* Equally difficult conceptual problems appear on the supply side. Note has already been taken of the fact that the word "locality" is used both in clause (1), which contains the formula for fair rents, and in clause (2), which states the rule for discounting scarcity. The relationship between these two clauses is not altogether clear. Clause (2) provides certain assumptions about supply and demand which are to be accepted in making the "determination," and this determination appears to be the determination of fair rent required in clause (1). But locality cannot be both considered and disregarded at the same time.

One approach to this ambiguity is to view the statute as having mandated a two-step process: market rents are first determined under clause (1), and then discounted for scarcity under clause (2). This approach was taken in the early days of the act; the market rent was first assessed, and an acceptable discount was then arrived at to represent the scarcity element. This approach has now been discredited,[16] but substantial problems of interpretation still remain.

These problems of interpretation can be clarified by using the Hampstead example. During debates on the act the Hamp-

---

[15] PARL. DEB., H.C. STANDING COMM. F, RENT BILL 623-31 (1965).

But note the comment in CIRCULAR 75/72, § 23, that "any inflation of the value of poor quality accommodation in town centres which could properly be attributed to the pressure of demand from tenants with low incomes working in the central area should be disregarded." The circular applies to fair rents in council housing.

[16] FRANCIS REPORT, at 58.

stead rent problem was usually conceptualized as one of imbalance; there was not enough housing in Hampstead to satisfy the many people who wanted to live there. As a result, rents in Hampstead rose.[17] This conclusion is correct if it means that rents are higher in Hampstead because it is a relatively small place with a limited quantity of housing. (The supply curve in Hampstead shifts to the left, and rents go up. See Figure 1.)

But other neighborhoods in London have in comparison with Hampstead an equally limited housing supply, yet rents there are not as high as they are in Hampstead. One possible explanation of this inconsistency lies in the demand curve. Tenants seeking accommodation in Hampstead may simply have more money available for housing, either because they are wealthier, or because they are willing to devote a higher proportion of their income to rent. In this event, the height of the demand curve would rise, and rents would rise accordingly for the same supply, again as in Figure 1. What this analysis suggests is that a limited housing supply and the character of the social and economic class seeking to live in a neighborhood will both affect the level of rents that is considered "fair" under the statute, a point to which we will have cause to return again.

But high rents in Hampstead are also affected by other factors that contribute to the character of the locality, an influence which is reflected in the supply curve. First, Hampstead is close to the center of London and most of its housing is in good repair. Secondly, the Hampstead neighborhood has desirable amenity; its elevation is good, and it is located near Hampstead Heath, a large and attractive park. Amenity is a housing output like any other, with the difference that it is both limited and fixed in quantity. Therefore, those who purchase amenity will have to pay a higher rent for it, and any housing which enjoys it will go up in value.

The statutory fair rent definition permits consideration of all of these factors. State of repair is explicitly mentioned, and the statute would appear to permit consideration of the neighborhood's distance from the center by authorizing a consideration of "locality" in clause (1). Parliamentary debate also made it clear that this term was also to permit a consideration of amenity.[18]

---

[17] Standing Comm., *supra* note 15, at 653-55.
[18] *Ibid. See also* 715 PARL. DEB., H.C. (5th ser.) 704 (1965).

Difficulties are again presented, however, by the failure of the statute to deal with the height of the demand curve, that is, with the amount which families seeking housing in the locality are willing to spend for rent. We noted earlier that rent officers made a downward adjustment in the height of the demand curve of persons seeking housing for the elderly on the ground that incomes of these people generally are lower. Fair rents are also lower proportionately. Higher amenities in Hampstead will attract would-be tenants who have higher demand curves than those seeking housing elsewhere. Therefore, an upward adjustment should be made in the height of the demand curve of people seeking housing in Hampstead. Clause (1) of the statute justifies this result to the extent that it permits consideration of the locality in which the housing is located. Locality factors are used to adjust both the demand and supply curves, and rents are set higher in the case of Hampstead.

But what about the injunction in clause (2) that scarcity in the locality is also to be taken into account? If "locality" for the purpose of applying clause (2) is the same as "locality" for the purpose of clause (1), then the effect of clause (2) will be to adjust rents in Hampstead to remove any impact on rents which the higher amenity in Hampstead, and the higher demand curve of those seeking housing in Hampstead, has produced. The problem was raised in parliamentary debate,[19] but no satisfactory answer was given. As a practical matter, the problem has been handled by considering "locality" as it appears in clause (2) in a much wider geographical sense than it is considered in clause (1).[20] The result is that rents in a desirable area such as Hampstead are not discounted for scarcity on the grounds that the locality in which scarcity is tested under clause (2) is so wide—all or almost all of London, at present—that there is no scarcity!

Another explanation may help. If the locality for testing scarcity in Hampstead is all of Greater London, then the effect will be that in the locality as so defined the quantity of housing will be greater and its average amenity less. As a result, there

---

[19] *See* note 15, *supra*.

[20] For example, rent assessment committees in London have taken the word locality in clause (2) to mean "the area within which persons likely to occupy this class of accommodation, having regard to their requirements and work, would be able to dwell." FRANCIS REPORT, at 61. *See also id.,* at 86-89.

will be no imbalance of supply and demand in Hampstead, in the language of clause (2), and no need to adjust rents in that area, which is the locality for purposes of applying clause (1). Rents within London will therefore be allowed to vary by district.

One consequence of this approach will be a certain distortion in rents which arises out of commuting patterns. In our discussion of Figure 1, we noted that distance from the center was an important influence on rent. Distance from employment centers has a comparable effect. Assume a large factory employing large numbers of low-income workers in a South London neighborhood. Rents in the immediate neighborhood of the factory will tend to be high, reflecting the shorter commuting time needed to reach the factory. Under clause (1), this factor can be taken into account when setting rents for that locality, and these rents would then be discounted for scarcity if the locality for purposes of considering scarcity under clause (2) is the neighborhood in the vicinity of the factory. But the employment center influence disappears if one considers London as the appropriate locality for determining scarcity under clause (2), because all of London is then considered the "center" for employment rather than just the immediate area of the factory. No scarcity element will be imputed to rents in the neighborhood of the factory, and fair rents will not be lowered. Workers in the plant will then have to look elsewhere than the immediate neighborhood of the factory for accommodation they can afford, or pay the higher rents in the factory neighborhood. If they elect to rent cheaper housing elsewhere, they will have to pay more in commuting costs. This increment in commuting costs will not be reflected in rents actually paid, but realistically it is an additional housing "cost" which is imposed by the need to commute. One way to handle this problem is to ignore the increased demand for houses in the immediate vicinity coming from workers who work in the factory,[21] on the ground that it is due to the personal circumstances of the factory employees, but this approach is inconsistent with the approach taken in evaluating the demand of elderly people as a class for elderly housing.

---

[21] *See* FRANCIS REPORT, at 62. In a circular giving advice for the determination of fair rents in council housing, the national housing department defines "locality" as "an area within reasonable commuting distance" of a place of work. CIRCULAR 75/72, § 23.

Whatever the impact of the fair rent standard on rents within London neighborhoods, the application of the statute to the Greater London area as a whole has led to rents lower than what they would have been in an open market. On what basis this reduction is made is not clear, but one approach is to make different assumptions in applying the fair rent standard to Greater London than are made in the rest of the country. For example, it could be assumed that more housing is available in London than is actually the case. London's housing supply would then be increased and rents would be correspondingly lower. Another alternative is to assume away the higher amenity and locational advantages generally present in London housing. Similar assumptions could be made in other urban areas suffering from intense housing pressures.

3. Operation of the System in Practice

The difficulties which are present in the conceptual basis of the fair rent standard have been somewhat overcome in practice.[22] For example, as a register of fair rents has built up in various parts of the country, rent officers and committees often assess the fair rent of a dwelling under review on the basis of fair rents set for comparable dwellings in the area. Evidence of fair rents for comparable dwellings was held to be the "best evidence" of fair rent in the *Tormes* case, a lower court decision,[23] but the court may not have interpreted the statute correctly. One problem is that the statute requires a fair rent determination as of the date the fair rent is registered. Rents used as comparables would have been determined at an earlier date, and to this extent the use of a comparable fair rent without updating goes contrary to the statute, a point forgotten in the judicial opinion just cited.

Another problem with the comparables method is that it may lead to bootstrapping. For example, a landlord or group of landlords interested in setting a high level of fair rents for their properties may simply pick as a precedent-setting case a dwelling in which they have a compliant tenant who does not present much argument in opposition.[24] Rents set in this and similar proceedings can then be used as comparables in subsequent determinations before rent officers.

---

[22] *See, e.g.*, FRANCIS REPORT, at 57-58.
[23] Tormes Property Co., Ltd. v. Landau, [1970] 3 All E.R. 653 (Q.B.).
[24] For examples of this practice see 826 PARL. DEB., H.C. (5th ser.) 102-03 (1971).

Limitations on the scope of judicial review will then foreclose the courts from reviewing the earlier rent which is being used as a comparable. Only questions of law may be raised in appeals of fair rent determinations, and so in the *Tormes* case, in which the landlord argued that the rent set for the comparable dwelling was too low, the court replied that the earlier rent had to be assumed to be correct in law. As the court pointed out, the comparable rents to which reference was made had been set for the same property, owned by the same landlord, and were not appealed in the earlier ruling. In other words, the court was denying the landlord an opportunity to make a collateral attack on the determination in the earlier case.

But resort to comparables is not the only method of fixing a fair rent. Rent officers and rent assessment committees are not required to use it,[25] and they in fact rely on a variety of criteria, such as value for property tax purposes, economic return, historic cost, and market rents.[26] Some of these criteria may appear incompatible with the purposes of the statute, but this eclectic approach has been upheld by a court opinion[27] which has accorded these agencies wide leeway in the making of the fair rent determination. This approach to the judicial review of administrative determinations is typical of English practice, and has tended to isolate the decisions of rent-setting agencies from the potentially corrective impact of judicial scrutiny. Nor is much additional insight into the working of the system to be gained from the work of the appellate tribunals, the Rent Assessment Committees. Some of these committees, such as the London Rent Assessment Panel, do publish selected decisions that are considered to have a precedential value, but they are largely factual recitations and do not discuss the conceptual principles on the basis of which the decision was taken.

These same tendencies toward a lack of articulation of the decisional basis for fair rent decisions are evident in the handling of the all-important scarcity issue. Very little direct evidence is presented at rent determination proceedings which bears on this issue, and rent officers and committees tend to rely on their own

---

[25] Metropolitan Properties Co. (F.G.C.), Ltd. v. Lannon, [1968] 1 All E.R. 354 (Q.B.), *rev'd on other grounds,* [1968] 3 All E.R. 304 (C.A.).

[26] FRANCIS REPORT, at 58-59; CIRCULAR 75/72, §§ 24-28.

[27] Anglo-Italian Properties, Ltd. v. London Rent Assess. Panel, [1969] 2 All E.R. 1128 (Q.B.).

expertise in assessing the effect of scarcity on fair rents.[28] In one court decision in which this method of reaching a fair rent determination was challenged the ruling of the rent assessment committee based on their own expertise was affirmed.[29] For information on the impact of the statute on rent levels we must rely on general appraisals of the system, which suggest that fair rents range about 20 percent lower than the market rents that would have been charged for the same properties.[30]

Inflation presents a final problem, as some method must be found to revise rents periodically to take account of increases in costs and taxes. While not explicitly provided for in the rent regulation statute, a method to revise rents to take account of inflation is available in the statutory provision that fair rents may be reviewed every three years.[31] One court has also held that evidence of inflationary trends may be taken into account in advance when a fair rent is set for the statutory three-year period.[32] As a result, and assuming that the parties continue to resort to the fair rent machinery, corrections for inflation should be made in due course and the disparity between fair rents and market rents should not increase. On the other hand, to the extent that market inflation is due to elements of scarcity value not present when the rent was first set, landlords may expect that the statutorily determined fair rent will not capture all of the inflationary push that the economy has generated.

B. Conversion of Controlled to Regulated Tenancies: The Problem of Housing Improvement

One of the difficulties with rent control and rent regulation systems is that they often set a rent standard that does not take the state of repair of the dwelling into account, or that does not allow a sufficient incentive which will induce the landlord to make necessary repairs and improvements. There is no such

---

[28] FRANCIS REPORT, at 59.

[29] Crofton Inv. Trust, Ltd. v. Greater London Rent Assess. Comm., [1967] 2 All E.R. 1103 (Q.B.).

[30] FRANCIS REPORT, at 62.

[31] Rent Act, § 45(4).

Note that the government imposed a temporary freeze on all rent increases beginning with legislation enacted in 1972. THE PROGRAM FOR CONTROLLING INFLATION: THE SECOND STAGE, CMND. NO. 5205 (1973).

[32] Metropolitan Properties Co. (F.G.C.) v. Lannon, *supra* note 25.

incentive or allowance in the English rent control legislation, and the problem is handled under the language of the rent regulation statute by allowing the state of repair to be taken into account when the fair rent for the dwelling is determined.[33] This approach permits a downward adjustment to take account of the dwelling's state of repair, but it does not necessarily guarantee that landlords will repair and improve their dwellings in order to be able to charge a higher rent. Neither may the rate of return guaranteed by the fair rent standard produce enough income or provide enough motivation to the private landlord to repair his dwelling, since fair rent determinations on an average are below market rent levels. In the council housing sector we shall see that the situation is not as acute, since local authorities are authorized to carry forward working balances in their accounts which can be applied to repairs. But dwelling repair is not compulsory, even in the council housing program. The English housing subsidy program will therefore subsidize substandard accommodation in the private sector, whenever an allowance is paid to a tenant who lives in a dwelling in an unsatisfactory state of repair.

Additional inducements for the repair and improvement of housing are provided, however, by other legislative incentives and controls. First, there are several programs for housing improvement which have been adopted independently of the rent regulation and housing subsidy structure. Second, an incentive for repair and improvement is provided by the rent regulation statute in its provisions for the conversion of a controlled to a regulated tenancy. We will look at these techniques in this order.

In brief, there are three major statutory programs that are aimed at the repair and improvement of substandard housing.[34] The first centers on a provision of the housing act which provides that a dwelling is subject to an order of demolition if it is statutorily unfit and if the necessary repairs are not made. This statute provides a list of factors, such as lack of stability and

---

[33] *Cf.* McGee v. London Rent Assess. Panel Comm., [1969] 113 SOL. J. 384 (Q.B.), holding the tenants not responsible for damage by fire which occurred when they vacated a house inhabited by a poltergeist.

[34] This discussion is based on Mandelker, *Strategies in English Slum Clearance and Housing Policies,* 1969 WIS. L. REV. 800.

Local governments may also adopt "control orders" which allow them to carry out repairs on rooming houses. Housing Act, 1964, ch. 56, §§ 73-91.

lack of repair, which are to be taken into account when a determination of unfitness is made.[35] But this finding requires that a dwelling be in a very much more serious condition than a dwelling would have to be in order to violate the standards contained in a typical American housing code. For this reason, and because the English are much less prone to compel the repair of dwellings, especially those that are owner-occupied, compulsory repair without subsidy is not as common a practice in home improvement programs as it is in the United States. We should note, however, that unfit dwellings may also be treated as a group and then cleared as part of a slum clearance area.[36] As we shall see, these repair and clearance powers assume a special importance under those provisions of the statute which authorize a conversion from a controlled to a regulated tenancy.

The second statutory program provides for two types of improvement grants to local authorities, owner-occupiers, owners of rental property, and tenants having at least a five-year lease.[37] These grants have been proportionately available on a much greater scale in England than in the United States, and have had a proportionately greater impact on the housing improvement program. The first type of improvement grant, called the standard grant, is awarded as a matter of right and provides for basic amenities, such as sanitary facilities and a hot water supply. The second type of grant is awarded for improvement of dwellings to a standard satisfactory accommodation for a stated period, which is at least ten years at the present time. These grants, neither of which is means-tested, provide one-half of the cost of the improvement in the usual case. They are made by the local authority, which then recovers three-fourths of the grant amount, from the national government.

Finally, the statutes authorize so-called General Improvement Areas,[38] known as GIA. Both housing rehabilitation and environmental improvements may be carried out in a GIA, and both housing improvement and area improvement grants are available

---

[35] Housing Act, 1957, 5 & 6 Eliz. 2, c. 56, § 4.

[36] *Id.*, pt. III.

[37] Housing Act, 1969, ch. 33, pt. I.

In economic development areas the grant now meets three-fourths of improvement costs. Housing Act, 1971, ch. 76.

[38] *Id.*, pt. II. For descriptions of several typical GIAs see Architects' Journal Information Library, June 10, 1970, at 1447-70.

to assist in the GIA program. A GIA may not be combined with a slum clearance area in the same project, although nothing in the statute prevents the designation of GIA and slum clearance areas side by side. Demolition of individual dwellings may also be carried out inside a GIA.

This brief review suggests that the machinery available to secure housing improvement is not as strong or effective as it could be. To date, the GIA concept is not fully tested, implementation of GIA programs has been slow, and even the effectiveness of the comprehensive system of English improvement grants has been doubted.[39] Interviews with local authorities indicate that the national government stands ready to fund whatever level of improvement grants is necessary, a distinct difference from American practice. The problem flows instead from the general economic weakness of the private rental sector, which seems unwilling to respond even to this financial incentive toward better housing conditions. Most of the improvement grants have been taken up by local authorities and owner-occupiers, and not by private landlords.[40] But the housing in these sectors is least in need of improvement.

The reason that private landlords are unwilling to accept improvement grants may be that they must pay one-half of the cost of the improvement themselves in most areas. While they are entitled by statute to increase rents in order to recoup a fair return on their investment, the statutory machinery for obtaining this rent increase has been cumbersome, and low tenant incomes have discouraged some landlords from taking the steps to make the increased charge. To the extent that landlords do make repairs and improvements, therefore, some or all of this cost will be shifted to the tenant unless there is a compensatory payment in the subsidy. A housing program must thus be prepared to subsidize substandard housing unless it is willing either to compel tenants to pay for the cost of housing improvement or to subsidize that cost directly. In that event, subsidy costs will rise proportionately. The English approach to this problem definitely appears to be a compromise.

---

[39] *See* Meacher, *Tinkering with Twilight Homes,* 18 NEW SOCIETY 20 (1971). However, from 1967 to 1971 the number of unfit houses in England and Wales declined by one-third. Press Statement, Improvement in National Housing Stock, May 23, 1972, at 1 (Dep't of Environment).

[40] *See* 821 PARL. DEB., H.C. (5th ser.) 389-90 (1971).

We noted that the English have also provided an incentive to housing improvement in the method that has been afforded for the conversion of a controlled to a regulated tenancy. A controlled dwelling may be converted, that is it may be treated for statutory purposes as a regulated tenancy. In this event it must be in good repair, taking into consideration its age, character and condition, and must have all the standard amenities—those for which the standard improvement grant is available.[41] Before the landlord can have his dwelling converted he must obtain a certificate of qualification from the local authority, and the certificate may be issued provisionally subject to the landlord's bringing the dwelling up to the prescribed statutory standard. Moreover, if a provisional certificate is issued, and if the tenant does not consent to the repairs which are necessary to bring the dwelling up to the statutory standard, a court may order the repairs to be done, and in making such an order "shall not take into account the means or resources of the tenant."[42] What this provision means is that a landlord may repair his dwelling beyond the means of his tenant, who may then be forced out. The Labor party objected to this provision. Improvement of lower grade properties in order to attract a higher class of tenants is already common in many older neighborhoods. It was argued that this provision would simply accelerate this neighborhood transformation process, and thus encourage class stratification. The government response was that any increase in rent as the result of such repairs would be absorbed by the new housing allowance for private tenants.[43] Whether this is so will have to remain for examination until the new housing subsidy system can be explored more fully. What is to be underlined here is that this change in the method of decontrol may have an inflationary effect on rent levels, may alter neighborhood living patterns, and may also result in higher housing subsidies.

In addition to these provisions the legislation also provides for a gradual conversion of *all* controlled tenancies to regulated tenancies under a schedule which takes into account the rent of the dwelling.[44] That is, the more expensive controlled tenancies

---

[41] Housing Finance Act, 1972, ch. 47, § 27(1).

[42] *Id.*, § 33(4).

[43] Parl. Deb., Standing Comm. E, Housing Finance Bill 1082-98 (1972) [hereinafter cited as Standing Comm.].

[44] 1972 Act, pt. IV.

will be decontrolled first, and the less expensive tenancies will be gradually decontrolled later. This provision should give some pause. We noted earlier that a large percentage of the controlled tenancies are substandard. While the statute since 1969 has permitted the decontrol of controlled tenancies that are in a state of good repair, as defined above, the rate of decontrol under these provisions had been slow.[45] Now all controlled tenancies are eventually to be converted to the rent regulation system, and fair rents determined.

There is one exception. Unfit houses subject to a notice of demolition or slum clearance order are to be exempt from decontrol.[46] This exemption is reasonable, but objection was taken to its scope on the ground that dwellings in many localities, even though unfit, are not subject to clearance or demolition orders because of time lags in the implementation of local programs.[47] As a result, decontrol will be applied to dwellings which are subject to removal as unfit for habitation, and the rent act machinery will have to be relied upon to set a rent which takes the condition of the dwelling into account. Except for this slum clearance and demolition exception, the gradual decontrol of all controlled tenancies, notwithstanding their condition, will tend to undercut the other programs of housing improvement. Decontrol also shifts the level of rents in the controlled private sector to the higher fair rent levels which are applied in the rent regulation system. Landlords may expect a fairer return, but what impact this change will have on tenants in private accommodations will depend on the nature of the housing subsidy, which will be examined in the next chapter. We must first discuss, however, the way in which the legislation applies the fair rent standard to council housing.

C. Fair Rents for Local Authority Dwellings

1. Policy Problems

From a very wide perspective, the fair rent system as applied in the private sector is a compromise. Market rents cannot be charged, and private landlords are denied some of the increment

---

[45] STANDING COMM., at 1150-51 (only 7000 dwellings). *See also* FRANCIS REPORT, at 96-8.

[46] 1972 Act, § 36.

[47] STANDING COMM., at 1231-37.

to the rental value of their properties whenever fair rents do not reflect the amenities of location. In the public sector the rationale for applying the fair rent standard is not as clear, and its application to council housing has been hotly disputed. The argument has been made that, as council housing receives the benefit of national and local subsidies, it serves a social purpose which should be reflected in the rents charged, and that a market-related rent standard such as the fair rent standard does not properly reflect this social purpose.

In this discussion, we will accept the fair rent standard as the starting point for our discussion, and then attempt to determine in what ways the fair rent concept is and is not compatible with the purposes of the council housing program. Two sets of issues are involved here. We must first look at the way in which the application of the fair rent concept to council housing achieves parity and equity as between different sectors of the housing market, and among different regions in the country. We will next look at the impact which fair rents are likely to have internally on the council housing program. This discussion should help us to determine how appropriate the fair rent standard is for council housing, and whether any other more suitable alternative is available. Underlying this discussion is one central fact. The extension of the fair rent standard to council housing will clearly lead to substantially higher rents, a change in the housing program which has led to vehement opposition, both from the Labor party, and from local housing authorities and their tenants.

We have already noted that rents in council housing have historically been set independently of any rebate which is given to tenants who live in the housing projects. This pattern is confirmed even more strongly by the 1972 legislation, under which fair rents are set nationally for all council dwellings, and a rebate is available to the tenant who needs it no matter where he happens to live. Although the amount of the subsidy is tied to the fair rent that is charged, the availability of the subsidy and the applicability of the fair rent standard in both the private and public sectors is intended to remove any previously existing disparities between these two parts of the rental market. As the government White Paper which introduced the 1972 housing legislation pointed out, one purpose of the reform was to provide "fairness between one citizen and another in giving and receiving help towards housing costs."[48] The hope is that consumer choice in housing will be broadened, and that council housing rent policies will no longer impede the mobility of those tenants who previously believed that they could not give up the bargain which their council housing unit represented. The question which we will discuss here is whether or not the application of the fair rent standard to both private and council-owned housing can actually achieve the parity that is intended.

One problem that must be faced in any attempt to achieve parity between council housing and private rental housing is that additional costs are imposed on council housing to achieve community benefits which are not limited to the housing program.[49] For example, council housing has been used extensively for redevelopment purposes on slum clearance sites. Land costs are higher in redevelopment areas, and these costs are reflected in higher rents for council housing and in higher housing subsidies. A new slum clearance subsidy, to be discussed later, does shift some of this cost to the national, rather than the local government, but the cost of using slum-cleared land still must be absorbed by the housing subsidy system.

Other differences between council housing and privately rented housing also limit the extent to which the fair rent standard can achieve parity between these two sectors. One difference is that private rental housing may not be in the same part of the city as council housing, so that differences in the locality in which each type of housing is located make comparisons difficult. Age differences are another problem, as the private rental housing supply is much older, and is also dwindling in amount.[50] Much council housing has been constructed in recent years, during which land prices have been rising at a more rapid rate than the composite cost-of-living index. This trend has been in evidence even outside slum clearance areas, which were discussed above.

---

[48] FAIR DEAL FOR HOUSING, CMND. NO. 4728, at 1 (1971) [hereinafter cited as FAIR DEAL].

[49] Some of these considerations are detailed in a memorandum submitted by Manchester in the MINUTES OF EVIDENCE TAKEN BEFORE SUBCOMM. B OF THE HOUSE OF COMMONS ESTIMATES COMM., Sess. 1968-69, Vol. III, at 651-60.

[50] NATIONAL BD. FOR PRICES AND INCOMES, INCREASES IN RENTS OF LOCAL AUTHORITY HOUSING, REP. NO. 62, at 22 (1968). This was an advisory board created under a temporary national law which regulated prices and incomes in an attempt to hold back inflation. The report contains a valuable review of local authority rent-setting practices.

Whether this above-average increase in land costs can be discounted under the fair rent formula is an open question.

Regional differences in rents determined under the fair rent standard present another complication. Here the difference lies between rent levels in London and the southeast, and rent levels in the rest of the country. From the beginning, the fair rent standard has contained a built-in preference for housing in the London region, where the discount for scarcity is highest. Now this preference is to be extended to publicly owned housing in the Greater London sector as well. One consequence of this policy is that it counteracts the impact which the rent rebate for council tenants has on labor mobility, for the application of the fair rent standard to London area council housing discounts to some extent the impact which London scarcities might have had on council housing rent levels. From a planning point of view, moreover, the high discount which disregarding scarcity brings to London housing counteracts the general thrust of English national planning policy, which has been to encourage new housing and other development in areas outside the southeast region. We will return to this point later.

The extent to which the fair rent standard is biased in favor of London housing is evident from a consideration of two alternative rent standards which have been considered for council housing.[51] The first alternative standard would base local authority rents on historic costs. In the London area, however, as housing needs are greater, local authorities are building proportionately more housing than local authorities elsewhere, and rents in this new housing reflect the present high construction cost levels. Application of the historic cost standard to London housing would therefore gradually raise the rents on London housing to points higher than they would be under the fair rent approach. Another standard that has been suggested would relate rents to replacement costs rather than historic costs. Rents would then include a sinking fund for the replacement of existing housing as it deteriorates and is demolished. Again, as London housing needs are greater, this standard would also result in higher rent levels in the London area.

There are other problems with historic or replacement cost. Using the replacement cost approach, for example, would mean

---

[51] *Id.*, at 23.

charging present-day tenants for the housing needs of future generations, an allocation of burden which many consider undesirable. Just to take one problem, replacement rents would then have to include an amount sufficient to cover the increased construction costs that inflation will impose on replacement housing.[52] To charge the present generation of housing consumers the cost of future inflationary increases which are imposed by cost tendencies in the general economy appears undesirable.

While the fair rent standard faces some difficulties in achieving parity between the private and public rental sectors,[53] parity with the owner-occupied sector cannot even be attempted so long as the price of owner-occupied housing remains uncontrolled. Nevertheless, the extension of the fair rent standard to council housing will have important effects on the relationships between all rented housing and owner-occupied housing, and we will make some comment on this issue here. In its White Paper which preceded the 1972 legislation, the government listed as one of its aims "a fairer choice between owning a home and renting a home,"[54] and there is no doubt that the Conservative government translates fairness in this context as a preference for home ownership over renting as the desired form of tenure.[55] Since the application of the fair rent standard to council housing will have the effect of generally increasing rents for council houses, some critics of the 1972 act claim that its intent, in part, is to force higher-income tenants in council housing to buy homes as an alternative. If this shift occurs, it will have several important effects on housing policy. The average incomes of council tenants will move downward, and these tenants will require more housing subsidy because they will not be able to pay as much in rent. To the extent that rent officers and committees consider the incomes of the class of tenants living in council housing, a trend toward lower incomes among council tenants may also lead to lower fair rents. If local authorities attempt to meet these problems by assigning the older and cheaper dwelling units to their poorer tenants, they will only stratify their projects by class, thereby inviting all of the problems which class stratification has brought

---

[52] *Ibid.*
[53] For a contrary claim see STANDING COMM., at 1427-33.
[54] FAIR DEAL, at 1.
[55] *Id.*, at 4, 5.

to American public housing. The problems will be compounded to the extent that local authorities site their new units away from high amenity, desirable neighborhoods in order to hold down their land costs. At the same time, since no direct housing subsidy is provided for owner-occupation, a substantial shift to owner occupancy will in turn reduce the level of direct subsidies which are needed for rental housing. But the indirect subsidy which is available to homeowners through tax forgiveness on home mortgage interest will increase proportionately.

Another change will be a relative shift in the extent to which historic cost levels determine the general level of housing expenditure. Homeowners enjoy historic housing costs if they stay for substantial periods of time in one dwelling, and mobility rates in general are much lower in England than they are in the United States. When the homeowner does move, he captures the price increase which inflation has added to his home, and this profit helps him to buy a new home at the higher price levels that inflation has brought to the housing market. Fair rents, on the other hand, may be reviewed and adjusted upward every three years.

2. The Statutory Fair Rent Formula as Applied to Council Housing

The fair rent standard is applied to council housing by one of the titles of the 1972 act,[56] but there are some important procedural[57] and substantive differences. With reference to the procedural changes, recall that fair rents in the private sector are first to be determined by a rent officer, with a further appeal to a rent assessment committee if either party is dissatisfied with the rent officer's determination. Proceedings before the rent officer and committee are not strictly adversary, but participation by both landlords and tenants is provided. While the statute does not provide for an appeal to the courts, appeals on points of law have been allowed under ministerial order.

Somewhat different procedures have been provided for council housing. Local housing authorities are first to draw up a provisional list of fair rents, and these lists are to be made available to tenants, who may make written representations concerning these rents to the authority. The authority "shall consider" any

---

[56] *See* pt. VI. For advice from the national housing department on the application of fair rents to council housing see CIRCULAR 75/72.

[57] The administrative machinery is created by §§ 51-57.

such representation, and may change any rent "which in their opinion should in consequence" be changed.[58] These provisional rents are then to be submitted to rent scrutiny boards appointed from the regional rent assessment committees, which may alter or accept the provisional rents that have been submitted by the local authorities. The authorities (but not the tenants) may make written representations concerning the rents to the rent scrutiny boards, which "shall have regard to those representations" in making their final determinations.[59] While no judicial appeal is provided by statute it is expected that appeals to the courts on points of law will at least be allowed to local authorities from decisions by the rent scrutiny boards.[60] Finally, fair rents for council dwellings need not be set on an individual basis, but may be set by reference to representative or sample dwellings in the council's housing supply.[61] The reason for this change from the procedure applicable to privately rented dwellings is that council dwellings are usually grouped in large estates, all of which have been built at approximately the same time.[62] As in private rental housing, there is to be a triennial review of rents.

What the act provides, therefore, is an informal administrative procedure in which both tenants and authorities have a limited opportunity to make known their views on council rents, a procedure similar to what some courts have required in American public housing.[63] While the statute stops far short of providing a full adversary proceeding, it does insert an outside rent-fixing body which, for the first time in English practice, mediates between the tenants and their authorities. Nevertheless, the statute still does not require procedural parity between private and public tenants, as private tenants enjoy a greater right to participate in the proceedings leading up to the fair rent determination. In addition, while appeals will be allowed from fair rent determinations by rent scrutiny boards in the public sector, it is not yet clear whether council tenants will be able to appeal these decisions. This question will be settled by a national administrative

---

[58] § 53(5).
[59] § 56(4).
[60] STANDING COMM., at 1908.
[61] § 55.
[62] *See* STANDING COMM., at 2059-64.
[63] *See* Hahn v. Gottlieb, 430 F.2d 1243 (1st Cir. 1970).

order. Notice also that council tenants do not have the statutory right to make representations to rent scrutiny boards.

Substantively, the statute applies the fair rent standard to council housing, but with two changes. One change requires the rent scrutiny board, when determining a fair rent for a council dwelling, to assume "that no person seeking to become such a [council] tenant can expect any special preference."[64] As the debate on this clause pointed out, local housing authorities are required by statute to accord certain preferences in the admission of tenants to council housing, as for example to persons occupying substandard houses, or having large families.[65] The clause was included to make it clear that these preferences were to be disregarded when fair rents for council housing were determined. There are some difficulties with this explanation, however. One is that the clause as explained is narrower than its language. All tenants accepted in council housing are preference tenants to the extent that admission is based on a system of priorities relating to housing need and other factors.[66] Since this is so, the clause might have been considered unnecessary, as the fair rent standard already directs the rent-setting authority to disregard the "personal circumstances" of the tenant. The clause may gain additional justification, however, in view of the practice of rent officers to consider the circumstances of a class of tenants in certain cases, as in the case of housing built for the elderly. The clause prohibiting consideration of any preference accorded to council tenants can thus be justified as a legislative attempt to preclude consideration of any factor which is common to council tenants as a class, such as lower than average incomes.

Interpretive problems are also raised by the second substantive change which was made in the application of the fair rent standard to the public sector. As the statute reads, consideration is to be given in fixing fair rents for council housing "to the return that it would be reasonable to expect on it [the council dwelling] as an investment" if a like consideration were to be made in a rent determination for a private dwelling.[67]

The purpose of this second modification in the fair rent standard is also puzzling. Again, the explanation was that the purpose

---

[64] § 50(2).
[65] STANDING COMM., at 1618.
[66] The point was made in debate. STANDING COMM., at 1620-22.
[67] § 50(4).

of the provision was to place council housing on the same footing as private housing.[68] As our earlier discussion indicated, however, it was not the intent of the rent act to introduce rate of return as a criterion under which fair rents for private housing were to be determined. Indeed, it was indicated that rate of return was not to be considered, at least not without a discount for scarcity. Cases such as the *Tormes* case[69] permit resort to rate of return as an element to consider in determining a fair rent, but none of the decisions have held that it should be the determining factor.

If rate of return is now to be considered in determining fair rents for council housing, it reintroduces the difficulties which the rejection of historic and replacement cost as the basis for determining council housing rents was supposed to avoid. No rate of return can be calculated except with reference to a capital base, and we have already noted the difficulties which either an historic cost base or replacement cost base brings. In the case of council housing the problem becomes even more complicated since some of the capital cost of that housing reflects planning and other qualitative judgments dictated by community needs. For example, council housing may purposely be built in desirable areas of high amenity in order to better disperse the council housing supply. To capitalize these extra costs into the rate base for purposes of calculating a rate of return appears improper. Neither will the higher land costs resulting from this factor necessarily be attributed to the influence of scarcity in the "locality" in which the council housing is located.

In summary, the introduction of a rate of return test in the determination of council house rents simply complicates the application to council housing of a rent determination standard which was already full of difficulty. We will explore in the next chapter the impact which the fair rent standard, in conjunc-

---

[68] STANDING COMM., at 1702. The clause was debated at length. See STANDING COMM., at 1695-1764.

[69] *See also* Crofton Investment Trust v. Greater London Rent Assess. Comm., [1967] 2 All E.R. 1103 (Q.B.), suggesting that the rent necessary to produce an adequate rate of return is only to be considered as a ceiling. These cases were discussed in debate. STANDING COMM., at 1744-48. *But cf.* Learmonth Property Inv. Co., Ltd. v. Aitken, [1971] Scots. L.T.R. 349 (Sess. Ct.), holding under the identical Scottish law that rate of return is a factor to be considered. The *Learmonth* case is discussed in Miller, *A Dear Searcher into Comparisons*, 17 J. LAW SOC'Y SCOTLAND 113 (1972).

tion with the housing subsidy system, has had on the council housing program. But we should first summarize some of the consequences which adoption of the fair rent standard has for English housing subsidy policy.

D. Summary

Throughout this book, the role of rents in adjusting the distribution of housing costs has been stressed. In the private sector, the English have chosen to shift some of these costs to the owner of rental housing through the adoption of a fair rent standard. While the fair rent standard does not necessarily deny the landlord a market rent, it does so in London and other areas of high scarcity, and in these cases it socializes some of his return away from him. The statutory fair rent formula also contains conceptual weaknesses, especially in the way in which it treats the demand and supply sides of the housing market. While the statute appears to legislate an aggregate approach to demand and supply, this kind of aggregation does not correspond with reality. Instead of a single market for housing, there are sub-markets disaggregated by the type of housing consumers who compete for housing, and by the type of housing supply that is available. While administrative practice under the rent act tends to take account of different types of housing demand, there is no statutory basis for this practice, and its impact is unclear and difficult to control.

On the supply side, the statute does permit a disaggregation of housing by "locality," but the statute does not make it clear just how "locality" is to be defined. So far as geographic sub-markets in sensitive areas such as London are treated as separate localities for purposes of applying the discount for scarcity, fair rent levels will either be higher or lower depending on such factors as location, amenity levels, and the like. Present practice which treats all of the Greater London area as one locality tends to leave undisturbed the high rents in areas such as Hampstead, where local conditions drive rents up. Since Greater London rather than Hampstead is the locality for applying the scarcity rule, rent differences among different areas within London are simply ignored. As between London and the rest of the country, however, the effect of the fair rent standard is to produce generally lower rents for the London area.

Fair rents have now been extended to the council housing sector, ostensibly to achieve parity with private rental housing, even though the discussion has suggested that parity has not and cannot be achieved through such an extension. The basic reason for this disparity lies in the nature of the fair rent standard itself. This standard makes allowances for the age and location of a dwelling, and because council housing is both newer and often located in different areas of the community than private rental housing, parity between the two sectors will be difficult to achieve. Extension of the rent standard to council housing will also create other distortions in the council housing program. As fair rents will lead to comparatively higher rents for the more desirable housing, local authorities may tend to place their more affluent tenants in this housing to avoid high subsidy costs. If this shift occurs, class stratification in council housing will increase, a change which many consider unfortunate on social grounds.

The basic issue to be faced in the rent regulation system is the decision to apply a market-related rent test to council housing in the first instance. In theory, the application of such a standard should increase consumer choice, as rents reach parity with housing costs in the owner-occupied sector, and as all rents within the rental sector tend to converge. In practice, this kind of parity does not seem possible, and the problem of parity between council and private rental housing has already been discussed. Parity with the owner-occupied sector appears even more difficult, partly because the cost of homes remains uncontrolled, and partly because homeowners enjoy an historic cost advantage which is denied to renters. We also suggested that adoption of the market-related fair rent standard for council housing was inconsistent with the implementation of community objectives in the council housing program which are not directly related to housing, but which nonetheless increase housing costs. These costs qualify more properly for total national subsidy rather than for inclusion in the rent charge.

In balance, the role of council housing in the English housing program still remains unclear, even after the 1972 reform. In the United States, the present solution in public housing is to connect an income-determined tenant rent with a cost-related housing subsidy. Under the impact of the Brooke Amendment, rents are set as a percentage of income, and any operating costs not met from rents are supposed to be subsidized in full. In England, we shall see that an income-related housing expenditure test has partially been adopted for tenants, and that a cost-related subsidy has been made available to local authorities. But the impact of these subsidies on tenants and on local authorities is largely determined by the impact which the fair rent standard has on rent revenues. The use of these very different criteria as the basis for a housing subsidy and rent regulation may create a lack of fit which distorts the housing objectives which the program is meant to achieve. The question of whether and to what extent this distortion occurs takes us to a discussion of the cost-related and needs-related subsidies in the next chapter.

Chapter VII

A "FAIR DEAL FOR HOUSING": THE HOUSING SUBSIDY SYSTEM IN ENGLAND

Besides extending rent regulation to council housing, the 1972 legislation dealt with other disparities in the housing subsidy program. As we have noted, the burdens and benefits of the housing subsidy program had grown disproportionate. Taxpayers in some local authorities made contributions to their council housing program, while taxpayers in other local authorities made none at all. Council housing rents varied considerably from one local authority to another, and not all authorities provided rent rebates to their tenants. Furthermore, no subsidy help of any kind was available to tenants in private rental housing.

In order to remedy these disparities, several changes were introduced by the 1972 law. Local tax contributions were reintroduced on a mandatory basis so as to assure a fair local assumption of housing subsidy costs throughout the country. New national subsidies have been made available to relieve local authorities from rising operating costs and the high expense of slum clearance programs. Finally, rent rebates based on a model national plan have been introduced in order to correct the present indiscriminate pattern of council housing rents, and to make certain that subsidies are made available to tenants in council housing who need them. For the first time, housing subsidies have also been brought to tenants in private rental housing through a rent allowance subsidy which is in most respects identical to the rent rebate program for tenants in council housing. The cost of these rent rebates and rent allowances is shared by the national government and the local authorities.

This chapter will analyze these new rebates, allowances, subsidies, and local tax contributions, and will also consider the relationship between housing subsidies and other income support programs, such as the English program of welfare assistance. We will concentrate on the impact of the subsidy system on council housing, partly because the subsidies available for council housing are more extensive, and partly because the legislative provisions for council housing rent rebates and private tenant rent allowances are nearly identical. Where differences occur they will be noted.

A. Elements of the Rent Rebate System

The new statutory rent rebate system, which preserves the characteristic pattern of council housing rents, is a process in which an unrebated rent is first determined for the dwelling under the fair rent standard, and a portion of that rent is then rebated to the tenant if the tenant is not able to pay the fair rent. We first need to look at the way in which the rent rebate is calculated, which includes four essential elements:

(1) Calculation of the rent rebate payable to the tenant begins with a statutory needs allowance, which is generally the same as the statutory family budget for items other than rent which is used in welfare assistance, known in England as Supplementary Benefit.

(2) The tenant pays a *minimum rent* which is either a percentage of the fair rent that has been determined for the dwelling, or a prescribed statutory amount, whichever is the greater.

(3) The difference between the minimum rent and the fair rent is rebated to the tenant, subject to a statutory *maximum rebate,* and the local authority receives a national subsidy to cover part of the rebate cost if there is a deficit in its Housing Revenue Account.

(4) Specific statutory provisions take care of areas of exceptionally high rent, and another provision takes care of the situation in which the rebated rent paid by the tenant is considered excessive.

These essential elements of the rebate system will be discussed in turn. At this point the important comment should be made that the English rent rebate does not reduce the tenant's rent to a fixed portion of his income, as in American public housing. As a result, there is no guarantee under the law that a tenant will not pay an excessive amount for rent after his fair rent and rent rebate have been determined. The government has given what is known in English parliamentary terms as an assurance that no tenant with one or more children whose income is at or below the statutory needs allowance will pay more than about ten percent of his income for rent.[1] But the extent to which this promise can be kept is limited by the amount which the government is willing to budget for the subsidy program. Higher rents, together with a higher rate of unemployment, would make this assurance a difficult one to keep.[2]

Inequities have also been built into the rent rebate system because of its reliance on the fair rent standard. Rents for comparable local authority housing will vary by locality, reflecting the degree of amenity and counterbalancing scarcity that is built into the fair rent standard. Similar families in similar housing will be treated differently, depending on the accident of geographic location, and low-income families in high rent council housing may find their rent burdens excessive. Whether the rent rebate system can provide the "fair deal" which its sponsors claim, considering these limitations, raises some very real questions. Let us test these observations by looking at the different elements of the rent rebate system in more detail.

1. The Rent Rebate and the Minimum Rent

The minimum rent concept is at the heart of the rent rebate system since, generally, the rent rebate meets the difference between the fair rent determined for the dwelling and the minimum rent which the tenant is required to pay. Different standards are provided for calculating the minimum rent and rebate for tenants who are working and tenants who are receiving Supplementary Benefit. We will begin our discussion with the working tenant and consider Supplementary Benefit tenants later.

---

[1] PARL. DEB., STANDING COMM. E, HOUSING FINANCE BILL 739 (1972) [hereinafter cited as STANDING COMM.].

[2] *See* Jessup, *A Fair Allowance?*, 19 NEW SOCIETY 650 (1972).

Under the statute, the minimum weekly rent is presently set at $2.50, or 40 percent of the fair rent, whichever is greater.[3] The monetary minimum was selected because it is equal to 40 percent of present average council housing rents in England and Wales.[4] (Monetary sums have been converted into approximate American dollar equivalents.) If the tenant's income is equal to the statutory needs allowance he pays the minimum rent, and the difference between the minimum rent and the maximum rent is rebated. If he earns more or less than the statutory needs allowance the minimum rent is adjusted upward or downward. What happens to the tenant who earns less?

For him the minimum weekly rent is reduced at the rate of 25 cents for each dollar that his actual income is below the needs allowance. No rent is payable at all if this reduction is equal to or exceeds the minimum rent. The statutory provisions can thus be reduced to a formula:

Where: M = the minimum rent payable
F = the fair rent;
N = the statutory needs allowance; and
I = the tenant's income, then:
$M = .40F - .25(N-I)$.

No rent is payable at all when $M = 0$, or a negative quantity. A sample calculation, based on current average rent levels, is reproduced in the footnote.[5] While the formula is attractive in the sense that it produces no rent at all for many tenants whose incomes are under the statutory needs allowance, two important qualifications must be made. The most important is that the marginal increase in rent at these levels is fixed at 25 percent of each additional dollar earned up to the statutory needs allowance. As we will see, this marginal increase rate is higher than

---

[3] Housing Finance Act, 1972, ch. 47, Sch. 3, pt. I, § 10(1).

[4] STANDING COMM., at 739.

[5] Assuming current average rent levels of $6.25 per week for council housing, and given the statutory needs allowance of approximately $50.00 per week for a couple with two children, no rent is payable at all by a family of this size if their weekly wage is $40.00 or less. Substituting these quantities, the formula works out approximately as follows:

$M = .40\,(\$6.25) - .25\,(\$50.00 - \$40.00)$
$M = \$2.50 - .25\,(\$10.00)$
$M = \$2.50 - \$2.50$
$M = 0$

it is for tenants whose incomes are over the statutory needs allowance. A second point is that fair rents in many areas, especially London, may be so high that the minimum rent payable is oppressive.

The possibility that hardship might arise because of high minimum rents is further increased by the fact that, with few exceptions, it is the tenant's gross income that is considered when a decision is made whether his income is less than, equal to, or in excess of the statutory needs allowance.[6] There is no deduction for medical and employment expenses, and the income considered to be available to the tenant is taken as his gross income before payment of national income tax and national insurance contributions; these contributions are substantial. Only certain government benefits are disregarded, and earnings of the tenant's wife, not to exceed $6.25 weekly. (This last deduction is also available to a woman tenant who has no husband.) On the other hand, the lack of more generous deductions has been defended on the ground that the statutory needs allowance was set high enough to make them unnecessary.[7] If this is the case—and the needs allowance can be administratively revised periodically—then the absence of an extensive list of deductions may not be as oppressive to tenants as it appears.

Other features of the law mitigate the effect of unduly high minimum rents. On application by a local housing authority, the national housing department may make changes in the level of the minimum rent and the maximum rebate. The minimum rent may be lowered or the maximum rebate increased whenever the "general level" of rents in the authority is "exceptionally high by comparison" with rents of "other" housing authorities.[8] Additional rebates authorized under this provision are shared like any other rebate between the national government and the local authority.

The statute also authorizes local authorities on their own initiative to grant a higher rebate than that provided by the law if they "consider that . . . personal or domestic circumstances are

---

[6] Sch. 3, pt. I, § 9. All statutory references are to the Housing Finance Act, 1972, unless otherwise indicated.

[7] STANDING COMM., at 812: ". . . takes broad account of basic expenses of employment such as taxation and national insurance."

[8] § 29(5). The department intends to exercise its powers under this section only in "exceptional circumstances. . . [where] large numbers of tenants may not get all the help that they need." CIRCULAR 74/72, § 9.

exceptional."[9] Just how far, and in what circumstances, this authority can be used was not made clear in the debate.[10] The clause is apparently limited to individual circumstances of hardship rather than general conditions of lower than average income within a particular local authority. Moreover, the total of all rebates paid by a local authority may not exceed by more than ten percent the amount of rebate which is authorized by the national plan.[11] While the point is not entirely clear from the law, the additional rebates granted for exceptional circumstances must be kept within the ten percent tolerance if they are to qualify for national subsidy.[12] Ultimately, the answer to the hardship problem will lie with the national housing department, for the department is authorized by statute to make changes in the model rebate plan.[13] The government[14] has stated that it will rely on this administrative power to make the entire housing allowance system more generous if widespread cases of personal hardship develop that cannot be taken care of within the statutory tolerance.[15]

We have been talking so far about tenants whose incomes are below the statutory needs allowance. For tenants whose incomes exceed the statutory needs allowance the computation of rent is easier. These tenants simply pay the minimum rent plus 17

---

[9] § 21(1). A local authority may also vary the provisions of the model national plan for rent rebates. § 21(3). For example, local authorities can make changes in the deductions which are to be allowed from the gross income of the tenant on which the minimum rent is calculated. See CIRCULAR 72/74, § 11. In no event may the local authority vary the rent rebate plan so that the tenant receives less than he would have received under the model plan. Any change which the local authority makes in its rent rebate plan must also be made in its rent allowance plan.

[10] See STANDING COMM., at 903-52.

[11] § 22(1).

[12] See STANDING COMM., at 959-60. The point is confirmed by CIRCULAR 72/74, § 12, and is applicable as well to any variations which local authorities make in the model national plan. See note 9, *supra*.

[13] The model rebate plan is in a schedule to the act, and the statute authorizes variations in its provisions by administrative regulation. § 20(2).

[14] STANDING COMM., at 934.

[15] Note that the statute does not allow the tenant to appeal from the local authority's decision on his application for rebate. However, a tenant "may make representations to an authority concerning a determination which they make in relation to him." Sch. 4, pt. I, § 15(2). Apparently the determination includes the decision to grant or deny a rebate as well as a decision to increase the rebate in view of personal circumstances. The authority is to "consider" the representation, and may alter or confirm its original determination.

cents of each dollar by which their income exceeds the statutory needs allowance.[16] Wealthier tenants, therefore, enjoy a lower marginal rate of rent increase than poorer tenants, a distinction which generally corresponds to the tendency of rents to decline as a percentage of income as incomes increase. But no governmental assurance was given for this group, comparable to that given for tenants earning less than the statutory needs allowance, that rents would be held to a fixed proportion of income.

This rebate system also carries the possibility that tenants may be able to inflate their subsidies to unmanageable proportions. With the difference between the fair rent and the required minimum rent subsidized, individual subsidies will be increased if the tenant selects a dwelling whose fair rent is substantially higher than the minimum rent he can afford to pay. This problem is partly handled by the absolute monetary limit which the statute places on the amount of the rebate payable and which applies to both council and private tenants. In addition, the local authority can limit the subsidy for council house dwellings by assigning their poorer tenants to dwellings which carry a lower fair rent.

No such controls exist in the private rental market in which the tenant is permitted to select his own dwelling. For this tenant, an additional statutory limitation has been added. The local authority may "consider whether they ought in all the circumstances" to reduce the amount of rent allowance payable if the tenant occupies a dwelling "larger than he reasonably requires," or if, because of its location, the dwelling carries a rent which is "exceptionally high by comparison with the rent payable under comparable private tenancies of similar dwellings in the authority's area."[17] This restriction is somewhat startling in its implications for freedom of housing choice, and it would also seem to contain a potential for real tenant hardship. As the provision reads, the rent allowance is to be reduced in the cases indicated even though no alternative suitable accommodation is available to the tenant. However, the national housing department has now stated that rents should be reduced under this

---

[16] Sch. 3, pt. I, § 11(3)-(5).

[17] Sch. 3, pt. I, § 17. In addition, if no fair rent has been registered for the tenancy, the local authority is to "disregard any sum of rent . . . which is in excess of their estimate of the likely fair rent." CIRCULAR 72/74, § 51.

provision only if "the tenant could in fact reasonably be expected to obtain other accommodation in the area."[18]

2. Rebates to Tenants on Supplementary Benefit

In an earlier chapter we saw the complications and difficulties that arose in American public housing in its treatment of welfare tenants. Part of the difficulty came from the fact that both welfare administration and public housing administration are decentralized, with little opportunity to work out a uniform policy at the national level. Other problems arose from the fact that rent levels are generally much lower in public housing than they are in the private market, so that welfare tenants in public housing often receive a rent bargain, at least in those authorities which do not charge them a disproportionate rent.

Most of these problems in England have been eliminated under the rent rebate system. Disparities in rents between the private and public sector have been removed by determining both private and council housing rents under the fair rent standard. Problems that arose in the United States in the case of working welfare tenants are eliminated in England to some extent. Income support for tenants who work full time is not covered by the Supplementary Benefit system, but by another benefit program which will be discussed later. Moreover, since the Supplementary Benefit and the rent rebate are both calculated from the same statutory needs allowance, disparities in treatment under the two programs do not arise.

Our earlier discussion had indicated, however, that problems had arisen in deciding how much of the housing cost for tenants on Supplementary Benefit should be borne by the housing subsidy. Many housing authorities had not been giving rebates to welfare tenants, a situation which required a settlement at cabinet level that placed responsibility for the housing costs of welfare tenants

---

[18] CIRCULAR 72/74, § 48. In addition, the tenant's age and health, and the length of time for which the tenant has held the tenancy, are also to be considered. For example, the Circular suggests that an infirm widow who is now living alone in a large dwelling in which she has brought up her family should not be moved. The Circular does not require that the alternative accommodation meet minimum housing standards, however. An earlier national circular which provided guidance for voluntary local rebates had suggested that the tenant's rent should be reduced only if he failed to accept alternative accommodation at a lower rent. CIRCULAR 46/67, Appendix, § 20.

on the Supplementary Benefit system.[19] This allocation has been altered by the 1972 legislation.[20]

The statutory adjustment that has been adopted for tenants on Supplementary Benefit works as follows: For the first eight weeks the council tenant's entire "going" rent is taken into account by the Supplementary Benefit program. The "going" rent is the rent chargeable to the tenant, and may be a rebated rent if this is the rent payable. After that period, the basis for calculating the rent and rent rebate changes. Since the statutory needs allowance provided by the housing act is the same as the needs allowance provided under the Supplementary Benefits Act, the rebate from that time on is the amount by which the fair rent exceeds 40 percent of that rent, or the statutory weekly minimum of $2.50, whichever is greater. This formula applies in the ordinary case in which the Supplementary Benefit tenant has been earning more than the amount of benefit he receives.

Note the effect which this formula has on the wage earner who has to resort to Supplementary Benefit for more than eight weeks. If his wage before unemployment was higher than the Supplementary Benefit needs allowance, his rent is reduced. Remember that for each dollar by which the tenant's income exceeded the statutory needs allowance his rent had been increased by 17 cents. When the tenant becomes unemployed and is awarded Supplementary Benefit equal to the statutory needs allowance, his rent will fall by that additional amount. What about the tenant whose income prior to his unemployment was less than the Supplementary Benefit? Under the law relating to Supplementary Benefits, the benefit paid to the unemployed worker in this case is equal to his wage prior to his unemployment, an adjustment which is known as the "wage stop."[21] In this event, the rebate under the housing act is to be calculated on the basis of his prior wage, under the assumptions legislated for working tenants whose incomes are less than the statutory needs allowance. In this case the tenant's rent will be calculated as it was before, and his rent will not increase.

Because of the way in which rents are budgeted under the Supplementary Benefit program, the problem of welfare rents

---

[19] For discussion of these problems see STANDING COMM., at 861-69.
[20] Sch. 3, pt. II; CIRCULAR 72/74, §§ 58-71.
[21] Ministry of Social Security Act, 1966, ch. 20, Sch. 2, pt. II, § 5.

which are excessive for the recipient does not arise in the English system. Under the law applicable to Supplementary Benefits, all of the rent is taken into account by the benefit payment, including property taxes, and the rent and taxes are added to the flat statutory benefit which is provided under the program to meet other needs.[22] There is an exception, as the Supplementary Benefit statute states that the rent paid by the benefit recipient must be "reasonable," although what is meant by "reasonable" is nowhere defined. As a result, unreasonable rents may be disregarded in determining the amount of the benefit.[23] In these cases, either the benefit will be reduced or the recipient will be moved to cheaper accommodation, although removal is not allowed if hardship will be created.

In practice, rents have been determined to be unreasonable only in about one percent of all of the cases in which supplementary benefit has been awarded, and the power of the Supplementary Benefit agency to reduce rents has now been further circumscribed by the national housing act. Whenever council housing rent rebates or private housing allowances are paid under the housing act, the power to reduce rents or compel removal may not be exercised under the Supplementary Benefits Act.[24] As a consequence, the Supplementary Benefits agency must accept the council rent which is determined by the rent scrutiny board, and the fair rent which is payable on the private dwelling. In addition, as noted above, legal authority to disregard unreasonable rents in the private sector has been transferred to the local housing authority. Since the rent in excess of the minimum weekly rent is now to be met from the housing subsidy, this reallocation of power to determine what rents are reasonable appears proper.

In effect, for the American system of fixing maximum housing allowances which is typical of some state welfare programs, the English have substituted an administrative power to disregard unreasonable rents in individual cases. The pervasiveness of rent control in England, together with low rates of unemployment in recent years, have also tended to minimize the problem of excessive rents, especially since the English have not budgeted their supplementary benefit awards at less than actual need. Should

---

[22] *Id.*, § 13.

[23] SUPPLEMENTARY BENEFITS COMM'N, DEP'T OF HEALTH AND SOCIAL SECURITY, SUPPLEMENTARY BENEFITS HANDBOOK 15-16 (1971).

[24] Housing Act, Sch. 9, § 6.

higher rates of unemployment become persistent, the problem of high rents for Supplementary Benefit recipients may become more acute.

Another problem posed by the housing needs of Supplementary Benefit tenants arises from the statutory decision to shift a high proportion of their rent rebate costs to the housing subsidy system. Since some of the rent rebate must be met from local taxes, the argument can be made that it is improper to shift to the local authority the cost of an income support program which arises out of national poverty rather than local housing needs. As low-income families needing Supplementary Benefit support are often concentrated, as in the United States, in the older and inner areas of urban regions, their housing subsidy is shifted to local authorities in these areas if a local tax contribution is required. Local taxpayers will then be taxing themselves to alleviate their own poverty, and the system will be regressive. These issues of cost distribution will be discussed in more detail below.

3. Relationship of Rent Rebates to Other Income Support Programs

Besides Supplementary Benefits, a wide range of additional benefits is also available to lower income families in England. These benefits include free school dinners, free welfare milk, and exemption from the minimum health service charges. These benefits, like the rent rebate, are means-tested, and either disappear over certain income levels, or taper off gradually. Another benefit, the family allowance (FAM), is not means-tested and is payable to all families. It includes payments for the second and any additional children. However, the level of national income tax has been adjusted so that FAM is recovered from all families who are required to pay the tax. Consequently, FAM is important as a benefit only to those lower income families not paying income tax. For this reason, it is deducted as a resource when Supplemenary Benefit awards are made. Recent suggestions by the Conservative government indicate that FAM will be replaced by an income tax credit program which will at the same time also reduce the need for Supplementary Benefits and other income support programs. But the principle of government support of lower income families through income allowances will be preserved.

The large number of welfare programs that are available in England presents problems of coordination with the housing subsidy. In particular, a serious marginal disincentive problem is created by the fact that all of these programs, many of which use a means-tested eligibility requirement, serve the same income groups. Eligibility of these groups for benefits is related to income, as in the rent rebate program. As incomes rise, all or many of these benefits are lost simultaneously, or else the package of benefits tapers off so quickly that the marginal "tax" on each dollar earned is excessive. Lower income families may find that for each dollar of additional income earned they may lose up to 75 to 80 cents or more of benefits. In some cases the marginal "tax" may be more than 100 percent.

Two of these collateral income support and welfare benefit programs which particularly affect housing subsidies and which will be considered here are the program of rebates to lower income families for local property taxes, and the Family Income Supplement, or FIS. The Family Income Supplement legislation was enacted about the same time as the national system of rent rebates was adopted. It arose out of a gap which was created by the Supplementary Benefit statute. Recall that Supplementary Benefit is not payable to persons in full-time work.[25] When it became apparent that many families were headed by full-time wage earners who earned less than the Supplementary Benefit allowance, the Family Income Supplement statute was enacted to meet this need.[26] The group to be covered by the FIS program, about 200,000 households containing some 500,000 children,[27] is not a large group in a total population of around 50,000,000, and seems even smaller when compared to the 2,000,000 persons receiving Supplementary Benefit.[28] Nevertheless, the FIS group represents a relatively large proportion of the younger, working population, a group whose housing needs are still growing and are difficult to meet. The relatively small size of the FIS group

---

[25] An increase in family allowances would not have alleviated the problem. Family allowances could not provide the scale of help that was needed, and in any event, poverty was not limited to large families. Moreover, many of those who are in need would have been forced to pay back any increased family allowance through their income tax. See the speech by the Secretary of State for Social Services in 806 PARL. DEB., H.C. (5th ser.) 218-24 (1970).

[26] The legislation also eases the wage-stop limitation on Supplementary Benefit. Family Income Supplements Act, 1970, ch. 55, § 13. If the Supplementary Benefit recipient was earning less than the Supplementary Benefit allowance prior to his unemployment, his benefit will now be equal to his previous wage plus any amount he would have received from the FIS program.

[27] PARL. DEB., *supra* note 25, at 217.

[28] *See* Bosanquet, *Banding Poverty,* 19 NEW SOCIETY 448 (1972).

prompted the government to set up a benefit program which would be easy to publicize and administer, however. This need for simplicity has, as we shall see, created some problems in the housing sector.

Like the rent rebate, the FIS benefit is calculated from the gross income of the applicant. The few deductions which have been provided from gross income are limited to a few of the national benefits disregarded under the rent rebate system, but there is no disregard of any part of the wife's income.[29] The basis for the FIS grant is the statutory "prescribed amount."[30] FIS recipients receive one-half of the difference between the prescribed amount and their gross income. As the statute is written, the prescribed amount is a fixed sum, with power in the social security minister to substitute higher prescribed amounts by regulation.

The need to specify a statutory prescribed amount as the basis for the FIS benefit arose out of the government's decision to simplify the administration of the program. To calculate the statutory prescribed amount the government took the Supplementary Benefit allowance, and added an assumed amount for working expenses, income tax, and national insurance contributions. It also added an amount for rent which was based on average rents in the entire country, and then deducted FAM. While it simplifies the administration of the program, this approach creates some problems in relating FIS to the rent rebate system. Most of the problem centers in the fact that FIS, unlike Supplementary Benefit, does not pick up all of the rent charged when that rent is in excess of the national average used in establishing the statutory prescribed amount for FIS. As a result, recipients of FIS will have to rely on the rent rebate program to meet any excess rental costs in these cases. Since the government has given assurances that no tenant whose income is below the statutory housing needs allowance will pay more than ten percent of his income for rent, this assurance apparently extends to FIS recipients as well. To make good on this pledge, the government will have to exercise its authority under the housing act either to increase the rebate for FIS recipients paying high rents, or to decrease their minimum rent.

---

[29] Stat. Instr. 1971, No. 226, § 2(5).
[30] FIS Act, § 2.

The other program affecting housing costs which should be discussed now is the rate rebate, or property tax rebate, program. Recall that tenants in England pay property taxes, even in council housing. Legislation enacted in 1966 now provides for a partial rebate of property taxes to all lower income families. These families, along with the families receiving Supplementary Benefit who have all of their property taxes taken into account in their benefit, now make up about 18 percent of all households in England.[31] Since property taxes average from four to six percent of income in addition to rents, and may even equal rents for some accommodation in some areas of Central London, the impact of the tax rebate program on housing costs can be considerable.

Like FIS, the property tax rebate program is fairly simple.[32] Application for rebate is made to the appropriate local authority, which approves or disapproves the rebate, but is then reimbursed for three-fourths of the cost of the rebate by the national government. The rebate is calculated as follows: A fixed amount is first deducted from the property tax, and the taxpayer must pay that amount. Two-thirds of the tax remaining is rebated for all taxpayers whose incomes are below the statutory income limit. This limit is based on gross income, and has been raised by regulation so that it is now about the same as the needs allowance for rent rebates. Previously it was somewhat below this level. Property taxpayers above the statutory income limit must pay an additional 25 cents toward their taxes for each dollar by which their incomes exceed the income limit. Before the income limit was raised, the tax rebate tapered off rather quickly, and disappeared altogether at income levels well below the average wage.[33] In an average case, the rebate appeared to be about one-half of the tax payable for taxpayers below the income limit.[34]

Although the tax rebate should be attractive to tenants, they have not been its primary beneficiaries, as homeowners claim the rebate in much greater numbers.[35] The fact that taxes are met in

---

[31] THE FUTURE SHAPE OF LOCAL GOVERNMENT FINANCE, CMND. NO. 4741, at 32 (1971).

[32] General Rate Act, ch. 9, § 49, Sch. 9.

[33] See FINANCE, *supra* note 31.

[34] *Rate Rebate Statistics*, 116 LOCAL GOV'T CHRONICLE 2087 (1971). For a general discussion of local property taxes see COMM. OF INQUIRY INTO THE IMPACT OF RATES ON HOUSEHOLDS, CMND. NO. 2582 (1965) (Allen Report).

[35] See *Rate Rebate Statistics, supra* note 34.

full by the Supplementary Benefit program may provide part of the explanation for this tenant lack of interest, as a high proportion of the poorer tenants receive Supplementary Benefits. FIS benefits do not include property taxes, however.

Another important factor affecting the comparative lack of tenant interest in the tax rebate program is the system of national support grants to local governments.[36] Recall that almost 60 percent of the local revenue needs of local governments are met in England through a system of national grants that would be called a general revenue sharing program in America. These national grants, which are to some extent correlated with local need, reduce taxes in the older, inner city areas in which tenants are more likely to live. This reduction in local taxes makes an application for tax rebate less worthwhile.

Nevertheless, changes in the housing situation may lead to an increase in tenant interest in the property tax rebate program. Tenants may begin to claim more property tax rebates in order to offset the higher rents which result from an extension of the fair rent standard to council housing. Tenants are also being resettled by slum clearance and rehousing programs into newer dwellings for which the property tax will be much higher. The tax rebate would also be made more attractive under proposals that have been put forward which would increase the number of eligible taxpayers as well as the amount of rebate at lower income levels.[37]

We made reference earlier to the marginal disincentive which the wide variety of means-tested welfare benefit programs imposes. Now we should note that the cumulative marginal loss of FIS, property tax rebate, and rent rebate can be substantial as incomes rise.[38] For wage earners receiving both FIS and rent rebates, for example, the marginal loss is 75 cents for each additional dollar earned. While the steps that are needed to remedy this problem lie outside a discussion of housing subsidy policy, we need to keep in mind the impact of the marginal disincentive problem on the content and structure of the housing subsidy system.

---

[36] Nevitt, *How Fair Are Rate Rebates?*, 18 NEW SOCIETY 1000 (1971).

[37] *See* FINANCE, *supra* note 31.

[38] *See* Lynes, *Family Income Supertax*, 17 NEW SOCIETY 770 (1971).

The final problem arising under the rent rebate and other income support programs which needs to be considered is referred to in England as the problem of "take-up." Because all of the programs we have been discussing so far, except family allowances, are means-tested, their benefits are not conferred automatically but require both an application and a review of income status before an award can be given. Unless eligible applicants actually apply for these benefits and "take them up," the programs will not be used and will not have fulfilled their purpose. The extent of take-up in these programs varies. The FIS program is too new to evaluate for take-up, and property tax rebates are provided under a formula too complicated to enable eligibility and potential take-up to be estimated. Experience with the older voluntary rent rebate systems operated by local authorities does not provide a reliable guide to the take-up that can be expected under the national rent rebate plan, because of differences among the earlier voluntary plans, and the lack of national publicity for them. Estimates have nevertheless been made that the take-up rate for rent rebates may be as low, nationally, as 30 percent. If this estimate proves to be accurate, then the low take-up will severely undercut the program, especially as fair rents will be chargeable regardless of whether the tenant applies for rebate or not. Substantial rent increases both in the council and private sectors will then work real hardship on tenants who qualify for rebates but who do not claim them.

B. Housing Subsidies to Local Authorities

We have so far discussed only part of the housing subsidy picture, the rent rebates available to council housing tenants. Rents charged to tenants together with any subsidies available to local authorities from the national government must together produce enough revenue to cover the cost to local authorities of operating their housing units. This requirement has been legislated by statute, and has been imposed on the council housing program through the Housing Revenue Account, or HRA, which the statute obliges all local authorities to keep.[39] The statute also

---

[39] Housing Finance Act, 1972, ch. 47, Sch. 1. For discussion see MINISTRY OF HOUSING AND LOCAL GOVERNMENT, HOUSING REVENUE ACCOUNTS (1969) (Report of the Working Party).

requires the Housing Revenue Account to be kept in balance, a requirement that can be expressed by means of a simple formula:

$CR = DEB$, when
$CR = $ Credits to the HRA, and
$DEB = $ Debits to the HRA.

Let us look next at the subsidies, payments, and expenditures that enter into the credit and debit sides of the Housing Revenue Account.[40] We can start with the credit side:

$CR = M + RE + RC + RF$, when
$M = $ the minimum rent,
$RE = $ the rent rebate, which is contributed by the local authority,
$RC = $ the rising costs subsidy, and
$RF = $ the local tax contribution, if any.[41]

Notice that the minimum rents paid (M), together with any rent rebate (RE), together make up the fair rent which is chargeable. As some 40 percent of all council housing tenants are estimated to be entitled to rebate,[42] the remaining 60 percent will pay the fair rent in full. While the rent rebates payable to those tenants entitled to them are initially to be met by the local authority, it will be partially reimbursed for the cost of these rebates by the national government.[43] A national subsidy is also available to meet part of the cost of the rent allowance to private tenants, which is also paid initially by the local authority. Ultimately, the statute contemplates that 75 percent of the cost of rent rebates will be borne by the national subsidy, but this subsidy is payable only when necessary to eliminate a deficit in the Housing Reve-

---

[40] The 1972 Act also provides for several transitional subsidies to ease the change to the new subsidy system. *See* FAIR DEAL FOR HOUSING, CMND. NO. 4728, at 27-8, 30 (1971). While these transitional subsidies are of some importance on a temporary basis, they are to disappear within a few years, and we may disregard them for purposes of our analysis. *See also* STANDING COMM., at 368.

[41] This formula greatly oversimplifies the statute in order to clarify the major elements that enter into the subsidy system. For example, the formula ignores other (though minor) miscellaneous income which may be credited to the HRA, Sch. 1, pt. I, § 1, and other transitional national housing subsidies which are available to local authorities on a temporary basis. The slum clearance subsidy, to be discussed more fully below, is excluded because it does not relate directly to housing.

[42] STANDING COMM., at 429.

[43] *See* Housing Finance Act, §§ 6-8

nue Account in order to bring it into balance. Any authority which rebates its rents to any extent can expect to generate deficits in its account, however. Payment of the national rent allowance subsidy to meet the cost of rent allowances to private tenants is not limited to the elimination of a deficit in the Housing Revenue Account, which only governs the financial affairs of council housing. The cost of rent allowances to private tenants will be met in full by the national government for a transitional three-year period, after which 20 percent of the cost of this subsidy will be met locally. After the statute has been in operation for ten years, the national housing department is also authorized to increase or decrease the national share of both the rent rebate and rent allowance subsidies, but not to an amount which is less than two-thirds of the total. But rent rebate and rent allowance subsidies paid by the national government are paid into the local authority's general fund, and not into its Housing Revenue Account. The rent rebate subsidy, however, does support part of the rent rebate payments which the local authority initially makes to its tenants. Local authority rent rebate or housing allowance payments in excess of the minimum tariff laid down by the statute, but subject to the statutory maximum, fall entirely on local taxes.[44] Additional local tax contributions are also required in any year in which the HRA shows a deficit. These contributions will be discussed later.

A subsidy for rising costs (RC) in council housing is required because the fair rents that are charged for council housing may not meet operating costs in full. Like the rent rebate subsidy, it is only payable to eliminate deficits in the Housing Revenue Account, but the rising costs subsidy is payable directly to the credit of the Housing Revenue Account.

The formula for the rising costs subsidy can be expressed as follows:

$RC = C_{ys} - C(ys-1) + CUMC$, when

C_{ys} = costs for the year in which the subsidy is calculated, and

$C(ys-1)$ = costs for the previous year, and

CUMC = all previous cumulative cost increases.[45]

---

[44] §§ 6(2), 7(2) (rent rebate); 8(2), 20(8) (rent allowance). For discussion see text at notes 8-12, *supra*.

[45] *See* § 4.

The statute then limits the amount of the previous cumulative cost increases which the subsidy meets by providing, in general, that rising costs subsidy which is based on a cost increase occurring in any year is not payable for more than five subsequent years.[46] As in the case of the rent rebate subsidy, 75 percent of the rising costs subsidy is ultimately to be met by the national government; the rest must be met by a contribution from local taxes. In order to regulate the amount of the rising costs subsidy, controls have also been placed on the amount of expenditure which the local authority may incur, and which can be met through the rising costs subsidy payments. These controls will be explained below, in connection with our discussion of the debit side of the Housing Revenue Account.

We should also note that the statute confers considerable discretion on the housing minister to vary the terms of the subsidy. This discretion may be exercised only after the 1981-82 fiscal year or, in other words, at a point in time ten years subsequent to the enactment of the legislation. After this time, the minister by order may direct:

(1) that subsidy will not be payable for a specified portion of any annual increase in costs; or

(2) that the national contribution to rising costs may be increased or reduced, subject to a two-thirds minimum; or

(3) that cumulative increased costs accrued for earlier years will continue to be subsidized when otherwise, according to the statutory rule, they would have been disregarded.[47]

These powers have been conferred in the alternative, and may be exercised singly or together. For example, the minister might reduce the amount of rising costs which qualifies for subsidy, while

---

[46] Again, the statutory provisions have been simplified for purposes of this presentation. See, e.g., note 47, *infra*.

[47] See §§ 4(3), 4(5), and 4(7). See also STANDING COMM., at 314-15.

With reference to the payment of subsidy for accumulated costs, the statute provides as follows in § 4(6): (1) subsidy based on any of the years from 1972-73 to 1976-77 shall not be paid for the year 1982-83 or any subsequent year, and (2) subsidy based on the year 1977-78 or any subsequent year shall not be payable for more than five years, including the base year. This sudden withdrawal of subsidy under the first clause of § 4(6) was criticized. STANDING COMM., at 331-40. However, the housing minister may direct by order that neither of these limitations applies, and may by order substitute a less restrictive limitation. § 4(7). For example, he might specify that subsidy is payable beyond the cutoff point specified in § 4(6) for a cost increment which occurred in an earlier year.

at the same time allowing subsidy to be payable for earlier years that would otherwise have been disregarded. In general, however, the effect of these discretionary powers is to allow the minister to reduce the subsidy should it come to be excessive. In this event any deficit in the HRA would have to be made up by a local tax contribution. We might also note that wholesale legislative revision of the subsidy structure is likely to occur well before the ten-year period after which ministerial powers to change the amount of the subsidy can be exercised. Even so, the extent to which the statute protects the national government from excessive contributions to local authority housing costs is indicative of legislative concern over the continuing increase of national expenditure in the council housing sector.

We had started this discussion with the assumption that the Housing Revenue Account is in balance when:

$CR = DEB.$

So far, we have been examining the credit side of the HRA, the elements that go to make up the income side of the account. Now, in order to understand the basis on which rising costs and, as we shall see, other subsidies are payable, we need to understand the debit side of the account.

We can express the legal content of the debit side of the HRA as follows:

$DEB = D + E + WB$ when
$D =$ debt service charges, and
$E =$ operating expenditure, and
$WB =$ the allowable working balance.[48]

The crucial point to be made about each of these debit items is that the amounts to be debited for each are *fully subject to control by the national government.* For example, all local authorities must receive ministerial approval before borrowing funds for housing construction. While local authorities may borrow on the open market, the borrowing rate at which local authorities may borrow from other public agencies is determined by the national housing department.[49] Annual debt service payments toward prin-

---

[48] *See* Sch. 1, pt. I, § 3; pt. IV, §§ 14, 15. In addition, "rents, taxes and other charges which the local authority are liable to pay" are debited to the HRA. *Id.*, pt. I, § 3(1)(b).

[49] *See, e.g.,* CIRCULAR 62/71.

cipal and interest on these borrowed funds are debited to the account, and make up by far the major part of local authority spending on the debit side.

Annual operating expenditure (E) is also to be debited to the HRA and is defined to include "improvement, repair, maintenance, supervision, and management."[50] This definition, however, is not intended as an open-ended authority to incur expenditure authorized by the definition without national approval. In the section dealing with the rising costs subsidy, the statute provides that local authority expenditure for purposes of determining the amount of this subsidy shall be so much of the expenditure debited to the HRA as the housing minister "may from time to time determine as being reasonable and appropriate having regard to all the circumstances."[51] As a result, any expenditure by the local authority which is not authorized by the minister does not count toward rising costs subsidy, and must be met out of local tax funds.[52] This last provision also prevents the local authority from counting unauthorized expenditure toward a reduction of surplus. As we shall see, some of the surplus in the HRA is payable to the national government.

Since the delegation of authority to the national housing minister to determine allowable housing expenditure is so open-ended, some additional comment on the way in which this authority is intended to be exercised is in order.[53] For example, expenditures for the cost of "social and amenity" services are to be excluded on the ground that they should be self-supporting.[54] The government also intends to use its statutory authority to review local housing authority expenditure as a means of controlling building costs. Under previous legislation, as we have indicated, the minister was authorized to impose a cost yardstick on new construction. While this specific statutory authority has been withdrawn by

---

[50] Sch. 1, pt. I, § 3(1)(c).

[51] § 4(11).

[52] Sch. 1, pt. II, § 9.

[53] See the discussion in STANDING COMM., at 341-64. See also CIRCULAR 76/72, App. G.

[54] Id., at 346. It should also be noted that so-called "unproductive" loan charges, which arise in respect of a dwelling before rent is received, are also to be included and count toward eligibility for deficit subsidy. Id., at 122. These charges may be substantial. They were previously met in full by the local authority, an allocation which stirred considerable controversy. See HOUSING REVENUE ACCOUNTS, supra note 39, at 60-61.

the 1972 law, the intention is to impose a cost yardstick as part of the minister's broad statutory powers to define allowable expenditure. Previous legislation also required the HRA to carry an explicit housing repairs account. This statutory account is also abolished, but the intention is that an amount for housing repair may both be debited to the account and carried forward in subsequent years.

However, a statutory limit has been placed on the size of the working balance (WB) in the HRA which may be carried forward from year to year, and includes any amount that has been set aside for repairs.[55] While the statute is not entirely clear, it would appear that the local authority is entitled to maintain a working balance of $100 for each dwelling. This working balance may be decreased, but it may be increased only when new dwelling units are added to the local authority's supply. In that case, the local authority can add the statutory working balance to the Housing Revenue Account for each new dwelling. Otherwise, a working balance which is once used to meet expenses may not be replenished unless there are no subsidies or tax contributions payable to the HRA, an unlikely case.

While the intent of this limitation on working balances is to prevent local authorities from increasing their working balances in order to create a deficit in their account which will attract subsidy, the statute may pressure local authorities into a series of possibly unpalatable alternatives in order to meet their deficits. Local authorities can meet their deficits from the rising costs subsidy, but this subsidy requires a local tax contribution. Working balances can be drawn down, but these may eventually be exhausted. In this event, another alternative is an increase in rents, if an increase is possible under the fair rent formula. Any deficit not met by any of these means will fall on the local authority, for the statute requires an additional local tax contribution whenever the Housing Revenue Account is not in balance.[56] Generally, it may be expected that a local tax contribution to balance the account will be necessary whenever the rising costs subsidy is not sufficient to meet an increase in expenditure in full, or when

---

[55] See Sch. 1, pt. IV, § 14.15, and STANDING COMM., at 524-44. See also CIRCULAR 76/72, § 27.

[56] Sch. 1, pt. IV, § 16.

this subsidy when added to fair rents does not meet the cost of operation in full.[57]

Apart from the necessity to eliminate any deficit in its account, the local authority is also required to make a property tax contribution whenever "benefits or amenities" arising from the exercise of the housing function "are shared by the community as a whole."[58] While the purpose of this clause has not been further explained, it is apparently meant to require tax contributions toward recreation areas, roads, and other facilities in housing projects which benefit the entire community.

Some relief from local tax contributions to the housing account is provided, however, by a newly-enacted slum clearance subsidy. Previous legislation had provided for an annual subsidy to meet part of the additional annual debt service cost that was attributable to the need to build on expensive sites,[59] and these sites could be located in slum clearance areas. However, the English did not previously have a subsidy which, like the American urban renewal subsidy, meets part of the loss which usually occurs when land acquired in slum clearance projects is sold for redevelopment. In England, the selling price of cleared slum land may be five or ten times less than its acquisition cost. This loss in value occurs because redevelopment after clearance usually takes place at much lower densities, which are in turn reflected in a lower selling price. Previously, when slum-cleared land was used for local authority housing, the local authority was required to bring the land into the housing program at its acquisition cost and not at its sale price, and the extra cost of this slum-cleared land was a financial burden on its housing.

To moderate the impact on housing costs of slum-cleared land which is expensive to acquire, the act now provides a national subsidy which meets three-fourths of the loss incurred on the sale of cleared slum land for housing,[60] and is to be paid out in

---

[57] This statement does not take into account the transitional subsidies that are payable under the 1972 Housing Act, and which may reduce the need for local tax contributions during the interim period of change to the new and permanent housing subsidy system.

[58] Sch. I, pt. II, § 10.

[59] Housing Subsidies Act, 1967, ch. 29, § 10.

[60] *See* § 11; FAIR DEAL FOR HOUSING, CMND. NO. 4728 at 31-32. Actually, the statute is not limited to redevelopment for housing, and subsidizes any loss that occurs in the reuse of slum-cleared land.

a series of equal annual payments, not to exceed 60. While the slum clearance subsidy goes into the authority's general fund, and not into the Housing Revenue Account, it does have the effect of offsetting some of the loss which the local authority incurs when it uses its slum clearance powers to make land available for council housing.[61]

Although the local authority must make a contribution from local property taxes to balance its Housing Revenue Account whenever it is in deficit, it is also required to pay over part of any surplus in that account to the general credit of the national government.[62] We might first take note of the limited circumstances in which a surplus in the Housing Revenue Account can arise. No surplus can arise from payment of the rising costs subsidy, which is payable only as needed to bring the Housing Revenue Account into balance, nor from a local tax contribution to the HRA which is made for the same purpose. Surplus may arise indirectly from payment of the national rent rebate subsidy, since this subsidy partly reimburses the local authority for its rent rebate payments to tenants.[63] Otherwise, a surplus in the Housing Revenue Account can only arise when the fair rents collected from council housing tenants exceed expenditures, and produce a working balance which is in excess of the statutory maximum.

We should next consider whether the partial payment of surplus to the national government is acceptable as a matter of housing subsidy policy, keeping the source of the surplus in mind. Since the national rent rebate subsidy contributes to the surplus to the extent that it meets part of the difference between the minimum rents and the fair rents that are chargeable, repayment of any surplus can be justified as a return to the national government of its share of the rent rebate subsidy. Repayment of surplus is not linked to the amount of national rent rebate subsidy that the local authority has received, however, nor is there any statutory requirement that any surplus received by the national government

---

[61] The effect of the new subsidy is that the slum-cleared land is valued at its reduced sale price when it is used for housing, but that three-fourths of this loss in value is now to be met by the national government rather than the local authority.

[62] Sch. 1, pt. IV, § 17.

[63] The national rent rebate subsidy does not go into the Housing Revenue Account. However, it provides national subsidy support for part of the rents that council housing tenants pay into that account. Generally, on derivation of HRA surplus, see STANDING COMM., at 590.

must be used for housing subsidy purposes elsewhere in the country. Neither is it clear what effect the payment of housing surplus by the local authority will have on the national grant which is payable to the authority in support of its local expenditure functions. These considerations suggest that recapture of surplus may be connected more with national budget pressures than with housing subsidy policy, although surplus paid to the national government could of course be used to subsidize less fortunate local authorities elsewhere, even though the statute does not require this use of surplus money.

Repaid surplus is not kept by the national government in full, however, as one-half is returned to the local authority in which it arose. But, if a national subsidy for private rent allowances is payable to any authority, the amount of the rent allowance subsidy is to be deducted from the surplus before the 50-50 division is made. The effect of this allocation is to shift to the council tenants of that authority a share of the rent allowance which is payable to private tenants, at least to the extent that minimum rents paid by council tenants make up a share of any surplus which is generated in the Housing Revenue Account. This shift in financial responsibility for part of the rent allowance paid to private tenants does not occur, however, when council housing tenants in the authority receive Supplementary Benefit. For these tenants the minimum rent will be payable out of national taxation by way of the Supplementary Benefit system.

These observations lead us to a discussion of the distributive effect which English housing subsidies have on the financial responsibility for housing costs. How will housing costs be distributed as between national and local government levels, and between local council tenants and local taxpayers? These are some of the major questions with which we opened this book, and we should now examine the answers that have been given to these questions within the confines of the English housing subsidy system.

C. The Distributive Impact of the Housing Subsidy System

We can best study the contribution made to local authority revenues by national subsidies and payments, local tax payments, and minimum rents paid by council tenants by returning to our earlier analysis of the component elements which make up the credit side of the Housing Revenue Account. Recall that the credit side of the Housing Revenue Account was expressed in the following equation:

$$CR = M + RE + RC + RF.$$

That is, the credit side of the account includes revenue coming from minimum rents, the rent rebate which meets the difference between minimum and fair rents, the rising costs subsidy (if any), and the local tax contribution, if any. Taking the minimum rent charge first, we have explained that council tenants receiving Supplementary Benefits have their minimum rent paid by the Supplementary Benefits Commission, a national agency. All other tenants pay their minimum rents out of their incomes. Therefore,

$M = SB + CT$, when
$SB = $ minimum rents paid by the Supplementary Benefits Commission, and
$CT = $ rents paid by council tenants from private incomes.[64]

This analysis does not take account of payments toward rent which come from Family Income Supplement (FIS) payments. This omission appears justified in most cases by the fact that the FIS group is small and the national FIS contribution to earned income is marginal, so that FIS payments make only a small contribution toward rents.

On the basis of this allocation of minimum rents, and assuming the 25 percent local contribution toward rent rebates and rising cost subsidies which the legislation ultimately contemplates, equations can be developed which express the local and national contribution to HRA income. These equations take the national subsidy toward rent rebates into account, even though technically this subsidy is paid into the local authority's general fund:

$L = .25 (RE + RC) + RF$, when
$L = $ the local contribution, and
$N = .75 (RE + RC) + SB$, when
$N = $ the national contribution.

---

[64] This equation ignores private incomes of retired tenants that come from national pensions. While these payments, in a sense, come from national funds, the pensions are a form of insurance to which the tenant has previously contributed premiums out of his earned income.

Transposing these equations into the earlier equation which indicates the several contributions made to the credit side of the Housing Revenue Account, we find that:

$$CR = CT + L + N.$$

To what extent income credited to the HRA will be supplied by council tenants, local contributions, and national subsidies, will thus depend on two critical factors that affect council housing finances: the tenant mix in the housing projects, and the cost position of the local housing authority. Generally, the more affluent the tenants in the projects, and the lower the operating costs of the local authority, the greater the extent to which the cost of operating council housing will be shifted to tenant rents. How this rule operates can be illustrated by two extreme situations, neither of which approximates actual conditions in any local authority, but which illustrate how costs will tend to be distributed, given the nature of the subsidy system.

Let us begin with the affluent, low cost authority. Assume that in this authority all tenants pay the fair rent, and that no rising costs subsidy or local tax contribution is needed. In this authority, all of the cost of operating the projects will be met by rents paid by the tenants, so that:

$$CR = CT.$$

At the other extreme, assume an authority with high operating costs, and in which many of the tenants receive the national Supplementary Benefit. This example is not as extreme as it appears. Many inner area authorities have high costs, together with a comparatively poor tenantry. In this local authority, assuming that rising costs subsidy is payable but that no local tax contribution is otherwise needed to meet deficits, revenues to the HRA will be provided as follows:

$$CR = SB + CT + RE + RC.$$

Note that the contribution made by tenant rents in this authority will be minimal. Tenants receiving Supplementary Benefit will have their rents met in full from the benefit payment and the rent rebate. Tenants not receiving Supplementary Benefit will have to pay the minimum rent from their incomes, but the lower their incomes are the lower their minimum rents will be. Given the subsidy allocation between national and local governments, the local and national shares of the Housing Revenue Account in this local authority will then be as follows:

$$N = SB + .75 (RE + RC)$$
$$L = .25 (RE + RC).$$

Just how much of the cost burden will fall on the local authority in this case will depend on the rent rebate and rising costs subsidies that are needed. Assuming that this type of authority is located in an inner area, it is likely both to have high fair rents and high costs. As a result, the rent rebate and rising costs subsidies will be substantial, and 25 percent of these subsidies will have to be met from local taxes. If the Housing Revenue Account is not balanced by the subsidies that are payable, an additional local tax contribution will also be required to meet any deficit that arises. We had assumed that a contribution to meet a deficit in the authority's accounts would not be needed, but this assumption does not appear reasonable in an inner area authority of the type considered here, which is likely to have high costs not entirely met by national subsidies. We have also left the slum clearance subsidy out of our equations. As this authority is likely to be building housing on slum-cleared land, a national slum clearance subsidy will probably be available and will also require a local contribution.

From these calculations, then, it is possible to reach some general conclusions about the distributive impact that the English housing subsidy system is likely to have on housing costs. If we make the reasonable assumption that the tenant affluent and low cost authority is either suburban or located away from the Greater London area, then the subsidy system will be both income progressive and regionally redistributive if it captures housing revenues from these authorities. That is, as these affluent and low cost authorities develop surpluses in their accounts they will partly be paid back to the national government, and will be available (though not required) to finance subsidies payable to the less affluent and high cost authorities in the poorer inner areas and in the Southeast. On the other hand, if the poorer urban authorities develop deficits and require high subsidies, the system will be income regressive and will not be redistributive nationally. That is, the poorer urban authorities will have to levy property taxes on their own comparatively poor taxpayers in order to make up deficits in the housing account which are caused both by low incomes and high costs. They will also have to use local property taxes to make up the local share of rent rebate and rising costs subsidies. This share may be substantial, and remember that the English property tax is levied on tenants as well as owner-occupiers.

While high local property tax contributions in poorer authorities will be offset to some extent by national block grants to support local expenditure, the national block grant system is only partially based on local poverty conditions, and on the budgetary needs of local authorities. Moreover, in some of the inner boroughs of Greater London much and in some boroughs practically all housing is or soon will be council-owned. The authorities here will simply have to collect enough property taxes from their taxpayers to eliminate the deficits which these very same property taxpayers, as council tenants, have brought to the Housing Revenue Account. Rebates on property taxes paid by these tenants will provide some, but not total relief, from this property tax burden.

Rent allowances paid to private tenants may also impose a burden on local council tenants and taxpayers. Not only is a share of the rent allowance to be paid from local taxes after the first few years of the new subsidy program, but any surplus in the housing account is to be applied toward a reduction of that part of the private tenants' rent allowance which was met by national funds. If surpluses in the housing account are generated by rents paid by council tenants, these surpluses will be applied to the rents of tenants who live in private housing. These surpluses are likely to be generated in Suburban London or outside the Greater London area, in areas where private tenants are comparatively well-off and where most dwellings tend to be owner-occupied. In these areas, somewhat affluent council tenants may subsidize somewhat affluent private tenants, although the effect of this redistribution of income will in most cases be mitigated by the fact that in such areas the average rent allowance to private tenants will be comparatively low.

A final comment should be made about the effect of the housing subsidy program as it relates to the local government system in England, and the planning and development strategies that have been adopted as part of the national and regional planning effort. As the new subsidy legislation was going through Parliament in the 1971-72 session, a major reform of the local government system was also underway. In general, existing units of local government throughout the country have been consolidated to embrace larger geographic areas, a reform which will substantially reduce the number of local housing authorities in the housing program.

Just what effect this reform will have on the housing subsidy system will have to be seen. To the extent that local authorities are enlarged the new local governments may be more heterogenous in population than they were before. Poorer authorities will to some extent be combined with wealthier local authorities, and the income regressive effects of the housing subsidy program will be mitigated. The new local government structure will generally still maintain the present separation between urban and suburban areas, however, and to this extent even the new local authorities will reflect the income and housing tenure differences that presently exist.

Greater London has been omitted from the present reform, since its government was reformed and its area enlarged several years ago. At that time, the consolidation of the boroughs, the subunits of government in Greater London County, did in some cases merge poorer with richer areas. The new borough of Camden, which includes the former borough of Hampstead along with less affluent areas to the south, is one instance of such a consolidation. However, the major split in English local government still lies between Greater London and the rest of the country. As surpluses in Housing Revenue Accounts are likely to be generated outside the Greater London area, the housing subsidy system is likely to subsidize housing in Greater London at the expense of the rent of the country, at least to the extent that these surpluses are kept within the housing subsidy program. The reason is that the Greater London authorities are most likely to need national rising costs subsidies in addition to the rent rebate subsidy, and these subsidies would be payable to some extent from surpluses generated in local authorities elsewhere. Subsidy redistribution to other high cost housing areas is also likely to occur for the same reasons.

Redistribution of the housing subsidy to Greater London will also tend to undercut the larger planning and development strategies which the English have chosen to follow, as these strategies favor new growth and development outside Greater London. To the extent that the national housing subsidy program reduces the differential in council housing rents between London and the rest of the country which would otherwise prevail, the subsidy program will be working against these strategies. Given the urgent housing need in London, any other approach to the housing problem is probably unrealistic. Nevertheless, the impact of housing subsidies on planning for England and for the Greater London region must certainly be considered in any evaluation of the effect of these subsidies on overall national objectives.

D. Summary

Perhaps the greatest change which has been brought about by the new housing subsidy system is the shift which it has legislated in the distribution of housing costs. Under the new system, a much larger share of these costs is to be borne by tenants in local authority housing, and to some extent by the local authorities themselves. Indeed, we have seen that council housing tenants will contribute part of the cost of housing subsidies to tenants in private dwellings, at least to the extent that local authorities develop surpluses in their Housing Revenue Accounts.

This shift in the distribution of housing costs is the basis for the major criticisms which its opponents levelled at the system.[65] Application of the fair rent standard to council housing, and the requirement that local authorities meet a share of subsidy costs, have particularly been questioned. Spokesmen for the 1972 law defended the fair rent standard, partly on the ground that it is a proper method for making council housing rent determinations, and partly on the ground that a change to fair rents puts council tenants on parity with the private sector.[66] They justified asking local authorities to share in the rising costs subsidy as a way of disciplining local authorities to keep their costs down.[67] Charging part of the rent rebate subsidy to local authorities was then justified on the ground that some of the benefits from council housing accrue to local authority areas,[68] so that local authorities should contribute to the costs which the council housing program brings. All of these arguments have been refuted. Local authority

---

[65] This point was made several times by Labor Party members in debate at committee stage. *See, e.g.,* STANDING COMM., at 52-100.

[66] *See, e.g.,* STANDING COMM., at 1442.

[67] STANDING COMM., at 329.

[68] STANDING COMM., at 436.

costs would be monitored on post-audit, for example. Housing subsidies could also be viewed as part of a national program of income support, and from this perspective their allocation to the national level can be supported. Reasons for objecting to the application of the fair rent standard to council housing were discussed in the previous chapter.

To what extent housing subsidy costs will shift to tenants and local authorities will depend, as this discussion has demonstrated, on a variety of factors, such as the tenant mix in the projects. Tenant mix depends in turn on what tenants are admitted to council housing, a decision which has been left to local authorities. National employment and unemployment trends are another factor, and this analysis has assumed the continuation of generally low unemployment levels. Should the employment situation worsen on a more or less permanent basis, more of the tenants living in public and private rental housing will come to be supported by the national Supplementary Benefit program. In this event, an increasing share of housing subsidy costs will be met by the national government.[69]

The extent to which housing costs are shifted to council tenants will also depend on the impact which the new fair rent standard, combined with the rent rebate program, has on tenant rent levels. As we have indicated, no provision in the statute limits council rents to a proportion of tenant income. This omission was somewhat remedied by "assurances" given in parliamentary debate that reasonable minimum rent/income ratios would be maintained for council tenants receiving Supplementary Benefit. Promises of this kind are often made in English parliamentary practice as an alternative to legislative amendment, especially as English governments prefer to enjoy as much administrative discretion as Parliament will give them in administering legislation. Parliamentary assurances are published in parliamentary records, and although they are usually honored they can return to haunt the government that does not live up to its promises. Nevertheless, rising housing subsidy costs and growing employment difficulties suggest that compliance with the parliamentary promise to hold down rents may be difficult in times to come. More explicit legis-

---

[69] This conclusion would not be altered by a shift to the proposed negative income tax, although the program basis for national income support would then be different.

lative attention to the rent/income ratio may still be necessary, and the English may yet have their own version of the American Brooke Amendment.

To what extent, then, does the new legislation provide the promised help to "People in Need" as promised by the White Paper which announced the new subsidy system? We noted in the last chapter that higher rents for council housing, which will not be fully subsidized by the rent rebate plan, may force the more affluent tenants out of council housing altogether. Deprived of their rent bargain, some of these tenants may buy their council houses, as programs for the sale of council houses to tenants are growing more common. Other tenants will be forced into buying in the private home ownership sector. The extent of home purchase will be limited by the fact that rents are regulated while house prices are not, and continuing inflation in house prices may make home ownership a limited alternative. Moreover, since home ownership tends to predominate in outer suburban areas, tenants forced from council housing may have to move further out from the urban centers in which they previously lived.

To the extent that minimum rents rise excessively in relation to income, poorer tenants in council housing will find their economic circumstances increasingly worsened, and this group may have no realistic alternative. Home ownership is largely beyond their means, and the parity which the fair rent system has introduced means that rental accommodation will be no cheaper in the private than in the public sector. The only way out for these groups is a move to a dwelling whose rent has been kept low because it is in disrepair, a move which can only worsen their housing situation qualitatively.

Overall, then, the subsidy revisions legislated by the 1972 law have brought substantial changes to the housing subsidy program. For a long time the English program made subsidized housing available to a large part of the population with no attempt to differentiate among subsidy recipients on the basis of income. So open a program could be tolerated as long as subsidy costs remained manageable, but rising operating costs and higher housing standards have led to a corresponding increase in the subsidy burden. The 1972 legislation attempts to deal with this problem by concentrating the subsidy on those who need it, by charging higher rents to those for whom the subsidy is unnecessary, and by shifting part of the subsidy to local governments.

Whether these objectives can be achieved without radically altering the nature of the English subsidized housing effort will have to await the test of experience.

Chapter VIII

CONCLUSIONS AND PROSPECTS

This discussion of the English and American housing subsidy experience has concentrated on the redistributive function of housing subsidies in the allocation of housing costs.[1] The exercise of this function was approached in the first two chapters through an analysis of the major policy issues in housing subsidy programs, and these issues have been further illustrated in our more detailed discussion of publicly owned housing in the two countries.

In this chapter we will review the housing subsidy issues which we have previously explored, and then see how they relate to some of the policy issues in housing subsidy programs which we have not fully considered until now, but which deserve closer attention. Even though, as our earlier discussion indicates, we

---

[1] The impact of the housing subsidy system on housing costs is redistributive primarily because the important factors which influence the cost of providing housing are external to the housing subsidy program. Interest rate levels, and wage, construction and land costs are largely determined by economic factors in the larger economic market of which housing is only a part, and the housing subsidy system must accept the cost levels at which dwelling units are made available in the marketplace by the economic system. The only impact the housing subsidy system has is to redistribute the cost of this housing among housing consumers and entrepreneurs, and among the different levels of government which are involved in the housing subsidy program.

could pick almost any starting point, we will use for this purpose two issues which, because they are central to any housing subsidy system, provide a convenient frame of reference for our discussion. We begin first with the method by which the housing subsidy system makes its internal allocation of housing costs, concentrating on decisions about housing rents and quality. We look next at the choice of intermediary for distribution of the housing subsidy. This issue provides a useful starting point for analyzing the larger questions of freedom of housing choice which have been gaining increasing importance in public discussions of housing subsidy questions. An analysis of these two issues will serve as a basis to examine alternative legal structures for housing subsidies, and the way in which they can help the subsidy system to achieve its economic and social goals.

One final point needs to be made by way of introduction. While public attention in both countries has tended to focus alternatively and exclusively either on the quality and rent issue, or on the subsidy distribution issue, all of these factors, as we shall see, are interrelated in practice. The quality and rents of housing in the subsidized market will limit the extent to which subsidy recipients can exercise freedom of choice in the selection of their housing, no matter how the subsidy is distributed. How the subsidy is distributed will in turn affect rents and quality. If the subsidy is distributed by way of a public housing agency as intermediary, for example, greater public control can be exercised over the type and quality of the housing provided. Understanding the nature of these relationships between quality and rents on the one hand, and the method of distribution on the other, will help us to better see the policy alternatives that realistically appear to be open in the housing subsidy system.

A. The Quality Level and Rent Determination Problems in Housing Subsidy Programs

1. The Quality Problem[2]

As is typical of Western industrialized countries,[3] housing quality has been kept at comparatively high levels in both England

---

[2] We should note that upward adjustments of the quality level applied to subsidized housing will have more than a redistributive effect on the cost of subsidized housing to the extent that quality increases also increase the average cost of subsidized housing. In this event, quality increases for subsidized housing will have the effect of redistributing investment for housing between the subsidized

and the United States, at least as applied to newly constructed subsidized housing. High quality levels, and the tendency of publicly owned housing programs in both countries to concentrate on new high-cost construction, have together kept dwelling rents in these programs correspondingly high. As a result, these programs appear to be over-rigid in offering the subsidized housing tenant a limited freedom in his choice of housing and rents.

To provide less rigidity, the quality level of housing in subsidy programs could be modified in either one of two principal ways. In new construction, quality could be adjusted by relaxing durability requirements, or by insisting on less space and amenity in the dwelling. This approach would probably face substantial public opposition, however, in view of the growing demand for higher housing standards.

The other alternative for changing the quality level of housing in the subsidy program is to make greater use of the existing housing supply. Older housing commands less in the way of rent, partly because older housing was constructed at a time when housing costs were considerably lower. The difficulty with the use of existing housing in housing subsidy programs in both countries is that this housing is in different states of repair, and improvements in the quality of this housing have proved difficult to achieve. In the private sector, both countries prefer to rely on housing improvement programs which require a minimum of compulsory interference with private owners. These programs have not been noticeably successful. Their failure suggests that the private rental sector is incapable of developing the initiative that a program of improved housing quality demands, even when the needed funds are available.

---

and unsubsidized housing sectors, assuming that total annual investment in housing remains constant. For example, assume that quality levels for housing in the subsidized sector are reduced. In this event the average cost of subsidized housing will be reduced and, given our assumptions about constant investment, capital not spent in the subsidized sector will be attracted to the unsubsidized sector, where average housing costs will increase. Average costs of housing within the two sectors will change, but the average price of housing throughout the housing market will remain the same. The situation changes only if an increase in the quality level of housing in either sector attracts more capital into that sector. This increased investment must in turn be attracted away from other sectors of the economy unless the supply of capital for investment is also increased proportionately.

[3] *See* Downs, *Are Subsidies the Best Answer for Housing Low and Moderate Income Households?*, 4 URBAN LAWYER 405 (1972).

In the public sector, while subsidized rents should produce enough revenue to fund necessary repairs and improvements, both countries have found it necessary to provide additional subsidies for this purpose. Even in the English council housing program, which does not house just the lower income families, additional operating cost subsidies have been made available. These operating subsidies probably reflect a political decision that public support of housing maintenance and improvement requires a separate legislative judgment on what the level of these subsidies ought to be. Our discussion has indicated that housing subsidy programs are sensitive to heavy cost burdens, and will respond by lowering subsidies even though a reduction in housing quality below acceptable levels may result. Restrictions on the amounts made available for operating cost subsidies in both countries support this conclusion.

Since that part of the housing supply which does not meet minimum quality standards is at varying levels of acceptability, the question is raised of how to determine the level of housing quality which can qualify for subsidy support. A compromise on this question has been achieved in England, where housing of any quality is accepted for subsidy so long as an appropriate adjustment is made in the fair rent. Presumably, any housing which is so bad that it does not pass the fitness standards of the English housing statute will eventually be removed through demolition or slum clearance. This kind of compromise may have to be accepted in housing subsidy programs so long as cost pressures continue to be severe.

2. The Rent Problem

Rents for subsidized housing will tend to be comparatively high or comparatively low, depending on the quality level that is chosen for the housing subsidy program. No matter what quality level is selected, however, a decision must still be made on what rent should be determined for each level of quality in the subsidized housing market. These rents must then be divided according to an acceptable formula between the housing subsidy system and the tenant, who pays that part of the rent which has not been met by the subsidy.

Rents in the English and American housing subsidy programs are determined under two very different types of standards. The English council housing program uses a market-related rent standard, while in American public housing a federal rent ceiling has been imposed which bases rents on a percentage of income. Both rent standards are somewhat arbitrary in the criteria they have selected. For example, even though the American public housing rent standard adjusts the rent to the tenant's ability to pay, and to this extent avoids personal hardship, the 25 percent rent/income ratio is questionable as a rent ceiling which can be made applicable to the economic circumstances of all families in public housing. Legislative and administrative battles over the deductions and exemptions to be applied in the implementation of the Brooke Amendment only testify to the rigidity of an unqualified rent/income ratio as a rent formula. Neither has the federal rent ceiling yet altered the complicated methods under which rents are in fact determined by local public housing agencies. Moreover, the low rent ceiling in American public housing only exaggerates the difference in rent levels between the subsidized and unsubsidized housing sectors.

By way of contrast, the English fair rent standard provides an identical measure for both publicly and privately owned housing, though even the uniformity provided by this standard may be illusory. In addition, the fair rent standard has, if anything, a pragmatic rather than a conceptually justifiable basis, since it divides housing costs in a somewhat arbitrary manner between the owners of rental housing, the tenants, and the housing subsidy system. Thus fair rents "tax" away some of the return of the private landlord by authorizing rents which are substantially below market levels. Within the housing subsidy system, the fair rent standard and accompanying rebates do not produce a rent which is a constant percentage of income, and so the program may bring hardship to tenants in high-rent areas if the rents which they are required to pay are financially intolerable. Administrative exceptions provided by the statute, under which rents can be lowered and rebates raised, only introduce substantive confusion by way of the administrative flexibility which is permitted.

Achieving comparability in rents between subsidized and unsubsidized housing units while at the same time imposing a rent which takes only a reasonable share of the tenant's income is difficult to achieve without recourse to a rent standard based on income for those who are in need of a subsidy. The problem is compounded in a program like English council housing, to which admission is not based on income, and for which some method must be found under which tenants needing a subsidy can be charged a rent within their means. In this situation, a means-tested rebate based on income appears inescapable. Distinctions between tenants who need and who do not need a subsidy are not made in American public housing because this housing is limited to families of low income. But in this program an income test is applied to determine admission, continued occupancy, and the ceiling rent which must be established under Senator Brooke's amendment. Many local public housing agencies also base their rents on a proportion of income. Public housing projects are socially and economically stratified as a result of these requirements. Difficulties also arise in the United States since many families eligible for housing subsidies are denied these subsidies because the supply of public (and privately owned) subsidized housing is limited. These families must compete for housing in the unsubsidized private market, where rents may be higher for the same or comparable dwellings. This problem can only be avoided if housing subsidies are extended throughout the housing market, at income levels at which these subsidies are needed.

Any rent system which reflects the tenant's ability to pay will require a detailed review of the tenant's economic circumstances in order to determine what the correct rent ought to be. In this situation conflict arises between the demands of equity and the demands of privacy. The problem is compounded by a situation like that in England, where a high proportion of the population receives a subsidy and therefore requires a means test. An additional difficulty is presented if, as in England, the tenant who is eligible for the subsidy must also file a claim for it. Tenants may object to making application if a detailed review of their personal circumstances is required, and if many tenants do not claim the subsidy there will be considerable financial hardship within the system.

The only feasible alternative to a review of individual economic circumstances as the basis for determining rent is a rent standard which is calculated as an average, and which permits few variations. Flat welfare grants in the United States which include an amount for rent based on statewide or regional averages, and the national rent average which is used in the English Family Income Supplement program, are two examples of this approach. It avoids a detailed investigation of circumstances and is easy to administer, but at the possible cost of personal hardship in individual cases in which the housing subsidy is not sufficient to meet the housing cost which the recipient of the subsidy must bear.

B. The Direct Housing Allowance and Freedom of Choice Issues

1. The Nature of the Problem

Our discussion of rents and quality levels in housing subsidy programs has helped us to better understand the reasoning on which the argument for a housing allowance is based. Because rents for publicly owned dwelling units are fixed by the local authority which owns and manages them, and as quality standards in subsidized housing have been maintained at high levels, the subsidized tenant living in this housing may find that he is paying more for his dwelling unit than he would have liked. The argument is that if he is given a subsidy directly he will be able to find a wider quality range of housing units in the private market at potentially lower rents.

This advantage in freedom of choice which appears to favor a direct rental allowance will largely disappear in England once rents are regulated throughout the rental market under the fair rent standard. The same rent structure which is applicable to council housing will also obtain in the private market. The major difference between council housing and private rental housing in England will then lie in the age of the available housing; rents in the private rental market will tend to be lower as housing in that market is generally older. Therefore, most of our comments on the direct housing allowance in this section will apply primarily to the American situation, where a wider range of housing exists in a private rental housing market which is uncontrolled.

Nevertheless, the private rental market places limits on the impact of a direct housing allowance, even in the United States. Our analysis has suggested that any housing subsidy must take the market as it finds it, and that the availability of housing of different quality and at varying rents may in fact limit the freedom of choice of subsidy recipients even under an American housing allowance. Proponents of a housing allowance in America may have been misled by the fact that the American public housing effort is relatively new, as most of the units in the program have been constructed since the Second World War. In America as in England, the private rental market offers a greater range of housing choice primarily as housing in that market is older, and more varied by type of dwelling. Therefore, a direct housing allowance will reduce housing subsidy costs only if recipients of the subsidy choose private dwellings for which the cost of operation is less than the cost of operation of comparable but newer dwelling units which are in the public housing supply.

A paradox here is that a direct housing allowance which permits subsidy recipients to rent older and privately owned dwellings may also lead to more social and economic stratification in the housing market. Tenants receiving the direct housing allowance will nominally be free to choose any unit they want. But it is inconceivable that any housing subsidy system will long permit tenants to build up housing subsidy cost by choosing dwellings on which rents are comparatively high, and for which the unsubsidized rent paid by the tenant covers only a small portion of the operating costs. To avoid this situation, controls will have to be placed on the housing selection which the subsidy recipient is allowed to make, especially if the rents of direct housing allowance recipients are held to the same 25 percent rent/income ratio which the Brooke Amendment imposes on public housing. We noted that controls of this type exist in the English housing subsidy and welfare assistance programs, as the subsidy may be reduced for dwellings on which the rent is considered too high, considering the housing needs of the family. These controls also exist in American welfare programs, where welfare agencies have the authority to relocate welfare recipients to different housing in order to reduce their shelter costs. Whether these controls would be accepted within the context of a more widespread housing subsidy system remains to be demonstrated. They are not consistent with the greater freedom of choice which the direct housing allowance aims to achieve.

2. The Home Ownership Problem

Our discussion of the direct housing allowance alternative has so far assumed a housing subsidy which is available only for housing in the rental market. But a housing allowance which is limited to rental housing still does not provide that complete freedom of choice in the selection of housing for which proponents of the housing allowance argue, and which requires access to the home ownership market as well.

Some critics would reply to this argument by pointing out that home ownership by lower income families receiving housing subsidies may not altogether be desirable as a matter of social policy.[4] Those doubts may be reflected in the limited steps which both England and the United States have so far taken in providing a subsidy program for homeowners. Apart from a series of individual and ad hoc programs, neither country provides a method under which recipients of a subsidy in a rental housing program may move in an organized and directed way from renter to owner status. In England, the mortgage subsidy program which was described earlier provides some assistance toward home ownership for lower income families, the property tax rebate program affords some relief from property taxes, and many local authorities are beginning to sell council housing dwellings to council tenants. Direct loans from local authorities for the purpose of buying a home are another help, but the volume of these loans has not been large. A similar home mortgage subsidy program in the United States reached substantial proportions, but is in difficulty because the housing that was subsidized was not always satisfactory, and because recipients of the subsidy were not always able to keep up their payments. In addition, a program enabling the sale of public housing rental units to their occupants is in the experimental stage.

Any attempt to provide home ownership opportunities in housing subsidy programs more effectively and more systematically faces some overwhelming problems. One is that a housing subsidy which expands opportunities for home ownership will have to deal directly with comparability of cost between the rental and home ownership markets. Prices for homes in both countries have been increasing significantly. If home prices continue to be unregulated at the same time that rents are controlled in England, or kept below market levels in American subsidized housing programs, cost differentials in the two sectors will make it difficult to integrate owner-occupied housing into the subsidized housing system. A factor that could act against any attempt to regulate

---

[4] See Marcuse, *Homeownership for Low Income Families: Financial Implications*, 53 LAND ECON. 134 (1972).

home prices is that controls over the price of homes are politically unthinkable, even on the English scene.

While home ownership in both countries also requires the availability of capital to make a downpayment on the purchase price, would-be-owners who are recipients of housing subsidies seldom have the requisite amount. This problem has been solved to some extent in the United States, where federal mortgage insurance, and liberal downpayment and mortgage terms in the federally subsidized home ownership program, make it easier for housing subsidy recipients to take on home ownership. Legislation on home financing in England is not as far advanced. There is no national system of mortgage insurance, which makes entry into the home ownership market more difficult.

These observations may reinforce the criticism that home ownership may not be a viable alternative for recipients of housing subsidies. And we have not even covered all of the problems. For example, a commitment to ownership may reduce needed mobility in the labor market, and the fixed payments which are part of the home ownership obligation may be difficult for recipients of housing subsidies to sustain, especially those who do not earn regular and steady incomes. The high foreclosure rate in the American home ownership subsidy program confirms this possibility. Nevertheless, the national commitment to home ownership as a preferred housing tenure, a commitment which is evident in both countries, indicates that some attempt to fit housing subsidies to the home ownership market may yet be attempted. The difficulty so far is that the implications of the home ownership alternative for the housing subsidy recipient have not yet been faced as squarely as they should.

3. The Concentration-Dispersion Issue

Any consideration of a direct housing allowance as a substitute for the more conventional system of housing subsidies provided by public authority housing will also have to give some attention to the concentration-dispersion issue. When the housing subsidy is available only on housing units which are owned and managed by a public housing agency, the argument is made that the geographic concentration of subsidized housing is increased, with negative consequences for the program. American public housing ghettos are cited as the classic example of this situation. Yet concentration of the publicly owned housing supply would not be inevitable were it not for other factors. In American public housing the concentration of publicly owned subsidized units has primarily been due to the geographic limitations that have been placed on the jurisdiction of inner city housing authorities, the failure of most suburban municipalities to engage in public housing programs, and the resistance of residents in better residential neighborhoods to the construction of subsidized housing projects in their areas. This problem has been avoided in England because all local authorities have some council housing, and because admission to council housing is not based on an income test. Nevertheless, even the English council housing project is not always a welcome newcomer in a suburban residential neighborhood.

The argument has been made that the change to a direct housing allowance will permit a greater dispersion of housing subsidy recipients because they would not be confined to projects built explicitly for them by local public agencies. Once more, however, location patterns in the housing market suggest that dispersion may be more of a hope than a real possibility even under a direct housing allowance system. We have already noted that there is a locational split between rental and owner-occupied housing in both countries, with rental housing tending to be more concentrated in the inner and poorer sections of metropolitan areas. To the extent that the direct housing allowance is limited to rental housing, therefore, dispersion opportunities will be limited.

Even the extension of housing subsidies to include home ownership may not radically change this situation. Home mortgage subsidies have now been available in the United States for some time for both newly-constructed, existing, and rehabilitated homes. The subsidy recipient is entitled to a free choice of dwelling so long as the dwelling falls within the cost limits specified by the program and meets minimum housing standards. In theory, the program provides an opportunity for the dispersion of the owner-occupied dwelling units which come within it.

In practice, widespread dispersion of these housing units has not occurred. Studies by the United States Commission on Civil Rights have found that units subsidized under this program tend to be heavily concentrated. In particular, housing purchased by Negroes and other minorities tends to be located in existing ghetto areas or in areas which are in a state of transition between white and minority occupancy.[5] Even new housing constructed under this program is often located in areas which are or have become areas of minority concentration. If dispersion of the subsidized housing supply is to be actively pursued as an important social aim, this objective does not appear to be heavily influenced by the method through which the housing subsidy is distributed.

The English have so far avoided an extreme concentration of subsidized families in their council housing projects by not imposing an income test for admission. This system has been criticized on the ground that all rents in English council housing are subsidized by the national subsidy payment, and it is argued that this subsidy should only be given to occupants of council dwellings who need the subsidy. This windfall in the housing system has been seen as one of its most undesirable features by critics of the program, but the consequences of eliminating this windfall have not been fully appreciated.

Changes in the program legislated in 1972 will limit payment of the subsidy to those who are found in housing need, but admission to the projects will continue to be open to anyone. We have suggested that these changes in the English subsidy system may force the more affluent tenants out of the program. At the same time, since operating deficits incurred by local authorities will not be fully subsidized by the national government, local authorities may seek to decrease the number of tenants requiring rent rebates in order to avoid the local tax contributions which otherwise would be required to meet operating deficits. Poorer tenants may also be assigned to housing units which are older, carry lower rents, and therefore require a lower subsidy. An aggravation of these trends may lead to a subsidized council housing program which is as stratified as the American.

C. Some Policy Alternatives for Housing Subsidy Programs

This review of policy problems in housing subsidy programs has suggested only some of the many complex legislative and administrative issues which these programs present. If any conclusion can be drawn from this discussion, it is that no one alternative will solve all of the problems or satisfy all of the

---

[5] UNITED STATES COMM'N ON CIVIL RIGHTS, HOME OWNERSHIP FOR LOWER INCOME FAMILIES: A REPORT ON THE RACIAL AND ETHNIC IMPACT OF THE SECTION 235 PROGRAM (1971).

many social and economic interests that have a stake in these programs. Housing subsidy programs are likely to remain mixed, for neither country is likely to achieve a political solution to its housing subsidy effort which is either totally controlled by government decision-making, or which is totally free of government intervention. Total government controls of the type needed would require Draconian measures which no western democracy would tolerate for long. Just to achieve a better effort in housing rehabilitation would require the exercise of more compulsion in housing improvement programs than either country has so far been willing to tolerate. On the other hand, the need for some form of housing subsidy for some of the population argues against any solution to the housing problem which would leave the housing market totally free from public intervention. What is needed in housing subsidy programs is a balance between government and private action which appears most appropriate for the economic and political system to which it must be fitted.

On the basis of this discussion some general conclusions can be suggested. One is that while economic weaknesses in the private rental market are likely to continue and to become more severe, the elimination of this market or its replacement with some alternative form of ownership is unlikely in the immediate future. Indications are that the private market in rental housing in England may gradually disappear over time due to the inroads of slum clearance and demolition on an aging rental housing stock, but this process will be gradual. In the United States, the abandonment of privately owned, low-income rental housing has only just surfaced as a serious housing problem. While a public policy for this phenomenon has not yet crystallized, the prospects for strengthening the lower income private rental sector are not good.

Since the private rental sector in both countries will continue for some time to provide a substantial share of rental housing in the lower income market at the same time that the condition of that housing is likely to deteriorate further, the role of the local public housing agency in bringing new rental units on the market at locations where they are required to fill a housing need should not be disparaged. The English compromise, which retains the council housing program while adding a direct housing allowance for tenants not in the program, should be considered for adoption in the United States, in spite of the fact that housing quality and parity problems will continue to be troublesome in this kind of system. Parity is presently achieved in England by applying a uniform rent standard to both publicly owned and privately owned rental housing, and by then taking the quality of the housing into account when rents are determined. Housing of less than satisfactory quality is thus accepted into the program. This adjustment is also made in the American welfare assistance program. But inequalities between the subsidized and unsubsidized housing sectors are greater in America partly because there is no independent public control over the level of rents in private rental housing, and partly because rents in the public housing program have been set at comparatively low levels. Unless either country is willing to budget more of its national income for housing subsidies, and is willing to take bolder steps to insure the renovation of its existing housing supply, this compromise in policy objectives is likely to endure for some time.

In view of these and other complexities that have been discussed above, suggestions for changes in existing housing subsidy programs should be approached with caution. Our analysis has suggested, moreover, that incremental rather than major changes in housing subsidy systems would appear to be preferred until major changes in the housing subsidy program can also be accompanied by major changes in the housing market. Program changes which can create agencies that are able to move among the different sectors of the housing market, and in so doing overcome some of the obstacles that are presently found in the subsidy programs, should especially be given close consideration.

One change in program, which would be a useful addition to the range of techniques now available in either country, would provide for a public agency in the housing field which could take a more aggressive role in housing subsidy programs than has presently been the case. What is suggested here is the creation of a public agency which will function more as a housing broker and administrator than as a builder and manager of subsidized housing. Such an agency could provide a bridge between the subsidized and unsubsidized housing markets which will facilitate the ability of housing subsidy recipients to move from one market to the other, and which will help remove some of the disparity in rents which presently exists between the two sectors. This type of agency can also provide a firmer public incentive for the repair and maintenance of existing housing.

A program of this kind has already been adopted to some extent in a variation of the American public housing program which is known as leased public housing.[6] In this program, the local public housing agency enters into a lease with the owner of an existing housing unit for a substantial period, and then subleases that unit to a tenant who is eligible for the public housing subsidy. The difference between the rent agreed upon with the landlord and the rent payable by the tenant is then subsidized, just as the excess rent in a conventional public housing unit is subsidized by the conventional public housing subsidy. As a requirement to participation in the program, the landlord must agree to improve his housing so that it meets the maintenance, facility, and space requirements of the local housing maintenance code. This program has been able to provide a wide variety of housing types and categories in many cities, at a saving over what it could cost to subsidize the conventional public housing unit.[7]

The leased public housing program has many advantages. Controls over rents are provided by the requirement that the lease between the owner of the unit and the public housing agency be negotiated by and acceptable to the public housing agency before the housing unit is taken into the program. The guarantee afforded the private landlord by the long-term lease and the public housing agency's guarantee of payment should also encourage the landlord both to make the necessary repairs and improvements, and to take a lower rent than he would have demanded from an unsubsidized lower income tenant who cannot give him the same financial assurances. Since leases for these units can be negotiated for housing located anywhere in the housing market, the dispersal objective is also easier to achieve under this program. Subsidy costs are lower whenever existing units are utilized, although the program has also been used for units that are newly constructed and that are then taken into the public housing program.

Comparatively minor adjustments in the leased housing program could extend its scope while at the same time providing a greater flexibility in its operation. These adjustments would ex-

---

[6] Christensen, *The Public Housing Leasing Program: A Workable Rent Subsidy?*, 1968 URBAN L. ANN. 57.

[7] F. DELEEUW & S.H. LEAMAN THE SECTION 23 LEASING PROGRAM (U. S. Urban Institute 1971).

pand the subsidized tenant's freedom of choice, and accomplish many of the objectives which have been claimed for the more radical form of direct housing allowance. In the program as it is now operated, the public housing agency negotiates with the landlord to bring the unit into the program, and then selects a tenant for admission. Greater freedom of choice would be afforded to the tenant if he were allowed to select his own dwelling, subject to the approval of its condition and the negotiation of a lease between the landlord and the public housing agency. Leases would be negotiated after the tenant has selected his unit, and after the landlord has brought it up to program requirements. The leased public housing program has already moved in this direction in many areas, in which leases are negotiated with landlords who bring tenants already living in the property into the program. Purchase of the unit by the tenant is also authorized by the federal statute, and the purchase option could be expanded.

Moreover, the leased public housing program has the potential of becoming a de facto substitute for formal rent control if the program were extended throughout the housing market. Rents can be fixed by the local housing agency before a unit comes into the program, and rent increases which absorb some or all of the subsidy can be avoided. In the present American program, however, the level of rents to be negotiated is not determined by statutory criteria and is left up to the local public housing agency. Rent-setting problems under this system have not so far been critical because the number of units in the program is small, but if the program were extended widely throughout the market some method would have to be found to determine the unsubsidized rents to which owners of these dwellings would be entitled. Some public housing agencies have developed their own rent schedules, and to assist it in making these rent determinations the public housing agency could also carry out a market-wide inventory of rents which would give it a register of rents as of a fixed point in time. This rental inventory, which could be carried out at the same time as property is reassessed for tax purposes, could then be updated periodically in much the same way. In the alternative, rent controls adopted at the municipal level could provide a control on market rents. Several municipalities on the eastern seaboard have already moved in this direction. Municipal rent controls may prove to be politically feasible even though a more widespread rent control system may not, since they could be imposed selectively in those municipalities in which a need for such controls creates the political support for their enactment.

An expansion of the leased public housing program along the lines indicated would require only minor legislative changes in the United States, as local public housing agencies already possess most of the necessary statutory authority. Most of the changes that are needed are a greater emphasis on this program administratively, and additional funding. In England, the newly-enacted rent allowance for tenants in privately owned housing has some of the elements of the proposed program, since tenants may select their own dwellings, and rent control is imposed nationally. Some English housing authorities also make use of existing housing units, which they acquire in the open market. What is suggested in the English context is a more aggressive use of this program by local authorities, and provision of statutory authority similar to the American, under which dwelling units can be leased from private landlords rather than acquired outright.

The American leased public housing program has not been without its difficulties however. Financial irregularities which have developed have led to criticisms about its effectiveness.[8] The program has been expensive and difficult to administer as well. For example, leased dwellings at scattered locations are difficult to monitor and expensive to administer. Units are sometimes vacated without notice having been given to the housing agency, and may be vandalized before the agency can find a new tenant. Another problem is that expenses of administration would soar even more with the extension of the program throughout the rental sector, as proposed here, and control of the program would be even more difficult to achieve. These problems must be faced, however, if society is to develop any alternatives to the present system of massive housing projects at one location, all of which are under the ownership and management of a public local authority. Similar problems are present in a direct housing allowance program, as the allowance could be spent by its recipients on housing which is located anywhere in the housing market, at locations as widely dispersed as the location of units in the leased public housing program. These problems are minimized in

---

[8] *See* Palmer, *Section 23 Housing: Low-Rent Housing in Private Accommodation*, 48 J. URBAN LAW 255 (1970).

England only by the presence of national rent control and by the willingness of the housing subsidy program to accept housing of less than ideal standards.

Any attention to policy changes in housing subsidy programs will also have to consider the relationship of the housing subsidy program to other programs of income support. For example, widespread extension of the leased public housing program throughout the housing market in the United States would aggravate the problems of coordination between the housing subsidy program and the welfare assistance program which already exist. A higher proportion of welfare recipients would then live in some form of subsidized housing, and the problems of differential treatment between welfare recipients living inside and outside of the subsidized housing sector would be magnified.

The English solution to this problem is to delegate the authority to make housing determinations for welfare recipients within the housing subsidy system to the local housing authorities. This approach could help to provide more coordination between the two programs in the United States, especially as there is no state intermediary agency in the public housing program and the potential for the development of uniform national standards in that program is greater.

The impact of the housing subsidy on income support programs lies beyond the problems of coordination to which we have especially given attention, however. Any income support program will have a housing subsidy element, even the universal and national support grant which has been proposed in America and which the English now plan to achieve through their income tax system. How the housing subsidy element of that program is managed will in turn affect the level of subsidy which the general income support grant can provide. If the structure of the housing subsidy leads to an inflation in housing costs, as may occur under an American direct housing allowance which is distributed in a market not subject to rent control, the level of subsidy provided by the general income support grant will be substantially eroded. This problem is especially serious as housing is a consumption item whose costs are least subject to control by low-income consumers.

Attention also needs to be paid to the allocation of intergovernmental financial and substantive responsibilities within the housing subsidy program. Both England and the United States have provided national subsidies for housing costs, but at the same time have also permitted a substantial delegation of substantive authority to local public housing agencies with a minimum of national direction. As a result, significant aspects of public housing policy are determined at the local level. A good example of this delegation of authority to the local level is the delegation to local public housing agencies in each country of the authority to decide on tenant admissions and evictions, with little guidance from national legislation. Friction between national and local authorities then results if the national agency which is responsible for housing subsidies grows dissatisfied with local policies. Recent federal disfavor with the admission of large numbers of welfare recipients to public housing projects in the United States provides one example.

Some of the problems arising out of this delegation of substitute authority would be obviated by the elimination of the local government authority as a supplier of housing, in which event a local authority would act only as an administrative and distributing agency for the implementation of housing subsidies which would be financed nationally. Full national assumption of administrative authority for housing subsidy programs does not appear possible in either country, however. In the United States, even a recent attempt to establish a national rent standard in public housing proved impossible to accomplish. In England, the reintroduction of mandatory local contributions to housing subsidies makes it unlikely that local control of the council housing program will be reduced.

Substantial local autonomy in the operation of American public housing continues in the face of mounting evidence that substantial federal financial underwriting of the program will be necessary. The increasing limitation of public housing to lower income and welfare families has eroded the economic base of the program, so that federal subsidies in increasing amounts will be needed, just to meet operating costs. It will be interesting to see whether changes in the English council housing program will narrow the economic base of the population living in council housing projects as well, and if so whether this change will lead to a greater national assumption of costs in that country also.

D. Conclusion

No thoughtful observer of the American or English urban scene would contend that housing problems can be solved solely through the housing subsidy system, especially not in older urban neighborhoods in both countries, where serious underlying social and economic problems threaten the entire fabric of urban life. Yet problems of housing subsidy remain of central importance in any program which seeks to attack and remedy the housing problem.

Unfortunately, the rhetoric of public debate and argument often calls for an approach to housing subsidy programs which the legal and administrative system is not capable of delivering, and which national budgets are unable to finance. The more realistic look at our housing subsidy programs which we have undertaken should point the way to less dramatic but, in the long run, more effective approaches to the housing subsidy question. There are no easy solutions, although our discussion has suggested that the path of change lies in the direction of more and not less centralization of housing subsidy and related programs, and more and not less government intervention in the housing market. England has perhaps gone farther in this direction than has the United States, but even in that country the housing subsidy issue is by no means settled, and in both countries the housing subsidy system remains a compromise of conflicting and diverse policy objectives. Politically viable and financially acceptable solutions must be found. Otherwise, Cathy may never come home.

Selected Bibliography

The bibliography that follows contains selected references to books, articles, and other materials on housing subsidies in England and the United States that have been published in recent years, most of which have not been cited in the text. The development of a serious literature in the housing field in both countries has been hampered by the absence of an academic journal devoted to housing problems, although *Land Economics,* a well-established journal published at the University of Wisconsin, does carry articles on housing regularly. *New Society,* a semi-academic English journal covering a wide range of social policy issues, also publishes brief but extremely useful articles on housing matters. However, most of the periodicals explicitly devoted to housing in both countries are journals published by trade associations of housing officials, such as the *Journal of Housing* in the United States, and the various housing periodicals published in England.

A different source of publications on housing problems are the reports published by national commissions in both countries, most of which have been cited in the text. Important papers have also been published by congressional committees in the United States, and the federally funded Urban Institute has also published a series of valuable housing reports in recent years.

References have been arranged approximately in accordance with chapter topics. Within each heading, citations are made first to books and monographs, then to articles in periodicals, and finally to government and other miscellaneous publications.

1. REFERENCES OF GENERAL INTEREST

C.S. Ascher, The Administration of Publicly-Aided Housing (Internat'l Institute of Administrative Sciences: Brussels, 1971)

Hagman, *Revenue Sharing: American Lessons from the Anglo Experience,* 1972 Univ. Ill. Law Forum 300

I.R. Silver, Housing and the Poor (Canada Ministry of State for Urban Affairs, 1971)
> (Good discussion of housing need concept)

I.H. Welfeld, European Housing Subsidy Systems: An American Perspective (U.S. Dep't of Housing and Urban Development, 1972)

2. ENGLAND: IN GENERAL

F. Allaun, No Place Like Home: Britain's Housing Tragedy (From the Victim's View) and How to Overcome It (1972)
> (Written by a chief Labor Party spokesman on housing policy)

C. Buchanan & Partners, The Prospect for Housing (1971)

E. Burney, Housing on Trial (1967)
> (A study of colored immigrants in the Midlands)

A. Crosland, Towards a Labour Housing Policy (Fabian Tract No. 410, 1971)

J.B. Cullingworth, Housing and Labour Mobility (1969)

J.B. Cullingworth, Housing in Transition (1963)
> (Study of decline in rented housing in Lancaster)

J.G. Davies, The Evangelistic Bureaucrat: A Study of a Planning Exercise in Newcastle upon Tyne (1972)
(Case study of unsuccessful housing rehabilitation project)

N. Dennis, People and Planning: The Sociology of Housing in Sunderland (1970)

Fabian Society, Social Services for All? (1968)
(Includes articles on housing allowance)

J. Greve, Homeless in London (1971)

J. Greve, Private Landlords in England (1965)

T. Hart, The Comprehensive Development Area (1967)

J. Macey, The Housing Finance Act (1972)

R. McKie, Housing and the Whitehall Bulldozer (1971)

A. Nevitt (Ed.), Economic Problems of Housing (1967)
(Includes paper by Professor Cullingworth on governmental role)

A. Nevitt, Housing, Taxation and Subsidies (1966)
(Influential review of English housing policies)

A. Nevitt, Fair Deal for Householders (Fabian Research Series No. 297, 1971)

A.L. Schorr, Slums and Social Insecurity (1964)
(Has chapter on British housing)

P.A. Stone, Urban Development in Britain, Vol. I: Standards, Costs, and Resources, 1964-2004 (1970)

R. Wilson, Housing Finance (1967)

Donnison, *A Housing Service,* 18 New Society 936 (1971)

Forster, *Rate and Rent Rebates,* 116 Local Gov't Chron. 1877 (1971)

General Improvement Areas: Action Report, Community Action, April-May, 1972, at 11-30

P.H. Levin, *Population Trends, Housing, and the Overspill Problem,* GREATER LONDON COUNCIL INTELL. UNIT QTLY. BULL., No. 5, Dec. 1968, at 49

Meacher, *Tinkering with Twilight Homes,* 18 NEW SOCIETY 20 (1971)
    (Skeptical of housing rehabilitation policy)

Nevitt, *Meeting the Cost of Housing,* 7 NEW SOCIETY 6 (1966)

Nevitt, *How Fair Are Rate Rebates?,* 18 NEW SOCIETY 1000 (1971)

E. Sharp, *Housing in Britain,* 215 ESTATES GAZETTE 1026, 1133 (1970)
    (Review of housing problems in England by former Permanent Secretary of Department of the Environment)

Sherman, *Can Housing Be Taken "Out of Politics?",* 39 TOWN AND COUNTRY PLANNING 307 (1971)

Wilson, *How Labour Lost Its Grip (Housing),* 81 NEW STATESMAN 799 (1971)

CHARTERED LAND SOCIETIES COMM. OF ROYAL INSTITUTE OF CHARTERED SURVEYORS, A REVIEW OF HOUSING POLICIES IN ENGLAND AND WALES (1969)

CONDEMNED (1971)
    (Report by the Shelter society on slum clearance)

REPORT OF THE SELECT COMM. ON RACE RELATIONS AND IMMIGRATION: HOUSING, SESS. 1970-71 (1971) (Parliamentary Report)

ROYAL COMM'N ON LOCAL GOV'T IN ENGLAND, VOL. I: REPORT, CMND. 4040 (1969)

3. ENGLAND: COUNCIL HOUSING

D. EVERSLEY, RENTS AND SOCIAL POLICY (Fabian Research Ser. No. 174 1955)

G. GRAY, THE COST OF COUNCIL HOUSING (1968)

A.D. Silverman, Selected Aspects of Administration of Publicly-Owned Housing (1961)

Allen & Lamb, *Rent Rebates,* 112 Local Gov't Chron. 1202 (1967)

Bell, *Rent Rebates,* British Housing & Planning Rev., vol. 9, May-June, 1954, at 5
>   (Discusses rent rebate plans then in effect)

Blake, *New Directions for Council Housing,* 139 Surveyor 22 (1972)

Bucknall, *Housing Revenue Account and Subsidies,* 117 Local Gov't Chron. 1787 (1972)

Cowley, *Possible Basis for Fixing Rents of Council Housing,* Housing, vol. 6, May, 1970, at 6
>   (Rent-fixing prior to 1972 law)

M.J. Dear, *The Growth of London's Housing Stock,* Greater London Council Intell. Unit Qtly. Bull., No. 14, Mar., 1971, at 3
>   (Predicts future growth of council housing in this area)

Fleming, *Subsidized Housing in this Day and Age,* British Housing & Planning Rev., vol. 23, May-June, 1967, at 6

Housing, *Walker's Secret Hand,* The Economist, May 22, 1972, at 18

Housing with Heath, 134 Just. P. 878 (1970)

Jennings, *Geographical Implications of the Municipal Housing Programme in England and Wales, 1919-39,* 8 Urban Studies 121 (1971)

Jewell, *Local Authority Housing: Differential Rents Schemes,* 1961 J. Plan. & Prop. L. 75

Macey, *Housing Policy and Its Implications,* Housing, vol. 3, May, 1967, at 16
>   (Macey was formerly director of Greater London housing and is influential in housing policy)

ASSOCIATION OF MUNICIPAL CORPORATIONS, COUNCIL HOUSE RENTS: MEMORANDUM BY THE ASSOCIATION (1968)

CENTRAL HOUSING ADVISORY COMM., UNSATISFACTORY TENANTS (Sixth Report of the Housing Management Subcomm., 1955)

CENTRAL HOUSING ADVISORY COMM., COUNCILS AND THEIR HOUSES: MANAGEMENT OF ESTATES (Eighth Report of the Housing Management Subcomm., 1959)

J.B. CULLINGWORTH, REPORT TO THE MINISTER OF HOUSING AND LOCAL GOVERNMENT ON PROPOSALS FOR THE TRANSFER OF GREATER LONDON COUNCIL HOUSING TO THE LONDON BOROUGHS (1970)

M. HARRISON & A. NORTON, MANAGEMENT OF LOCAL GOVERNMENT, VOL. 5: LOCAL GOVERNMENT ADMINISTRATION IN ENGLAND AND WALES, AN ENQUIRY CARRIED OUT FOR THE COMM. ON THE MANAGEMENT OF LOCAL GOVERNMENT (1967)

REPORT OF THE COMM. ON LOCAL AUTHORITY AND ALLIED PERSONAL SOCIAL SERVICES, CMND. 3703 (1968)
   (Includes sections on housing)

A. RICHARDSON, PUBLIC HOUSING IN ENGLAND (N.Y.C. Community Service Soc'y, 1969)

UNITED NATIONS CENTRE FOR HOUSING, BUILDING AND PLANNING, HOUSING ADMINISTRATION IN ENGLAND AND WALES (1967)

4. ENGLAND: FAIR RENTS

LABOUR PARTY, ACTION: RENTS, REBATES (1967)

LABOUR PARTY, HOUSING: REPORT OF THE HOUSING POLICY STUDY GROUP (1969)

R. MEGARRY, THE RENT ACT (10th ed. 1967)
   (Leading legal text)

A. NEVITT, THE NATURE OF RENT CONTROLLING LEGISLATION IN THE UK (Centre for Environmental Studies, 1970)

Aughton, *Trouble With Fair Rents,* 117 LOCAL GOV'T CHRON. 1785 (1972)

Cullingworth, *The Twentieth Rent Act,* NEW SOCIETY, Dec. 10, 1964, at 8

Donnison, *How to Help the Poorest Tenants,* 13 NEW SOCIETY 86 (1969)

Haddon, *Francis Committee Report: Recipe for Conflict,* 3 RACE TODAY 132 (1971)

Hollamby, *The Fair Rents System,* 220 ESTATES GAZETTE 809 (1971)

Irvine, *A Cruel Choice for Tenants,* 81 NEW STATESMAN 298 (1971)

Macey, *Making Rents Fair,* 21 NEW SOCIETY 14 (1972)
    (An analysis favorable to the 1972 Housing Finance Act)

McLachlan, *How Rent Tribunals Work,* NEW SOCIETY, Aug. 8, 1967, at 16

Morris, *How Fair Are "Fair Rents?",* 16 NEW SOCIETY 947 (1970)

Parker, *Will We Get a Fair Rents Policy?,* 80 NEW STATESMAN 665 (1970)

Prohpet, *What Is a Fair Rent?,* 111 LOCAL GOV'T CHRON. 693

The Rent Act of 1965 in Practice, 134 JUST. P. 515 (1970)

Sophian, *Valuation of "Fair Rent,"* 1971 J. PLAN. & PROP. L. 262

Street, *Defending the Francis Report,* 17 NEW SOCIETY 536 (1971)

Worpole & Heo, *Rent Act in Brighton,* 12 NEW SOCIETY 641 (1968)

Zander, *The Unused Rent Acts,* 12 NEW SOCIETY 366 (1968)

CHARTERED SOCIETIES JOINT WORKING PARTY REPORT ON THE DETERMINATION OF FAIR RENTS AND THE CONSEQUENCES (1966)
    (Discusses application of fair rents to council housing)

DEPARTMENT OF PROFESSIONAL STUDIES, DIVISION OF BUS. ADMIN. (Ashford, Kent), VERBATIM REPORT ON THE RENT ACT (1967) (conference report)

THE IMPLICATION OF THE FRANCIS REPORT, TRANSCRIPT OF A CONFERENCE ORGANIZED BY SHELTER, Mar. 13, 1971

INTERIM REPORT BY THE RENT REGISTRATION GROUP, BRIGHTON RENTS PROJECT, RENTS IN BRIGHTON (1969)

NOTTING HILL HOUSING SERVICE, THE RENT ACTS AND THE HOUSING MARKET IN NORTH KENSINGTON (1970)

E.O. OLSEN, THE EFFECTS OF A SIMPLE RENT CONTROL SCHEME IN A COMPETITIVE HOUSING MARKET (Rand Institute, 1969)

5. ENGLAND: RENT REBATES AND HOUSING ALLOWANCES UNDER HOUSING FINANCE ACT OF 1972*

Allaun, *Housing: Labor's Answer to Tory Policy,* TRIBUNE, Dec. 3, 1971, at 5

Aughton, *A Second Look at the Housing Finance Bill,* HOUSING & PLANNING REV., vol. 28, Mar.-Apr., 1972, at 5

Forster, *Party Games with Public Expenditure,* 117 LOCAL GOV'T CHRON. 2315 (1971)
    (Estimates housing subsidies under new legislation)

Nevitt, *A "Fair" Deal for Housing?,* 42 POLITICAL QTLY. 428 (1971)

Nevitt, *The New Housing Legislation,* HOUSING REV., Mar.-Apr., 1972, at 60

Page, *Housing: How Fair?,* 18 NEW SOCIETY 376 (1971)
    (Argues for inclusion of furnished tenancies under the legislation)

Price, *Walker's Housing Package,* 82 NEW STATESMAN 73 (1971)

---

* Periodicals only.

6. ENGLAND: WELFARE PROBLEMS RELATED TO HOUSING LEGISLATION*

Barker, *The Family Income Supplement*, 18 NEW SOCIETY 240 (1971)

Bosanquet, *Banding Poverty*, 19 NEW SOCIETY 448 (1972)

Field, *Means Test Madness*, 82 NEW STATESMAN 434 (1971)

Field, *Welfare Rights and Local Action*, 3 RACE TODAY 219 (1971)

Lynes, *Family Income Supertax*, 17 NEW SOCIETY 770 (1971)

Stacpoole, *Running FIS*, 19 NEW SOCIETY 64 (1972)

7. UNITED STATES: IN GENERAL

H.J. AARON, SHELTER AND SUBSIDIES (1972)
: (Reviews federal housing programs and assesses economic impact of subsidies)

A. DOWNS, SUMMARY REPORT: FEDERAL HOUSING SUBSIDIES: THEIR NATURE AND EFFECTIVENESS AND WHAT WE SHOULD DO ABOUT THEM (1972)

J.P. FRIED, HOUSING CRISIS U.S.A. (1971)
: (Popular review)

D. MANDELKER & R. MONTGOMERY, HOUSING IN AMERICA: PROBLEMS AND PERSPECTIVES (1973)
: (Collection of readings on housing policies and programs)

G.S. STERNLIEB & B.P. INDIK, THE ECOLOGY OF WELFARE: HOUSING AND THE WELFARE CRISIS IN NEW YORK CITY (1973)

R. TAGGERT, LOW-INCOME HOUSING: A CRITIQUE OF FEDERAL AID (1970)
: (Review of federal programs)

Grebler, *A Problem of Social Priorities: Criteria for Appraising Governmental Housing Programs*, 50 AM. ECON. ASS'N PAPERS & PROCEEDINGS 321 (1960)

---

* Periodicals only.

Kristof, *Federal Housing Policies: Subsidized Production, Filtration and Objectives: Part I,* 48 LAND ECON. 309 (1972)

Morgan, *Housing and Ability to Pay,* 33 ECONOMETRICS 289 (1960)

Rapkin, *Rent-Income Ratio,* 14 J. HOUSING 8 (1957)

Rodwin, *Rent Control and Housing: A Case Study,* 27 LAND ECON. 314 (1951)
    (Boston rent control after World War I)

Ross, *A Proposed Methodology for Comparing Federally Assisted Housing Programs,* 57 AM. ECON. ASS'N PAPERS & PROCEEDINGS 91 (1967)

Schafer, *Slum Formation, Race, and an Income Strategy,* 37 J. AM. INST. PLANNERS 347 (1971)

BUILDING THE AMERICAN CITY: REPORT OF THE NATIONAL COMMISSION ON URBAN PROBLEMS (1968)
    (Report of commission headed by former Senator Douglas; contains chapters on public housing)

J.S. DESALVO, A METHODOLOGY FOR EVALUATING HOUSING PROGRAMS (Rand Institute, 1970)

FOURTH ANNUAL REPORT ON NATIONAL HOUSING GOALS, MESSAGE FROM THE PRESIDENT OF THE UNITED STATES, H.R. DOC. No. 92-319, 92nd Cong., 2nd Sess. (1972)
    (One of a series of reports required to be submitted annually; contains valuable statistics on housing production and subsidies)

Hearings on Housing Subsidies and Housing Policies Before the Subcomm. on Priorities and Economy in Government of the Joint Econ. Comm., Congress of the United States, 92nd Cong., 1st Sess. (1972)

I.S. LOWRY (ED.), RENTAL HOUSING IN NEW YORK CITY, VOL. I: CONFRONTING THE CRISIS (Rand Institute, 1970)

I.S. LOWRY, J.S. DESALVO & B.M. WOODFILL, RENTAL HOUSING IN NEW YORK CITY, VOL. II: THE DEMAND FOR SHELTER (Rand Institute, 1971)
    (Part of important series of studies by the Institute on housing in New York)

P. Marcuse, Housing Policy and Social Indicators (Univ. of Calif. Inst. of Urban and Regional Development, 1970)

L. Orr, The Welfare Economics of Housing for the Poor (Univ. of Wisconsin Institute for Research on Poverty, 1968)

Papers Submitted to Subcomm. on Housing Panels on Housing Production, Housing Demand, and Developing a Suitable Living Environment, Pts. 1 and 2, House Comm. on Banking and Currency, 92nd Cong., 1st Sess. (Comm. Print 1971)

> The following papers in this collection are especially of interest:
> Frieden, *Improving Federal Housing Subsidies: Summary Report*
> Isler, *The Goals of Housing Subsidy Programs*
> Kummerfield, *The Housing Subsidy System*
> Lowry, *Housing Assistance for Low-Income Urban Families: A Fresh Approach*
> Moskof, *Foreign Housing Subsidy Systems: Alternative Approaches*
> Newman, *Housing the Poor and the Shelter to Income Ratio*
> Schecter & Schlefer, *Housing Needs and National Goals*
> Thurow, *Goals of a Housing Program*

M. Rein, Welfare and Housing (Joint Center for Urban Studies, rev. ed. 1972)

Report of the President's Comm. on Urban Housing: A Decent Home (1968)

> (Thorough and influential report by committee appointed by President Johnson)

Staff of Joint Economic Comm., Congress of the United States, 92nd Cong., 2nd Sess., The Economics of Federal Subsidy Programs (Jt. Comm. Print 1972)

Staff of Subcomm. on Urban Affairs of Joint Economic Comm., 91st Cong., 2nd Sess., Housing, Development, and Urban Planning: The Policies and Programs of Four Countries (Jt. Comm. Print (1970)

J.R. Storey, Studies in Public Welfare, Paper No. 1: Public Income Transfer Programs: The Incidence of Multiple Benefits and the Issues Raised by Their Receipt, Subcomm. on Fiscal Policy, Jt. Economic Comm., Congress of the United States, 92nd Cong., 2nd Sess. (Jt. Comm. Print 1972)

8. UNITED STATES: HOUSING ALLOWANCES*

Dasso, *An Evaluation of Rent Supplements,* 44 Land Econ. 441 (1968)

De Leeuw & Ekanen, *The Supply of Rental Housing,* 61 Am. Econ. Rev. 806 (1971)
    (Discusses impact of housing allowance on housing prices and demand)

Olsen, *A Competitive Theory of the Housing Market,* 59 Am. Econ. Rev. 612 (1969)
    (Argues that housing allowance will stimulate new construction and add to supply)

Peabody, *Housing Allowances: A New Way to House the Poor,* HUD Challenge, July, 1972, at 10

Smolensky, *Public Housing or Income Supplements—The Economics of Housing for the Poor,* 34 J. Am. Inst. Planners 94 (1968)

von Furstenberg, *The Inefficiencies of Transfers in Kind: The Case of Housing Assistance,* 9 Western Econ. J. 184 (1971)

Comm. on Housing and Urban Development, N.Y.C. Community Service Soc'y, Rent Subsidies (1964)

F. de Leeuw, S.H. Leaman & H. Blank, The Design of a Housing Allowance (Urban Institute, 1970)

M. Friedman, On Housing Allowances (NAHRO Program Policy and Research Division, 1971)

---

* No books listed.

J.D. HEINBERG, THE TRANSFER COST OF A HOUSING ALLOWANCE: CONCEPTUAL ISSUES AND BENEFIT PATTERNS (Urban Institute, rev. ed. 1972)

S.H. LEAMAN, ESTIMATED ADMINISTRATIVE COST OF A NATIONAL HOUSING ALLOWANCE (Urban Institute, 1970)

MIDWEST COUNCIL OF MODEL CITIES, INTERIM REPORT: HOUSING ALLOWANCE PROJECT EVALUATION, KANSAS CITY, MISSOURI (1971) (prepared under contract with the United States Dep't of Housing and Urban Development)

E.O. OLSEN, AN EFFICIENT METHOD OF IMPROVING THE HOUSING OF LOW INCOME FAMILIES (Rand Institute, 1969)

Philadelphia Housing Ass'n, *Housing Grants for the Very Poor* (1966), *reprinted in* HEARINGS ON HOUSING AND URBAN DEVELOPMENT LEGISLATION AND URBAN INSURANCE BEFORE THE SUBCOMM. ON HOUSING, HOUSE COMM. ON BANKING AND CURRENCY, 90TH CONG., 1ST SESS. 317 (1968)

SAN FRANCISCO DEVELOPMENT FUND, THE MOVE TO HOME OWNERSHIP (1970)
    (Discusses housing experiment including temporary subsidy to renters)

9. UNITED STATES: PUBLIC HOUSING

R.M. FISHER, TWENTY YEARS OF PUBLIC HOUSING: ECONOMIC ASPECTS OF THE FEDERAL PROGRAM (1959)

L. FREEDMAN, PUBLIC HOUSING: THE POLITICS OF POVERTY (1969)

T.L. McDONNELL, THE WAGNER HOUSING ACT (1947)

G.Y. STEINER, THE STATE OF WELFARE (1971)
    (Contains chapters on public housing)

Bish, *Public Housing: The Magnitude and Distribution of Direct Benefits and Effects of Housing Consumption*, 9 J. REGIONAL SCIENCE 425 (1969)

Hirshen & Brown, *Too Poor for Public Housing: Roger Starr's Poverty References,* SOCIAL POLICY, vol. 3, May-June, 1972, at 28

Mulvihill, *Problems in the Management of Public Housing,* 35 TEMPLE L.Q. 163 (1962)

Nourse, *Redistribution of Income from Public Housing,* 19 NAT'L TAX J. 27 (1966)

Prescott, *Rental Formation in Federally Supported Public Housing,* 43 LAND ECON. 341 (1967)

Turnkey Public Housing in Wisconsin, 1969 WIS. L. REV. 231

H.M. BARON, BUILDING BABYLON: A CASE OF RACIAL CONTROLS IN PUBLIC HOUSING (Northwestern University Center for Urban Affairs, 1971)

COMM. ON HOUSING AND URBAN DEVELOPMENT, N.Y.C. COMMUNITY SERVICE SOC'Y, RENT AND INCOME POLICIES IN PUBLIC HOUSING (1968)

COMPTROLLER GENERAL OF THE UNITED STATES, PROBLEMS IN THE PROGRAM FOR REHABILITATING HOUSING TO PROVIDE FOR LOW-INCOME FAMILIES IN PHILADELPHIA, PA. (1971)

F. DE LEEUW & S.H. LEAMAN, THE SECTION 23 LEASING PROGRAM (Urban Institute, 1971)

J. MACEY, PUBLICLY PROVIDED AND ASSISTED HOUSING IN THE U.S. (Urban Institute, 1972)

E.O. OLSEN & J.R. PRESCOTT, AN ANALYSIS OF ALTERNATIVE MEASURES OF TENANT BENEFITS OF GOVERNMENT HOUSING PROGRAMS WITH ILLUSTRATIVE CALCULATIONS FROM PUBLIC HOUSING (Rand Institute, 1969)

UNITED NATIONS CENTRE FOR HOUSING, BUILDING, AND PLANNING, HOUSING MANAGEMENT IN THE UNITED STATES (1967)

von Furstenberg, *The Impact of Rent Formulas and Eligibility Standards in Federally Assisted Housing* in REPORT OF THE PRESIDENT'S COMM. ON URBAN HOUSING, TECHNICAL STUDIES, Vol. 1, at 103 (1967)

von Furstenberg & Moskof, *Federally Assisted Rental Housing Programs: Which Income Groups Have They Served or Whom Can They be Expected to Serve?* in REPORT OF THE PRESIDENT'S COMM. ON URBAN HOUSING, TECHNICAL STUDIES, VOL. 1, at 147 (1967)

Index

A

Aid to Families with Dependent Children (AFDC), 60-61, 65-66, 68-69, 71-76, 101-103
American public housing
See PUBLIC HOUSING
Annual Contributions Contract, 47-49, 82, 87, 90, 93

B

Brooke Amendment
introduction of, 84-85
early problems of, 85-90
and welfare tenants, 89-90, 98-105
in 1969 Housing Act, 91-92
administration of, 92-99, 211
and rent limitation, 86-87, 95-98
effect of, 99-101, 108, 111
and 1970 changes, 104-108
and proposed changes, 109-110

C

Controlled tenancies, 140-141
termination of, 160-161
Conservative Party
and housing policy, 124
Council housing, 7-8, 9, 131-133
admission to, 11, 39, 128, 133-136
rents in, 32-35, 39, 127-131, 139, 161-170, 211, 212
intergovernmental relationships in, 38-41, 131-136
and property taxes, 31, 129-131, 197-201
tenants in, 35, 37-38, 120-122, 165-166
subsidies for, 126-128, 188-197
and Fair rents, 161-170
location of, 216-218

D

Dandridge v. Williams, 74-76, 78, 103

E

English public housing
See COUNCIL HOUSING
Equal Protection of the Law
and welfare assistance, 73-76, 102-103
and public housing, 76-79, 102-103

F

Fair rents, 141-143, 170-171
determination of, 143-154
in practice, 154-156
in council housing, 161-170, 203-204
and private housing, 162-164
and London area, 145, 150-154, 164, 170, 177
and rent rebates, 175
Fair rents controlled tenancies, 139-155
Family allowances, 183
Family Income Supplement, 184-185, 187, 188, 198, 212

H

Hammond v. Housing Authority and Urban Renewal Agency of Lane County, 77-78
Housing allowances, 12-13, 19, 213-218
Housing and Urban Development, U.S. Department of
and public housing crisis, 82, 85
and Brooke Amendment, opposition, 88-91, 94, 104, 106, 108

INDEX

Housing and Urban Development, U.S. Department of (Cont'd)
  and Brooke Amendment interpretation, 92-99, 108
Housing conditions, 28-29
  and welfare recipients, 60-62, 70
Housing costs
  and personal incomes, 3
  and property taxes, 31
  and housing standards, 27-30, 49
  in public housing, 27-30, 49
  in welfare assistance, 60-62, 69-76, 89
  in council housing, 132-133, 193-194
  and housing subsidies, 3-4, 6, 26, 32-33, 81-84, 85, 121-122
Housing improvement
  and subsidies, 16, 18, 158-159, 209-210
  in England, 157-159
Housing ownership
  See OWNERSHIP OF HOUSING
Housing programs
  history of, 13-15
Housing Revenue Account, 129, 188-197
  deficit in, 194-195
  surplus in, 196-197
Housing shortages, 2, 14-15, 141, 143
Housing standards, 2-3, 27-28
  in subsidy programs, 15-17, 112, 208-210
  in public housing, 49
  in council housing, 133
Housing Subsidies
  definition of, 1-5, 41-42
  policies for, 218-226
  and housing costs, 3-4, 6, 26, 32-33, 81-84, 85, 121-122
  scope of, 5-8, 21-23, 41-42
  and method of distribution, 9-11

Housing Subsidies (Cont'd)
  and housing standards, 15-17, 112, 208-210
  and housing improvement, 16, 18, 158-159, 209-210
  and type of ownership, 17-18
  and rents, 19, 25-30, 33-35, 87, 91, 96-97, 111, 121-122, 210-213
  and rental housing, 7, 21
  financing of, 26, 40-41
  and regional impact, 201-203
  and welfare assistance, 35-38, 224-225
  and supplementary benefits, 197-201, 204
  and intergovernmental relationships, 38-41, 47-49, 121-126, 197-203, 224-225
  for public housing, 47-49, 85, 87, 90-92, 94-97, 106-110
  in England, 122-126
  for council housing, 188-197
  and property taxes, 190, 194-195
  effect of, 197-206

I

Income guarantees, 8-9, 12, 1 & 3
Intergovernmental relationships, 30-31
  and public expenditure, 30-31
  in public housing, 38-39, 45-49, 87, 89, 91, 95-97, 105-110
  and subsidies, 38-41, 121-126, 197-203, 224-225
  in council housing, 38-41, 131-136

L

Labor Party
  and housing policy, 124, 126, 130, 141

M

Maryland
  welfare rent problems in, 101 103

Massachusetts
  welfare rent problems in, 101

N

National Association of Housing and Redevelopment Officials (NAHRO), 92-104
National Tenants Organization, 93, 104
National Welfare Rights Organization (NWRO), 93, 98

O

Ownership of housing, 17-18
  in England, 120-122
  and fair rents, 165-166, 205
  and housing allowance, 214-218
  and subsidies, 18, 215

P

Property taxes, 30-32, 40-41
  and rental housing, 30-32
  and public housing, 45
  and council housing, 129-131, 197-201
  and housing subsidies, 190, 194-195
Property tax rebates, 186-188
Public housing, 6, 7, 10
  admission to, 11, 39, 49-52, 57-58, 62-65
  and property taxes, 31, 45, 49-52
  rents in, 32-35, 37, 39, 49-70, 76-80, 86-87, 91, 95-106, 109-111, 211-212, 222
  and welfare tenants, 35, 37-38, 58, 60-70, 76-80, 89-90, 98-105
  and leasing program, 220-224
  intergovernmental relationships in, 38-41, 45-49, 87, 89, 91, 95-97, 105, 110
  Annual Contributions Contract in, 47-49, 82, 87, 90, 93
  subsidies for, 47-49, 85, 87, 90-92, 94-97, 106-108
  financial crisis in, 81-84
  and management problems, 88, 91, 93-94, 109
  proposed changes in, 109-110
  location of, 216-218

R

Rate rebates
  See PROPERTY TAX REBATES
Rates
  See PROPERTY TAXES
Rental housing, 3, 7, 20-21, 29, 219-220
  rent/income ratios in, 25-30
  and property taxes, 31-32
  in England, 120-122, 140
  and housing allowance, 213-214
Rent allowances
  See RENT REBATES
Rent controls, 15, 19-20
  See also FAIR RENTS CONTROLLED TENANCIES
Rent/income ratios, 25-31, 211
  and housing standards, 27-28
  and property taxes, 30-32
  in public housing, 49-50, 53-56, 91, 95-98, 109-110
  and Brooke Amendment, 86-87, 89, 91, 95-98, 101
  and fair rents, 175
Rent rebates, 128-131, 174-188
  and fair rents, 175
  and minimum rents, 175-178
  and maximum rents, 179
  and Supplementary Benefits, 180-183, 187-188
  and Family Income Supplement, 184-185
  and housing subsidies, 189-190

Rents
   See also FAIR RENTS CONTROLLED TENANCIES
   in subsidized housing, 33-35, 39, 111, 210-213
   and rent/income ratio, 25-30
   in public housing, 49-70, 76-80, 86-87, 91, 95-106, 109-111, 211-212, 222
   maximums and minimums, 54-56, 96, 110, 175-180
   in welfare assistance, 60-62, 69-70
   and constitutional problems, 70-79
   inflation in, 81-84
   and Brooke Amendment, 86-87, 89, 95-103
   in England, 121-122
   in council housing, 127-131, 139, 211-212
Rhode Island
   welfare rent problems in, 101-103
Rising costs subsidy, 190-195
Rosado v. Wyman, 71-72, 75

S

Slum clearance subsidy, 195-196
Sparkman Amendment, 87, 90, 93
Supplementary Benefits
   See also WELFARE ASSISTANCE

Supplementary Benefits (Cont'd)
   and rent rebates, 180-183, 187-188
   and housing subsidies, 197-201, 204

T

Thomas v. Housing Authority, 64-65
Tormes Property Co. Ltd. v. Landau, 154-155, 169

W

Welfare assistance, 9, 35-38, 183-188
   See also SUPPLEMENTARY BENEFITS
   administration of, 36-38
   and subsidies, 37-38, 224-225
   housing costs in, 60-62, 69-76, 89
   constitutional problems in, 70-76
   budgeting in, 60-62, 71-76
   and Brooke Amendment, 89-90, 98-105
Welfare recipients
   in public housing, 35, 37-38, 58, 60-70, 76-79
   and rents, 60-62, 69-80
   and housing conditions, 60-67, 70
   and Brooke Amendment, 89-90, 98-105, 110